DOUGLAS W. MCADAM

(EDL)

Systems Network Architecture

A tutorial

Systems Network Architecture

A tutorial

Anton Meijer

Pitman

PITMAN PUBLISHING
128 Long Acre, London WC2E 9AN

© A Meijer 1987

First published in Great Britain 1987

British Library Cataloguing in Publication Data

Meijer, Anton
    Systems network architecture: a tutorial.
    1. SNA (Computer network architecture)
    I. Title
    004.6   TK5105.5

    ISBN 0-273-02842-1

ISBN 0 273 02842 1

Printed at The Bath Press, Avon

Contents

Introduction

Systems Network Architecture (SNA) was introduced by IBM in 1974. Since its announcement it has been gradually expanded and enhanced and today is the most widely accepted communications architecture. Around the world thousands of computer networks that conform to SNA have been implemented and are in operation. Not only IBM products are implemented according to the SNA rules, but a large variety of other manufacturers provide products that are either fully SNA-compatible or have at least some interface to connect to the SNA world. SNA may well be called the *de facto* standard.

Work on Open Systems Interconnection (OSI) is proceeding but the progress is in general not as fast as it is with SNA. The reason is obvious: SNA is developed under the control of one company with a strong product-oriented commitment. The OSI standardization work takes place in a more open, concensus-oriented environment, which necessarily means slower procedures. Furthermore, OSI is from its origins an *interconnection* architecture, which does not describe the internal workings of the participating systems. For a full network architecture, more is needed and this is provided by, for instance, SNA. It has been stated several times by IBM that OSI should be seen as complementary to SNA and – for that matter – any other proprietary architecture and not as a competitor.

Whether this is good or bad is not our concern in this introduction (nor in this book). It is only noted that the functionality of SNA at the moment is far greater than that of OSI. Many users and manufacturers base their networks on SNA as a (reasonably) stable architecture for the years to come. It is therefore necessary to understand the structure and the inner workings of this architecture at a conceptual level. This book is intended to be a tutorial for exactly that purpose. It aims at understanding and not at a presentation of facts, such as specific layouts of messages and so on. These can better be found in IBM reference manuals. Also, because of the architectural emphasis, the book does not cover specific implementations.

The history and the overall concepts of SNA are described in Chapters 1 and 2, to create an overall context for understanding. In Chapter 2 the layered structure of SNA is also introduced. In the following chapters each layer is treated in depth without going into too much specific detail.

Initially, SDLC (and the S/370 Channel architecture) were the main link controls for SNA. Today, however, an important role is becoming clear for the IBM Token Ring. Both SDLC and the Token Ring are therefore described in Chapter 3. Path Control, with the advanced functions in Virtual Route and Explicit Route Control, is the major layer that transports messages through an SNA network. The routing and flow control mechanisms are extensively discussed in Chapter 4.

The layers above Path Control 'reside' in the Logical Units. Their protocols govern the end-to-end communication between two partners. An understanding of these protocols is necessary to understand the advanced architecture of LU 6.2 (Advanced Program to Program Communication, APPC). They are discussed in Chapters 5 through 7. In Chapter 8 the various ways to define functionality for the users (the Logical Unit types) are described. These descriptions culminate in the discussion of Logical Unit 6.2, which is heralded by IBM to be its strategic direction for program-to-program communication.

Interconnection of networks is becoming more and more important with the increased use of communications. SNA Network Interconnection is the vehicle to interconnect two or more autonomous networks in a transparent way. In Chapter 9 SNA Network Interconnection is described.

The distribution architectures (DIA, DCA and SNADS) build on top of the services provided by LU 6.2. Together they provide the functionality required for the distribution of information ('documents') through a store-and-forward-like network. Sometimes they are regarded as part of SNA; other authors consider them related to SNA. DIA, DCA and SNADS are discussed in Chapter 10.

In the future, networks will become larger and larger, with potentially thousands of (small) nodes like personal computers. This necessitates a change in the architecture to allow for more flexibility in the configuration without elaborate definition. The way SNA is evolving towards Advanced Peer-to-Peer Networking is described in Chapter 11 as the future direction of SNA.

As I indicated above, the International Standards Organization defines standards for Open Systems Interconnection. This will allow for the interconnection of various architectures. Support of these standards (as far as their definition is complete) in SNA is described in Chapter 12, together with a brief comparison of SNA and OSI. Necessarily, this chapter is more closely related with implementation than any of the other chapters.

The material in this book has been developed for the various courses and seminars I have taught in the past years. (Part of it can be found in the first edition of *Computer Network Architectures*, which I published in 1982 together with Paul Peeters.) It can be used as a textbook for similar courses and in that case it should be used sequentially. It is my experience that the bottom-up sequence in the discussion of the layers is easier to follow than the top-down sequence. However, for the total picture, a brief top-down description is provided in Chapter 2. Those who are already familiar with the concepts of SNA may want to skip immediately to the more advanced chapters, Chapters 8 through 12. However, it has been my experience in many seminars that a review of the first seven chapters will prove beneficial.

A book is hardly ever written by one person alone in seclusion. There are always discussions with other professionals about conceptual and technical matters, which influence an author while he tries to structure his material. There is also the environment in which one should be able to keep up one's spirit during the 'ordeal' of completing a manuscript and where people are willing to help out with sometimes clerical detail. I would like to thank – without mentioning specific names – all those who have contributed to my thinking about SNA: friends I still have at IBM (even though I left the company in 1983), students who attended my seminars, and colleagues with whom I worked on various projects. As for the environment, who else could I thank but my wife, for her continuous encouragement (and the little extra push I needed many times). I owe a special thank-you to Ed van der Geest, for his help in the preparation of the index.

Alphen aan den Rijn, June 1987   Anton Meijer

---

to Cisca, Yvonne, Carine and Kumar

---

1 SNA history

Systems Network Architecture (SNA) was introduced by IBM in 1974. It is based on the philosophy of the distribution of a particular function to the place where it can best be handled. This distribution is made possible by the increasing use of very-large-scale integration (VLSI), which makes it more attractive to put a lot of 'intelligence' in terminal devices. The philosophy of distribution made it also necessary to reconsider the whole concept of computer communication networks: the basic functions that must be performed in such a network and the relationship between them. This was done in a way similar to the reasoning followed in the derivation of the OSI Reference Model several years later. It is therefore not surprising that there is a similarity between SNA and the Reference Model. This will be discussed in Chapter 12.

SNA was first made public through the announcement [1] of several products in September 1974. The major products were.

a IBM VTAM (Virtual Telecommunications Access Method)—the access method for telecommunications to run in the host system (IBM S/370).
b IBM NCP (Network Control Program)—the control program to run in the network controllers (IBM 3705 Communications Controllers).
c SNA versions of the IBM 3600 (banking applications) and IBM 3650 (retail applications) Cluster Controllers.

They were the first that were designed and manufactured according to the SNA architecture, which was said to be *the* architecture for future communications products. Since, in this book, we are concerned with architecture, we will not refer to specific IBM products in describing SNA. We will refer to the various stages of SNA through the 'generic' SNA release numbers. For an overview of the products included in these releases, the reader is referred to [1].

The first releases of SNA, known as SNA-0 and SNA-1, provided fairly limited function (Fig. 1.1). The main purpose was, however, to set the direction and the concept of an all-encompassing well-structured architecture. In these releases, a network could consist of a host computer, a channel-attached Communications Controller, and attached to it some of the Cluster Controllers. Neither the channel-attachment of clusters nor remote Communications Controllers were possible. In short, an early SNA network was a very limited tree network, in which the Communications Controller was not much more than a front-end, but it exhibited all the important concepts of SNA.

In the next major release, SNA-2, the most significant enhancements were (Fig. 1.2)

a   local attachment of Cluster Controllers;
b   remote Communications Controllers (but never more than one local and one remote in tandem);
c   attachment of Terminal Nodes (simpler than Cluster Controllers);
d   support of switched communication lines.

These enhancements, however, did not extend the scope of the architecture. That happened with the next release, SNA-3, also known as Advanced Communications Functions (SNA/ACF). Until that time, SNA was often said to be a 'centralized' architecture: a tree network with the network manager (SSCP—System Services Control Point) located in the root. This also implied that there could be only one general-purpose computer in the network. The network was more a 'terminal access' network than a 'computer' network. Now with SNA-3 it became possible to interconnect host computers via their local Communications Controllers (Fig. 1.3). Each of these host computers contains a System Services Control Point (SSCP). These SSCPs are responsible for the control of the set of resources allocated to them, thus constituting so-called 'control domains', or, briefly, *domains*. The SSCPs cooperate on a non-hierarchical basis, while, internal to the domain, the centralized management is adopted, as in earlier SNA networks. Another, very important feature of SNA-3 was the fact that, once a terminal is in 'session' with an application in a domain other than its own, the data traffic to that application bypasses the domain host. Domain host involvement is required only to establish the session or to terminate it.

In the next releases of SNA, SNA-4.1 and 4.2 or, in short, SNA-4, first some restrictions were removed that existed in earlier versions. One of the most important was the fact that from now on any number of Communications Controllers could be cascaded from a host. Previously, there could only be one *local* (channel-attached to the host) and one *remote* (attached to the local via a communication line). One could argue, however, that this restriction was more of an implementation nature than an architectural one. An important enhancement from an architectural point of view was the introduction of *parallel sessions*. Formerly, the SNA session entities (Logical Units) could only have one

2

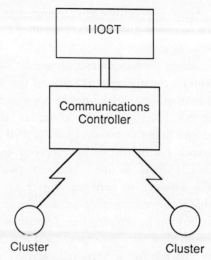

Fig. 1.1 SNA-1 Configuration

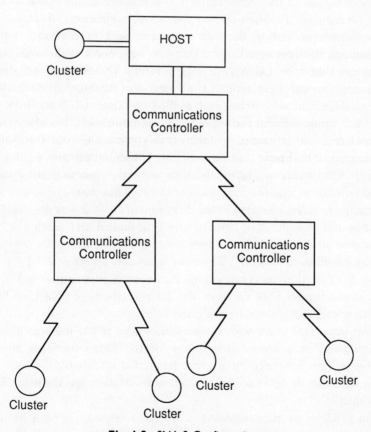

Fig. 1.2 SNA-2 Configuration

session between them. Especially for distributed transaction-oriented application subsystems, it is now defined how they can have more than one session at the same time.

The most important enhancement, however, was undoubtedly SNA-4.2. This release, mostly centered around the SNA Path Control Layer, added full networking capabilities to SNA, with inherent ability for future expansion [2,3]. The backbone of this release is the possibility to use more than one physical path (called an *Explicit Route*) between two network nodes and to have several end-to-end network connections (called *Virtual Routes*) between two network nodes, independent of the network in between (Fig. 1.4). Between adjacent nodes, it is possible to have multiple transmission links that can either behave as separate links or be grouped into *Transmission Groups* in such a way that a Transmission Group behaves as if it were one link.

SNA-4 was the last release of SNA that carried a generic number. Subsequent additions to SNA were announced without calling them a 'new release' of the architecture. The first major addition was in 1982 the *Advanced Program-to-Program Communication* (APPC). This announcement had to do with more extensive functionality for the communication between Logical Units. Its key point was the definition of Logical Unit type LU 6.2. It was a formal extension of an already existing Logical Unit type (LU 6) used for communication between Logical Units in subsystems, such as IBM's products CICS and IMS. The LU 6.2 announcement formalized this communication, but also made it available to other products, most notably various Cluster Controllers, which up to that time could not directly communicate with each other. (In architectural terms, before this time one of the communicating parties had always to reside in a host machine. That restriction was now formally relieved.) Related to the definition of LU 6.2 was the definition of Physical Unit PU 2.1. This Physical Unit looked very much like PU 2 that had already existed for a long time. Some characteristics were now more emphasized however. The most significant aspect of PU 2.1 nodes was the fact that they can communicate on a peer-to-peer basis, i.e. without a further SNA network. PU 2.1 is the basis of SNA/Low Entry Networking, which will be discussed below.

An important event with the announcement of LU 6.2 was also the publication of a *service description* for the functions. This allowed programmers to make an overall design for distributed systems and translate that design into the characteristics of each specific machine or product.

In 1983 yet another extension to SNA was defined, the *SNA Network Interconnection* (SNI). It allowed independent SNA networks to com-

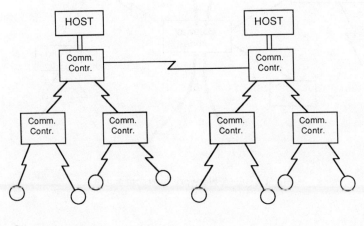

Cluster Controller

Fig. 1.3 SNA-3 Configuration

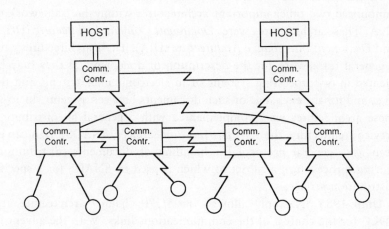

Cluster Controller

Fig. 1.4 SNA-4 Configuration

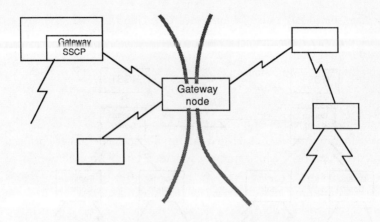

Fig. 1.5 SNA Network Interconnection

municate through a *gateway node* (Fig. 1.5). This is attractive when one wants to have networks, that are controlled by different organizations, communicate with each other. SNI also formed a temporary solution to a problem, which was not resolved until later in 1983: the limitation of the SNA address structure.

At the same time the LU 6.2 architecture was released, IBM also announced two other important architectures within the framework of SNA. These architectures were: *Document Content Architecture* (DCA) and *Document Interchange Architecture* (DIA). These architectures gave a general framework for the description of documents as they may be created in textprocessing systems or in electronic mail systems and the like, and for the exchange of such documents between systems. In 1983 these architectures were complemented with a general file-distribution service architecture: the *SNA Distribution Services* (SNADS). DIA can be seen as a general protocol for handling of documents (distribution, storing, processing), a subset of which is used by SNADS for a specific distribution service.

Until 1985 SNA only allowed the S/370 channel architecture and SDLC for the control of the communications links. With the advent of Local Area Networks, there came a widespread interest in the application of those networks in the SNA world. The two mainstream developments were the Carrier Sense systems ('Ethernet') mainly sponsored by Digital Equipment Corporation and Xerox and the Token Ring which was supported in the standardization bodies by IBM. In 1985 IBM finally announced its own implementation of the Token Ring Architecture. It is closely linked with the IBM Cabling System which was announced at an earlier date. Gradually, also because of PU 2.1 and LU 6.2, the Token Ring is finding its place in the SNA environment.

Until the mid-eighties, a basic restriction of SNA was the asymmetry between the two communicating partners and the restrictive topology of the 'peripheral network' around the SNA Communication Controller nodes. In 1985 the concept of *SNA/Low Entry Networking* (SNA/LEN) was introduced through some papers by IBM authors. This concept removes the restrictions that existed before. The peripheral network can be a meshed network, which may also include Local Area Networks or Public Data Networks (like X.25 networks), with a flexible, dynamic topology. Communications can be between partners anywhere in these peripheral networks. SNA/LEN networks can also be independent networks, i.e. without a 'traditional' SNA backbone network. At the time of this writing, IBM has formally announced this concept under the name *Advanced Peer-to-Peer Networking* (APPN), implemented on only one machine (S/36). The term SNA/LEN is used for the communication between adjacent 'small' machines. It is thus the basis on which APPN is built and will most likely be expanded further.

In the following chapters, we will first give a global overview of the SNA architecture and then discuss each of the layers in more detail. The amount of detail presented does not mean that a complete description of SNA is given, but it is used to explain SNA's most important aspects. For an exact and complete definition of SNA, the reader should refer to the appropriate IBM literature, e.g. [4, 5].

2 Architecture overview

2.1 Network structure

In an SNA network, all communication between end-users is via a port into the network, called a *Logical Unit* (Fig. 2.1). It means that the end-users themselves are not known to the network. As a matter of fact, even the interface between the end-user and the Logical Unit is not defined in the architecture but it is product, i.e. implementation, specific. The Logical Units perform all those functions for the end-users that are related to the communication between them: in the general terminology, all the session-specific functions. These Logical Units are then interconnected through a Path Control network that performs all those network

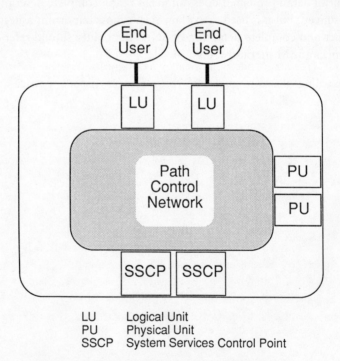

LU Logical Unit
PU Physical Unit
SSCP System Services Control Point

Fig. 2.1 End-users communicate through Logical Units

functions not specific for the session but oriented towards the transport-ation of messages from one Logical Unit to another.

The Logical Unit is only one of a class of communicating entities in the SNA network. In general, these are called *Network Addressable Units*, because they are identified in the network by a *network address*. The others are

a *Physical Units*. These interface the control functions in a particular physical piece of equipment to the network.
b *System Services Control Points*. These are used for the management and control of the network.

Communication between Network Addressable Units (NAUs) takes place through messages, which in SNA are called *Request Units*, and the responses to them, called *Response Units*. *Headers* that contain information relevant to a particular layer (or a number of layers) in SNA are added to these Request/Response Units. There are three different headers:

a *Request/Response Header*. This header contains control information regarding the state of the conversation between two communicating parties.
b *Transmission Header*. This is a header that contains control information related to the transport of the messages through the Path Control network.
c *Link Header*. This is a header containing control information regarding the movement of the messages in one particular link (normally SDLC).

Note that actually there is a fourth header, the *Function Management Header*, but this header is *part of* the Request Unit. It can be created by the Function Management Data Services to specify actions to be taken with the data in the RU.

A fundamental rule in SNA is the concept that no communication can take place if there is no *session* between the communicating entities, the NAUs. One of the NAUs is assigned the role of *Primary LU*, the other the role of *Secondary LU*. The session concept implies that both NAUs are simultaneously 'present', as with a telephone call. This is sometimes called 'synchronous' communication, as opposed to 'asynchronous' or 'store-and-forward' communication (the mail system). In SNA, asynchronous communication is provided at a higher level, through the use of SNA Distribution Services (SNADS).

Sessions can normally not be set up without the approval of a System Services Control Point. This means that for any Logical Unit to participate in a session, it must first be in session with an SSCP. Using this session, it can then request permission for other sessions. The Logical Unit may therefore be 'standing on several legs', one connecting it to the SSCP and the other(s) to one (or several) other Logical Unit(s). These 'legs' are called *half-sessions*. In Physical Unit 2.1 a session with an SSCP is not required, since the PU contains its own Control Point (see Section 7.3).

Sessions in SNA are identified by a *Session Identifier*, which is the ordered pair of addresses of the two communicating NAUs (Primary, Secondary). In general, this yields a Session Identifier which is unique in the network. Only in the case of *parallel sessions* (i.e. two Logical Units having more than one session between them) does this create a problem. Although other options were possible, the architects have chosen a solution which is consistent with the Session Identifier, but which uses more addresses. Every Logical Unit has at least one (base-)address assigned to it. This address is used for those sessions on which the LU is the Secondary. If the LU cannot initiate parallel sessions, it will use the base address also as the Primary address when it performs that role. However, if the LU initiates parallel sessions, an additional address is assigned to it for *each* session on which it is the Primary.

In Fig. 2.2 the structure of the Logical Unit is given, together with a horizontal structure of three layers:

1 The uppermost layer is the *Function Management Layer*, in which the services that support the end-user are located. The layer contains a number of NAU Services Managers that belong to the NAU itself and a set of *Function Management Data Services* for each half-session. These Function Management Data Services select the required services from the NAU Services Managers. They are, therefore, session-specific. For a Logical Unit, they define the Presentation Services available to the end-user.

The above description of the upper layer is only valid for the 'old' SNA. With LU 6.2 a new (better) definition of the structure of the upper layers is given. The old definition applies of course still for older LU-types and it can also still be used to describe the interaction with other NAUs (e.g. the SSCP).

In LU 6.2 the uppermost layer is the *Transaction Services Layer*. This layer is responsible for providing certain services to the SNA end user, i.e. an Application Transaction Program (Fig. 2.3). The next layer is *Presentation Services* and is concerned with 'presentation' in the broadest sense, i.e. not only the presentation of user data but also the interpretation and processing of the transaction program verbs ('command primi-

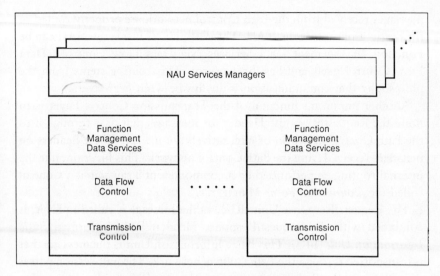

Fig. 2.2 Structure of a Logical Unit

tives' of the generic LU 6.2 interface). Presentation Services maps these verbs on Function Management Data or on relevant Data Flow Control mechanisms. In addition to these two layers, LU 6.2 also contains a NAU Services Manager. This Services Manager is considered to play a more general role than before and it sits alongside the layers. It manages their operation and the LU resources.

2   The next layer inside the Network Addressable Unit is the *Data Flow Control Layer*. This layer is concerned with the management of message exchange protocols. Responses received are correlated to the appropriate Requests that were sent earlier, using a sequence number or some other identification for the Request. If required, Data Flow Control can also manage the dialog between the two session partners by controlling which can send a message and when. In order to perform these functions, information must be exchanged between Data Flow Control elements in each half-session. Normally, that information is related to a particular request and thus contained in the appropriate header, in this case the Request/Response Header. Sometimes, however, it is necessary to exchange information that is not related to a specific Request/Response. Data Flow Control has its own Requests defined for that case.

3   The bottom layer inside the Network Addressable Units is the *Transmission Control Layer*, responsible for maintaining the session. It is aware of the identity of the session partners and it makes sure that

messages received from the Path Control network are properly routed to the destinations inside the NAU. The destinations inside the NAU can be Function Management Data Services (via Data Flow Control), Data Flow Control itself and Session Control. This routing stems from the philosophy that communication is always between *peer* layers.

Another important function of the Transmission Control Layer is to build the Request/Response Header for messages that pass through it to the Path Control network, or alternatively, to interpret these headers on messages received from the Path Control network. This function, like the internal routing, is performed by a component of Transmission Control called the *Connection Point Manager*.

The Request/Response Unit (RU), as the message is called in SNA, is combined with the Request/Response Header (RH) to form a *Basic Information Unit* (BIU). This Basic Information Unit is the message that is transported through the *Path Control* network. The half-session passes the BIU to the Path Control network, together with information pertinent to the destination of the message. In addition, some other information is passed, such as the message sequence number. The Path Control network uses this information to route the BIU through the network and deliver it to the destination.

Basically, the Path Control network consists of three layers, Path Control, Data Link Control, and Physical Control. Of these, Path Control is responsible for the selection of the 'next link' on the path towards the destination, Data Link Control for the transmission across that link, and Physical Control for the conversion of the 'bits' into the physical phenomena (electric pulses, light flashes, etc.) that are actually transported through the medium.

The Path Control layer can be looked at as consisting of three sub-layers:

a *Virtual Route Control Layer*, defining a logical 'pipe' between a source and a destination node.
b *Explicit Route Control Layer*, defining the actual routing functions, i.e. the path through the network.
c *Transmission Group Control Layer*, which will make a number of parallel data links appear as one link, i.e. including the guaranteed message sequence.

The Data Link Control Layer is in charge of uncorrupted message transfer across a physical link. In SNA this can be done through Synchronous Data Link Control (SDLC, a subset of HDLC) or the channel interface to the host. The channel interface is more related with

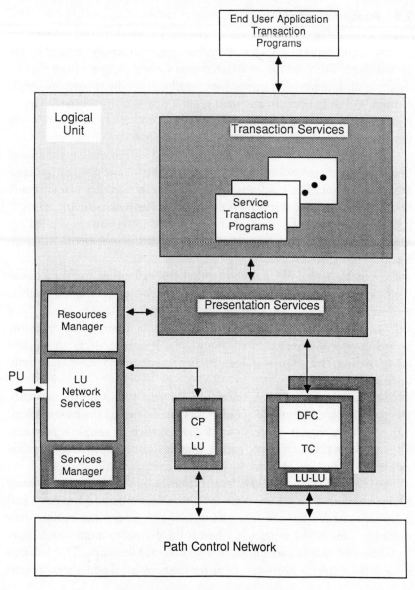

Fig. 2.3 Structure of Logical Unit 6.2

the architecture of the computer system than with the communications architecture. It is therefore not included in this book.

The Physical Control layer is not specifically defined in SNA, since applicable International Standards are used.

13

2.2 Function subsetting

An important aspect of SNA is the subsetting of functions defined by the architecture. The need for an architectured subsetting stems from the fact that not all functions can be implemented in all products (such as simple terminals), but in order to maintain general connectivity it is necessary to control the subsetting done in the products. Otherwise, a Pandora's box filled with incompatible subsets might be created.

Subsetting is defined in two areas of SNA. First, in the capabilities of Logical Units, by defining suitable protocol sets in each of the layers of the Logical Unit. These subsets are called *profiles* and they can normally be agreed upon when a session is established. Particular combinations of profiles for each of the layers that can be used in sessions are called *LU types*. Several LU types have been defined, all serving specific environments. These are discussed in Chapter 8.

Experience with SNA has shown that the definitions for the Logical Unit types are too much device-specific and create another level of proliferation of non-overlapping subsets. One aspect of LU 6.2 (which was mentioned before) is that it is supposed to be the only LU-type to survive in the long run. It uses a different method of subsetting, sometimes called the *base and towers* approach (refer to Section 8.1).

The second form of SNA subsetting is in the Path Control network. Here, the capabilities of the actual boxes are defined as the *Physical Unit Types*. They range from very simple boxes, such as simple typewriter-like terminals (PU type 1), to rather complex nodes, such as Communications Controllers (PU type 4) and Host computers (PU type 5).

The major subsetting at this level, however, is the subsetting between PU types 1 and 2 on the one hand (*peripheral* nodes) and PU types 4 and 5 (*subarea* nodes) on the other hand. Subarea nodes can be interconnected in a mesh-like topology, whereas the peripheral nodes could only be connected to a subarea node in a star-shaped network. This subarea node is then called a *Boundary* node for the peripheral nodes attaching to it.

With the announcement of LU 6.2, another type of Physical Unit, PU 2.1, was also announced. This Physical Unit has the potential for more flexibility in the peripheral network. It can also be used in a 'peer-to-peer' -network (i.e. two adjacent boxes).

3   Data Link Control

3.1   Introduction

The definition of IBM's Synchronous Data Link Control (SDLC) [6] was
the result of IBM's participation in the work of the International
Standards Organization to define new data link control procedures
[7,8,9]. For several reasons, IBM could not wait with its product
announcements until the definitions were completely settled and it
announced a 'starter' definition under the name Synchronous Data Link
Control. Later, when HDLC was accepted as a standard, minor changes
were made to SDLC to make it a subset of HDLC, with the exception of
the loop (see Section 3.6). These changes concern mainly terminology
and a list of them is provided in [6], together with a discussion of the
level of compatibility between SDLC and HDLC. Although the current
edition of [6] does not describe the HDLC Asynchronous Balanced
Mode of operation, this mode can be used by, for example, the new
Physical Unit 2.1. In order to provide a complete picture, we will
therefore also discuss Asynchronous Balanced Mode.

A significant extra feature of SDLC is the definition of the *loop*, which
has not been defined for HDLC. We will discuss the operation of the loop
in Section 3.6.

In this chapter, we explain SDLC in a fair amount of detail, to show
what is required for a reliable, error-free exchange across a medium that
is not necessarily reliable.

In SDLC, any control information that must be exchanged between
two stations is placed in specific fields in the transmission frame. These
fields are in a fixed position relative to the boundaries of the frame, as is
indicated in Section 3.3.

SDLC may be thought of as consisting of three sub-layers:

a   The first (lowest) sub-layer is concerned with the transparency of the
bit stream to be transmitted (see Section 3.2).
b   The second sub-layer is concerned with the format of the transmission, i.e. the imbedding of the data in a header and a trailer
containing the protocol information (see Section 3.3).

c The third sub-layer is responsible for the cooperation between the stations on a link such that orderly exchange is obtained (see Section 3.4).

3.2 Transparency

Since SDLC must be completely independent of the data transmitted, it will view that data as a transparent bit stream. Protocol information added by the other sub-layers is also regarded as just part of the bit stream. This means that the only requirement is to have some means to indicate the beginning and ending of a transmission. This is accomplished by the concept of a *frame*. A special bit sequence, the *Flag* sequence, has been defined that is used to indicate both begin-of-frame and end-of-frame. The flag is the unique bit sequence

  0 1 1 1 1 1 1 0

In order to ensure the uniqueness of this flag, a sending station will always monitor the bit stream being transmitted and whenever five consecutive ones are transmitted, an additional zero is inserted (bit stuffing). The receiving station will similarly monitor the incoming bit stream and after five consecutive ones the sixth bit is dropped if it is a zero. However, if this sixth bit is a one, either the Flag (the next bit must then be zero) or the sequence for abortive termination of the frame (at least seven ones) was received:

  0 1 1 1 1 1 1 1...

3.3 SDLC frame format

All transmissions in SDLC are in the form given in Fig. 3.1. This basic format is called a *frame*, which begins and ends with a flag, as explained above. The Information Field (I) in the frame is optional.

  The Address Field (A) and the Control Field (C) are in the basic format both 8 bits* wide. In the Extended Control format (see below) the Control Field is 16 bits long. The Frame Check Sequence (FCS) has always a length of 16 bits. According to international standard procedures, the octets in the SDLC frame—except those of the FCS—are

---

* Both SDLC and HDLC are bit-oriented. Groups of eight bits are therefore called *octets* instead of *bytes*. We will adhere to this terminology in the present chapter.

Flag (F)	Address (A)	Control (C)	Information (I)	Frame Check Sequence (FCS)	Flag (F)

Fig. 3.1 The basic SDLC frame

always transmitted with the low-order bit first. The FCS octets are transmitted with the high-order bit first.

Note that when two frames are sent immediately following each other, the end flag of one frame can also be the begin flag of the next frame. However, more flags in between the two frames are allowed.

Address Field

The first field in an SDLC frame is the Address Field. Whether the field contains the address of the sending or the receiving station depends on the particular class of procedures that is used (Section 3.4).

In unbalanced configurations, there are a *primary* and one or more *secondary* stations (see Section 3.4). Every secondary station is assigned a unique address. In addition, certain addresses may be assigned to more than one station. These addresses are called *group addresses*. Frames transmitted using a group address will be received by all stations in the group. The 'all ones' address is reserved to address all stations on the link. It is called the *broadcast address*. When a secondary station sends a response, it must always use its unique address.

Control Field

There are three different types of frame in SDLC:

a   I-frames (Information frames), used for data transfer.
b   Supervisory frames, used to control the *flow* of data. (The frame itself never contains data.)
c   Unnumbered frames, used to control the link itself. They may sometimes contain data.

The particular type of frame is indicated in the Control Field. The basic format of the Control Field is given in Fig. 3.2, the extended format in Fig. 3.3. Note that in the extended format the control field in the Information and Supervisory frames is two octets wide, instead of one.

The Unnumbered frame carries no counters and, moreover, is used to select the particular mode. It must therefore be of fixed format in both modes.

The letter symbols in the figures have the following meaning:

N(R)   Receive count.

N(S)   Send count.

         All stations maintain counters for the number of I-frames they have sent and received. These counters are transmitted in the Control Field of each I-frame. They are used to synchronize the stations at the frame level, i.e. to check the sequence of received frames and to acknowledge the reception of frames.

         In the basic format, the counters are 3 bits wide (refer to Fig. 3.2), thus giving a modulo-8 count. In the extended format (Fig. 3.3), the counters are 7 bits wide, giving a modulo-128 count.

         The counters are always used in a wrap-around mode. The effect is that a station may never have more than (modulo−1) unacknowledged frames outstanding.

P/F   Poll or Final bit. This is called the *poll bit*, the P-bit, when used in a command frame. (Refer to page 21 for a definition of commands and responses.) It indicates that the receiver must acknowledge this frame through a response frame carrying this bit as the F-bit, the *Final* bit.

S   Supervisory frame type indicator. It is used to identify which type of Supervisory frame is sent.

M1, M2   Modifier bits for the Unnumbered frames.

Information Field

The Information Field in an SDLC frame is optional in I-frames and mandatory on some unnumbered frames. On all other frames, it is prohibited. If it is present, its length must be a multiple of 8 bits, up to an upper limit implied by the error detection algorithm (FCS). An upper limit may also be set by implementations, based on buffer sizes in the stations.

Frame Check Sequence

The Frame Check Sequence is a cyclic redundancy check. A discussion of this technique is outside the scope of this book. A good explanation is

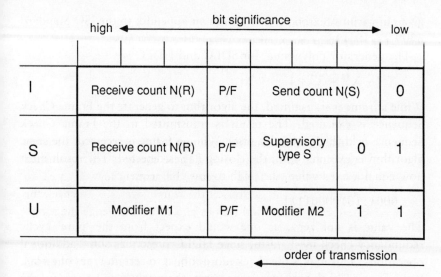

Fig. 3.2 Control Field: layout in the basic format

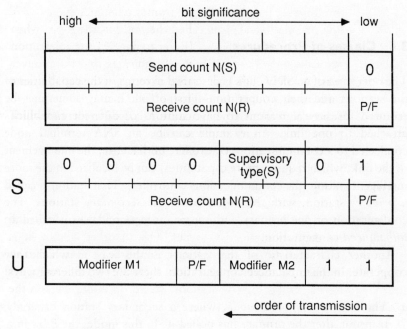

Fig. 3.3 Control Field: layout in the extended format

given in various textbooks and also in an appendix to the ISO Standard 3309 [7,10,11].

The generator polynomial for SDLC and HDLC is

$$X^{16} + X^{12} + X^5 + 1$$

While a frame is transmitted, the algorithm to generate the Frame Check Sequence is executed. The result is transmitted in the Frame Check Sequence field (high-order bit first). While a frame is received, the same algorithm is executed until the closing flag is detected. The result must now equal a fixed value, the (high to low) bit sequence

0001110100001111

The value is not zero, as one would expect from the 'pure' cyclic redundancy check mechanism, since HDLC prescribes some additional operations. This makes the check more robust to certain types of errors. If the Frame Check Sequence is incorrect, the receiver will disregard the frame completely. The loss of the frame will eventually be detected and retransmission initiated, using procedures as described in Section 3.5.

3.4 Classes of Procedures

The operation of an SDLC link is described in terms of the capabilities of the stations and their cooperation. First of all, it may sometimes be required for several reasons to have stations of different capabilities attached to one link. An example can be an SNA terminal node connected to a communications controller. In that case, the management of the link, which requires more capabilities, can be localized in the more intelligent station (the communications controller). That station is called a *primary* station, with the others being the *secondary* stations. The configuration of one primary and one or more secondaries is called an *unbalanced* configuration.

Another characteristic of the stations is the way in which they cooperate. In the unbalanced configuration, there are two different ways:

a The *normal response mode*, where a secondary station can only transmit after the primary has polled it. In this mode, the P-bit in a command frame is indicating permission to transmit. The F-bit in a response frame indicates the last frame of a transmisson.

b The *asynchronous response mode*, where a station (either primary or secondary) may transmit whenever it finds the link idle.

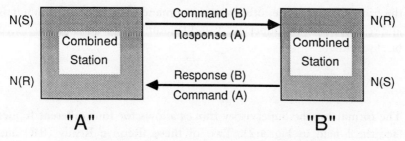

Fig. 3.4 SDLC Asynchronous Balanced Mode

In other cases (e.g. for Physical Unit 2.1), total symmetry between the stations is required. The stations have equal capabilities and are called *combined* stations (Fig. 3.4). Configurations using (two of) these stations are called *balanced* configurations operating in asynchronous mode.

Based on these functional capabilities of the stations, three *Classes of Procedures* have been defined in HDLC [9]:

1 Unbalanced operation in Asynchronous Response Mode (UAC).
2 Unbalanced operation in Normal Response Mode (UNC).
3 Balanced operation in Asynchronous Response Mode (BAC).

In Fig. 3.5 a summary is given of the command/response repertoire for two classes of procedures, UNC and BAC. This repertoire consists of a basic set which is mandatory for all implementations, and a number of optional functions. Most IBM SDLC products use the UN class. These products all support the basic functions, and some also support several optional functions. The ones used most widely are XID (1), REJ (2) and SIM (5). Physical Unit 2.1 allows the use of either UNC or BAC (also called ABM, Asynchronous Balanced Mode). For PU 2.1 products the use of XID is mandatory, since it is used to negotiate the class to be used between two stations.

Commands and responses

As indicated before, three types of frame have been defined in SDLC. These are the Information frame, the Supervisory frame and the Unnumbered frame.

A frame of any type is called a *Command* if it is sent by a primary station and a *Response* if it is sent by a secondary station. Combined stations can send both commands and responses. The difference is then indicated by the address in the frame. If it is the station's own address, the frame is a response, otherwise a command. The relevant commands and responses for the Supervisory and Unnumbered frames are discussed briefly below.

Supervisory frames

The format for the Supervisory frames allows for four different frames (see the S-field in Fig. 4.2). Two of these, Receive Ready (RR) and Receive Not Ready (RNR), are used on all types of link. The other two, Reject (REJ) and Selective Reject (SREJ), are only useful in Two-Way-Simultaneous communication. The Supervisory frames themselves are not included in the Send and Receive counts.

RR   Receive Ready. This frame is used whenever a station wants to tell its counterpart that it can receive I-frames. Normally, this is implicit when the Poll or Final bit is received in an I-frame. If there is no I-frame to be transmitted or if the other station cannot receive, then this RR frame can be used. Since this frame carries the Receive count of the sender, it can also be used as a separate acknowledgement when no I-frames can be transmitted.

RNR   Receive Not Ready. The Receive Not Ready frame is used by a station to indicate to the other one that it is (temporarily) unable to receive. It depends on the specific procedure class how and when the other station is notified that the station is ready again. The frame carries also the Receive count, to acknowledge the frames correctly received so far.

The next two Supervisory frames are of use in Two-Way-Simultaneous communication only.

REJ   Reject. This frame is used by a station to notify the other station of the fact that otherwise valid frames had to be rejected because of a sequence error. The Receive count in this frame is the Send count value expected in the next transmission.

SREJ   Selective Reject. This frame is used to indicate to the other station that a sequence error occurred, but that only the indicated frame needs to be retransmitted (unlike REJ where all the frames following must also be retransmitted). This is particularly useful when modulo-128 is used, to avoid substantial retransmission.

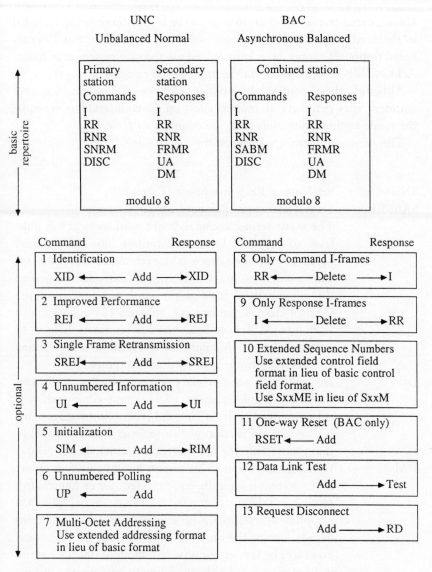

	UNC		BAC	
	Unbalanced Normal		Asynchronous Balanced	

basic repertoire

Primary station	Secondary station	Combined station	
Commands	Responses	Commands	Responses
I	I	I	I
RR	RR	RR	RR
RNR	RNR	RNR	RNR
SNRM	FRMR	SABM	FRMR
DISC	UA	DISC	UA
	DM		DM
	modulo 8		modulo 8

optional

Command	Response	Command	Response
1 Identification		8 Only Command I-frames	
XID ◄——— Add ———► XID		RR ◄——— Delete ———► I	

2 Improved Performance		9 Only Response I-frames	
REJ ◄——— Add ———► REJ		I ◄——— Delete ———► RR	

3 Single Frame Retransmission		10 Extended Sequence Numbers
SREJ ◄——— Add ———► SREJ	Use extended control field format in lieu of basic control field format. Use SxxME in lieu of SxxM

4 Unnumbered Information	
UI ◄——— Add ———► UI	

5 Initialization		11 One-way Reset (BAC only)
SIM ◄——— Add ———► RIM	RSET ◄——— Add

6 Unnumbered Polling		12 Data Link Test
UP ◄——— Add	Add ———► Test

7 Multi-Octet Addressing		13 Request Disconnect
Use extended addressing format in lieu of basic format	Add ———► RD

Fig. 3.5 SDLC Classes of Procedures: the two boxes at the top represent the basic repertoire; the numbered boxes are optional functions

Unnumbered frames are used to control the link without being included in the send and/or receive sequence counts. This implies that Unnumbered responses cannot be acknowledged via the receive sequence count. Acknowledgement is made via the appropriate response.

Although these commands/responses do not update the sequence counters, they may have an indirect effect on the counters. For example, the mode-setting commands reset the counters to zero.

The various unnumbered frames are

SNRM(E)   Set Normal Response Mode (Extended).

SABM(E)   Set Asynchronous Balanced Mode (Extended). The mode-setting commands are used to establish link-level contact and bring the stations into the required mode of operation from whatever mode they were in. The counters are reset to zero. The Extended version of the commands is used if the extended format of the Control Field is required (i.e. modulo-128 counters).

UA   Unnumbered Acknowledgement. This frame is used to acknowledge an Unnumbered frame if no other specific Unnumbered frame is defined as a response.

DISC   Disconnect. When a primary or a combined station wants to close the link, it sends a Disconnect command. It is acknowledged with an Unnumbered Acknowledgement, after which the receiver goes into Disconnected Mode. In that mode, only the mode-setting commands are valid.

DM   Disconnected Mode. This response can be used to report that a station is logically disconnected, for example, after receiving a DISC command. In that mode, the DM response will normally be sent in response to all commands, except the ones for mode setting. It may, however, also be sent in response to a mode-setting command if the station is not able or willing to perform the actions required for the mode setting.

FRMR   Frame Reject. A Frame Reject command or response is sent when invalid conditions are detected. These conditions can be

a   The Command Field is invalid for the repertoire implemented in the receiver.

b The Receive count is illegal, i.e. a frame is acknowledged that has not yet been sent.

c The Information Field is too long for the Receiver's buffers.

d The Information Field is not permitted for the frame type.

All these conditions cause a station to enter the Frame Reject State. In this state, all frames will be discarded until the station can send the FRMR. This exception state can only be reset by one of the mode setting commands.

In a balanced configuration, the FRMR can be sent by either station. In unbalanced configurations, it can only be sent by a secondary station.

The Information Field is 24 bits long (or 40 bits for the Extended mode).

The field contains the following information:

a Eight (or sixteen) bits Control Field, containing the Control Field in the frame that caused the FRMR.

b Eight (or sixteen) bits containing the Send and Receive counters in the format of the Control Field in an Information frame, with the Poll/Final bit set to zero. This is used to communicate to the receiver what the expected values of the counters are, which is especially important in the case of an illegal receive count.

c Four bits indicating the reasons for the FRMR, as explained above.

d Four padding bits, set to Zero.

The Unnumbered frames discussed above are part of the basic repertoire of SDLC stations (refer to Fig. 3.5). The remaining commands/responses discussed below are part of the optional repertoire.

UI   Unnumbered Information. The UI frame can be used to send data to one or more stations, independent of the normal flow of Information frames.

XID   Exchange Identification. The XID command and response is one of the few Unnumbered frames that carry an Information Field. The frame can be used between two stations in order to exchange station identification and the characteristics (capabilities) of the two stations

The layout of the I-field depends on the product type. In SDLC, four types of XID have been defined for use with SNA products. The format-0 XID contains only information on the (Physical Unit) type of the sending node and an IBM-defined node identification (product and station specific). This format is also the root of the other three formats, which have more detailed information about the characteristics of the nodes and the use of the link. XID format-3 is for instance used to negotiate the roles of two Physical Unit 2.1 stations (Section 4.5 and Chapter 11). The reader is referred to [12, 13] for a description of the various fields in these formats.

SIM   Set Initialization Mode. The SIM command is used when remote initialization of a station is required. The response to the SIM command is the Unnumbered Acknowledgement.

In the Initialization Mode, the required information (e.g. micro-code for the station) can be sent using Unnumbered Information frames. The actual initialization procedure is dependent on the particular product. It is controlled by the higher layers of SNA, in particular the management functions in the SSCP. The initialization cycle is terminated through the use of one of the mode-setting commands (SNRM, SARM or SABM).

RIM   Request Initialization Mode. The RIM response can be used by a secondary station in response to a mode-setting command if it is not yet capable of performing the required functions. The primary should follow up with a Set Initialization Mode (SIM) command to start the initialization sequence.

RD   Request Disconnect. This response can be used by a secondary station if it wants to terminate operation of the link. The primary should follow up with the DISC command (see above).

RSET   Reset. This command can be used by a station to re-initialize the flow in one direction only. This is unlike the mode-setting commands, which reset the flow in both directions. The command is only valid in the repertoire for balanced configurations.

UP   Unnumbered Poll. This is used to invite one or more stations on a link to respond. That response is optional contrary to when the Poll bit is used. The command is used only for the SDLC loop (see Section 3.6).

TEST   The Test command is used to invite the remote station to send a Test response. The frame may include an Information field, in which case this field is returned unmodified in the response.

3.5 Examples of SDLC sequences

In the following, a number of sequences is given to illustrate the use of SDLC. Most of the examples use the unbalanced, normal response mode class of procedure. In addition, the transmission facility is Half-Duplex, unless it is explicitly stated otherwise (Two-Way Alternate communication).

Use of the sequence counters

The sequence counters are used for the acknowledgement protocol. Both stations maintain a Send and a Receive counter. These counters are copied into the Control Field when a frame is transmitted. After the sender has successfully completed transmission, its Send counter is updated. When the receiver has checked that the received frame is OK (i.e. no error in the Frame Check Sequence) and the value of the $N(S)$ in the frame is equal to the expected value (which is its receive count $N(R)$), it updates its $N(R)$. In this way, both sides are kept in synchronism. The $N(R)$ in the frame indicates how many frames the sender had received at the time the frame was transmitted. It is therefore an acknowledgement of those frames.

It should be noted that the primary station in an unbalanced configuration must keep copies of the pair of counters for *each* secondary. In Fig. 3.6, an example is given of the use of the Send/Receive counters in the transmission of I-frames between a primary and a secondary station, with Two-Way Alternate communication.

Since the sequence counters are 3 bits wide, SDLC makes it mandatory to wait for a response (i.e. to poll the secondary) after at most seven frames have been transmitted since the last acknowledgement. Otherwise, ambiguity might result when the counter wraps around. Normally, the 3-bit counter is sufficient. On satellite links, with their high transmission rate but long propagation delay, it may be a serious limitation. For such cases, the extended format has been defined. In the extended format, the counters are 7 bits wide and the number of unacknowledged frames can therefore be 127.

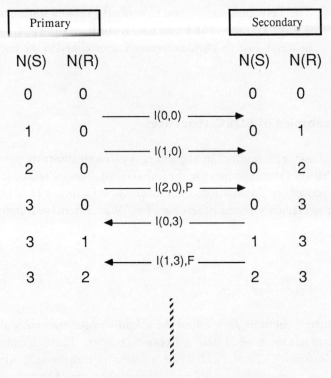

Fig. 3.6 Send and Receive counters in operation

Error signaling

In TWA communication the Receive counters can also be used for error signaling. The basic philosophy is that, whenever a station detects an error in a transmission (FCS error or wrong sequence number), it discards the frame and any frames that follow it until it has an opportunity to send (i.e. when it receives a frame with correct FCS and the P-bit on). It then sends its Receive count in an I-frame or in a Supervisory frame (RR or RNR), which tells the sender what the next expected frame is. Figure 3.7 gives an example of error signaling via the sequence numbers.

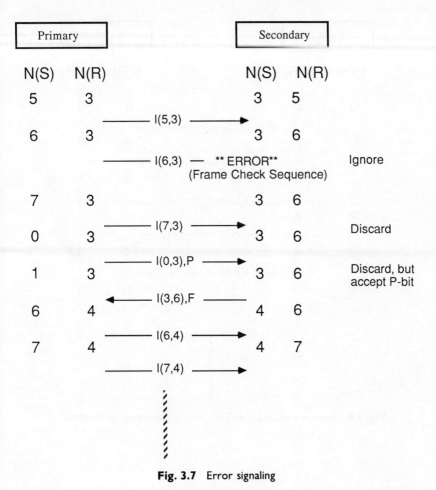

Fig. 3.7 Error signaling

When the error occurs in a frame that has the Poll bit on, the secondary cannot transmit and both stations wait for the polling time-out to expire at the primary station. After the time-out expires, the primary will normally send ⟨RR, N(R), P⟩ in order to find out what happened. After the secondary has responded with either an I-frame or a Supervisory frame, the two stations are again in synchronization.

In Two-Way Simultaneous (TWS) communication, it is no longer necessary that *both* counters agree since the transmissions in both directions overlap. The Receive count in a frame may run behind the station's Send count, since the station may have sent frames on the other

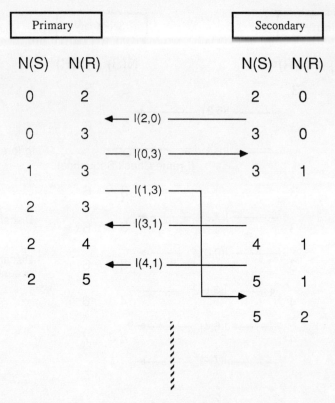

Fig. 3.8 Sequence counters in Two-Way-Simultaneous communication

channel that arrive after the other station sent its frame (Fig. 3.8). In this situation the Receive count does not indicate that frames were not received, but only that they were *not yet* received. The count can therefore be used as an acknowledgement for frames up to and including $N(R) - 1$ and these frames can thus be flushed from the sender's recovery buffers. The constraint of a maximum of modulo $n - 1$ unacknowledged frames outstanding remains applicable. The counters can, however, no longer be used to signal missing frames, and another technique must be used on these links. This is the Supervisory frame *Reject*, discussed on page 33.

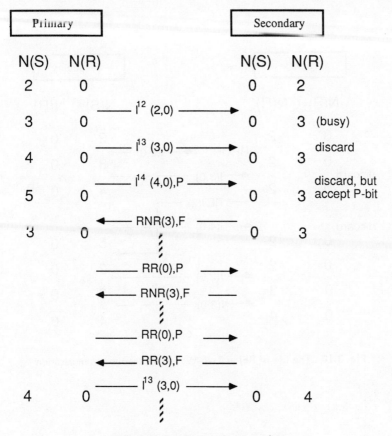

Fig. 3.9 Reporting a busy condition

RR and RNR

An example of the use of Receive Ready (RR) and Receive Not Ready (RNR) is given in Fig. 3.9. Assume that frame $\langle I^{12}, P = 0 \rangle$ filled all the buffers in the secondary and set the Receive count to 3. However, the secondary cannot signal to the primary that its buffers are full, because $P = 0$. Now, when the frame $\langle I^{13}, P = 0 \rangle$ comes in, the secondary will reject it (buffers full). Frame $\langle I^{14}, P = 1 \rangle$ is also rejected, but now the secondary can send (because $P = 1$) a $\langle RNR, N(R) = 3, F = 1 \rangle$. This tells the primary that the secondary accepted frames up to and including I^{12} but no more. The primary will now send $\langle RR, P = 1 \rangle$ at regular intervals, until the secondary can receive again and thus responds with $\langle RR, F = 1 \rangle$. The primary will then resend I^{13}.

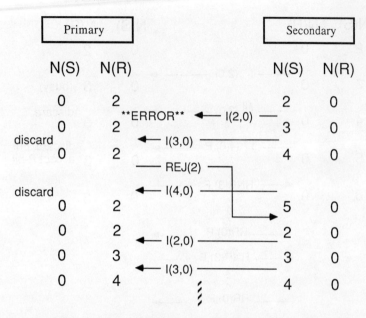

Fig. 3.10 The use of REJ in Two-Way-Simultaneous communication

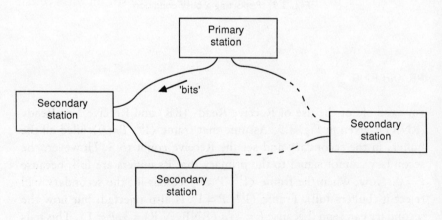

Fig. 3.11 Example of a loop configuration

Reject

When a station discovers that the Send count in a frame is not equal to its Receive count, it signals this in TWS communication with an REJ frame, $\langle REJ, N(R) \rangle$. The Receive count in the frame indicates to the other end which frames were received correctly. Figure 3.10 illustrates what happens when a link error occurs. Assume that frame $\langle I, N(S) = 2, N(R) = 0 \rangle$ never reaches the primary because of a link error. When the next frame $\langle I, N(S) = 3, N(R) = 2 \rangle$ arrives, the primary detects the wrong Send sequence number and sends $\langle REJ, N(R) = 2 \rangle$. All incoming I-frames are now discarded, until $\langle N(S) = 2, ... \rangle$ is retransmitted by the secondary and received by the primary. The secondary then continues from there on.

3.6 The SDLC loop

In SDLC normally secondary stations are connected to a primary station in a Half-Duplex, multipoint configuration. In such a configuration, it is necessary to send a specific 'poll' (permission to send) to each terminal attached and to wait for a response or a time-out, before the next station can be polled.

In a loop configuration (Fig. 3.11), all terminals form a ring in which they repeat incoming bit streams on their outgoing link. Data to be sent by a terminal to the primary can be included in that stream when certain protocol requirements are satisfied.

In the SDLC loop, the primary station manages the loop and it controls the *Poll cycle*. Normally, this cycle is started with frames sent by the primary to the secondary stations. This is followed by the unnumbered command UP (Unnumbered Poll) with the broadcast address and a special sequence *Go Ahead* which consists of a 0 and seven 1s:

0 1 1 1 1 1 1 1 ...

After that sequence, the primary maintains the idle condition on the outgoing link, by continuously transmitting 1s.

This whole stream is repeated by each station on the loop, but any station that recognizes its address in a frame will also copy that frame for its use. Stations that want to send frames to the primary must wait until they receive the UP command and after that the Go Ahead sequence. Once they see the Go Ahead sequence, it is the only moment in the cycle that they can transmit. They turn the seventh 1 into a 0, thus creating a Flag and then transmit their own frames instead of repeating the incoming stream of 1s. When the transmission is complete, the station resumes repeating the idle stream. The trailing 0 of the last Flag will form a new Go Ahead sequence with the first seven 1s of the idle stream.

The next station that wants to transmit will also detect the UP, but before it receives the Go Ahead sequence and can transmit, it must repeat all frames that stations 'upstream' have transmitted. The whole Poll cycle is complete when the Go Ahead sequence is received by the primary on its input channel.

In the above description the UP command was sent *after* the primary had completed its output to the secondary stations.

In some cases, it may be required to warn the stations in advance that a new Poll is coming, i.e. first send the UP command and then send the output. It will then be difficult for the primary to distinguish on its input channel what was its own output and what is input from the secondaries. For that reason, another special sequence was defined, the *Turn Around* (TA) sequence. This sequence consists of a flag followed by an all-zero address. It is therefore, not a valid frame and it will be ignored by the secondaries. The primary interprets it as a signal that all following frames are input frames. The output sequence from the primary in that case is:

UP, output frames, TA, Go Ahead, idle

and the input sequence:

UP, output frames, TA, input frames, Go Ahead, idle

In the description, we have so far assumed that all input was optional and at the discretion of the secondaries. All rules that normally apply to a primary-secondary relation are still valid, however. This means that in any output frame the Poll bit can be set, which means that the secondary *must* respond in that cycle. The rules for transmitting the response are the same as those for optional responses, i.e. the station must wait for the Go Ahead sequence and then immediately react.

3.7 The IBM Token Ring

The SDLC loop can be seen as an early example of a *token ring* with central control. The primary station acts as the controller and the Go Ahead sequence is the token. However, with the advent of Local Area Networks, the Token Ring concept has been expanded much further. After having been awaited for a long time, the IBM Token Ring was finally announced in 1985.

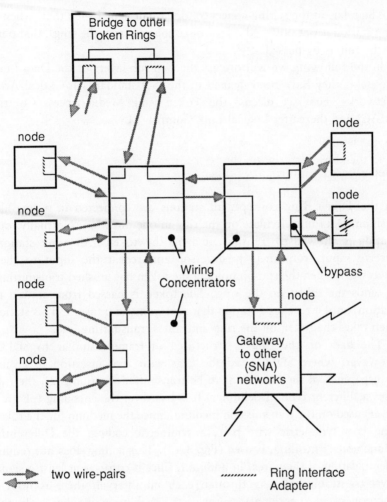

Fig. 3.12 Example of Token Ring topology

From an architectural point of view, the IBM Token Ring [14] conforms to the international standards for token rings, i.e. ISO 8802.5 for Media Access Control [15] and ISO 8802.2 for Logical Link Control [16]. What is specific to the IBM Token Ring, however, is the proposed wiring of the ring. It is based on the IBM Cabling System and provides for a ring, using star-wiring. Central in the concept is the wiring concentrator, from which the cables (two wire-pairs) emanate to the wall receptacles for the ring. In the wiring concentrator the cables are interconnected in such a way that a ring with one or more lobes is formed (refer to Fig. 3.12).

The relais in the wiring concentrators are designed such that, when a ring station is not powered on (or disconnected from the ring), that part of the ring is by-passed.

In the following we will discuss the two sub-layers of the Data Link Layer, as they have been defined in the ISO standards for Local Area Networks. First we discuss the Token Ring Media Access Control (MAC) and thereafter Logical Link Control (LLC).

Media Access Control

In the Token Ring concept, all stations are connected in a ring-like fashion. Data bits circulate on the ring in one direction. Normally, one station is allowed to transmit, it owns the 'token'. All other stations receive input from their predecessor and repeat the input to their successor. When the station holding the token has finished transmitting, it sends the token on the ring. The token is passed from station to station, until it reaches a station that also wants to transmit. This station then takes the token off the ring and starts transmitting, etc.

The data on the ring is structured in frames, similar to SDLC. However, where SDLC used the flags with zero insertion to ensure transparency of the bitstreams to be transmitted (Section 3.2), the ring uses a different type of delimiter. It is based on the encoding (physical layer) used on the transmission medium. Since the medium for the token ring is a symmetric wire pair, a symmetric coding, the Differential Manchester Encoding, is used (Fig. 3.13). This coding does not require identification of the wires. In addition, since it enforces at least a signal level transition half-way through each bit interval, there is no DC component in the signal (average = 0). A binary one has only this transition, whereas a binary zero also has a transition at the bit boundary.

The delimiters used on the ring are violations of the encoding scheme and can thus not be valid data. The violation of a one-encoding is called a J-symbol, the violation of a zero-encoding a K-symbol. The starting delimiter consists of the sequence

J K 0 J K 0 0 0

Similarly, the ending delimiter consists of the sequence

J K 1 J K 1 0 x

The x-symbol is either one or zero, depending on whether a station detected an error (see below).

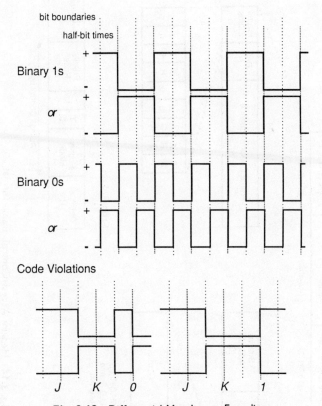

bit boundaries

half-bit times

Binary 1s

or

Binary 0s

or

Code Violations

J   K   0   J   K   1

Fig. 3.13 Differential Manchester Encoding

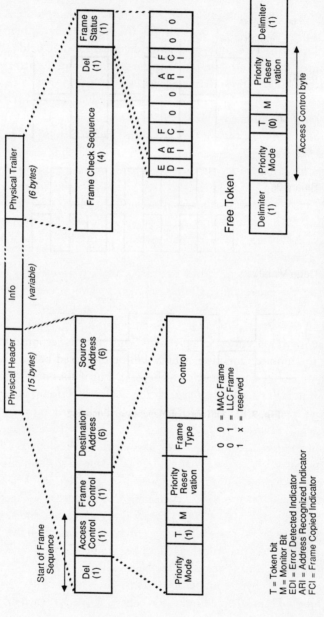

Fig. 3.14 Medium Access Control: frame format

T = Token bit
M = Monitor Bit
EDI = Error Detected Indicator
ARI = Address Recognized Indicator
FCI = Frame Copied Indicator

The MAC frame The MAC frame format is shown in Fig. 3.14. It has three main components: the Physical Header, the Information and the Physical Trailer. The Physical Header starts with the delimiter, followed by a byte called *Access Control*. It contains the *Token*, a one-bit field. If the frame is in use (i.e. contains information) this bit is set to one. A *Free Token* consists of just the starting delimiter, the Access Control byte with the Token bit set to zero and the ending delimiter. Other fields in the Access Control byte are a one-bit Monitor counter and two three-bit Priority fields, which will be discussed below.

The next byte defines the type of frame, whether it contains MAC frames, used in the management of the ring, or Logical Link Control (LLC) frames. Finally, the header contains two address fields: the Destination Address and the Source Address. According to the ISO standard, these addresses can be either two bytes or six bytes long, but in the IBM Token Ring the long form is used. Similar to the addressing in SDLC, the structure of the addresses makes it possible to use individual addresses or group addresses. In addition, it is possible to distinguish between universally administered addresses (e.g. by the manufacturer) and locally administered addresses.

The locally administered addresses are particularly interesting, since they 'override' the universally administered ones. This is used to create so-called 'functional addresses'. These addresses are used for functions that are assigned to a particular station, without the other stations having to know which station at a given instant of time is responsible. An example is the monitor function, which will be discussed below. There can be one and only one monitor on the ring, but if the monitor fails, another station will take over. Through the use of functional addresses other stations need not keep track of who is the active monitor.

The Physical Trailer consists of a four-byte Frame Check Sequence, the ending delimiter and a Frame Status byte. For the Frame Check Sequence an algorithm is used that is similar to the algorithm used in SDLC, except it involves 32-bit polynomials instead of 16-bit. Whenever a station—independent of whether it recognizes its address—detects an FCS error, it will turn on the last bit of the ending delimiter, thus signaling to the sender that an error has occurred somewhere on the ring. The FCS covers the frame starting with the Frame Control byte (the Access Control field is not included, see below).

The Frame Status byte contains two flags: the Address Recognized Indicator and the Frame Copied Indicator. The first one is turned on by a station that recognizes its address; the second one is turned on if that station could also successfully copy the frame from the ring. Since these bits (and the Error Detected Indicator) are modified while the frame passes along the ring, they are not included in the FCS mechanism. They are thus vulnerable and in order to give a minimum error detection, they are repeated in the second half of the byte. If the bits are inconsistent, the sender at least knows that there is some kind of problem somewhere.

The Ring Monitor Unlike the SDLC Loop, control over the access to the ring is totally distributed for the Token Ring, using the token mechanism. Each station has the same responsibilities to acquire the token before it sends and to release the token when it is finished sending. There are, however, a number of management-related control functions that cannot be easily distributed. There has to exist a unique function that continuously checks whether the ring performs as intended and verifies whether every station follows the rules. This function is performed by one station, which is called the Monitor. Normally every station on the ring can act as the Monitor, but only one at a time will be active. The others are the 'standby monitors'.

An important function of the monitor is to check the operation with respect to the token. Due to station malfunction, a token may accidentally be lost. Or a transmitting station may fail to take the frame it transmitted off the ring, thus causing a busy frame to circulate continuously. The monitor uses the Monitor Count bit in the Access Control field to detect a 'continuous busy' frame. Whenever a frame with the Token bit set to one (and Monitor Count zero) passes the monitor, the monitor sets the Monitor Count bit to one[*]. If the monitor detects a frame with token busy and monitor count on, it removes that frame from the ring and issues another free token.

The potential loss of a token is detected through a time-out. If the active monitor does not receive the (free or busy) token within the time-out, it sends a CLAIM__TOKEN MAC frame with a broadcast address as the destination. If this frame returns with its own address as the source, it has successfully reclaimed the token and may issue a new one.

Another responsibility of the Monitor is to ensure a proper minimum delay on the ring. Since the token frame has a length of 24 bits, the minimum delay (*latency*) for a bit to travel round the ring must be 24 bits, otherwise a free token could not circulate. The active monitor

---

[*]The change of this bit (and also of the priority reservation bits—see later in this section) is one reason why the Access Control field is not included in the FCS calculation. Changing these bits would destroy the FCS. Another reason is that the free token, in order to keep it short, does not have the FCS field. It does, however, make the AC field vulnerable. In particular, the token may be lost because of a transmission error.

Inserts a *latency buffer* of 24 bits, so the delay is guaranteed, independent of the number of stations active on the ring.

The procedures described above assume the proper operation of the monitor. But, of course, a monitor station may also fail. Therefore, the monitor is required to issue an ACTIVE__MONITOR__PRESENT (AMP) MAC frame at regular times. If it fails to do so, a standby monitor will issue the CLAIM__TOKEN frame in order to take over. If it succeeds, it is the active monitor from there on. All stations on the ring may act as standby monitors. They report their presence also at regular intervals using the STANDBY__MONITOR__PRESENT (SMP) frame.

The AMP-SMP procedure is also used to determine the actual sequence of stations on the ring. The active monitor sends the AMP frame and uses the broadcast address in the destination address field. The first downstream station recognizes the broadcast address, but finds the ARI and FCI bits zero. This means that it is the first station to receive the frame and thus the source address indicates its Nearest Active Upstream Neighbour (NAUN). The station remembers this address and sets the ARI and FCI bits to one. (All other stations use the frame only to reset their monitor active timers.) When the station next receives a free token, it transmits an SMP frame with the broadcast address. The next station on the ring finds the ARI and FCI bits zero and thus establishes its NAUN address and so on. Finally the active monitor receives an SMP frame with its NAUN address and the neighbour notification procedure is complete.

Knowledge of the NAUN is necessary when (part of) the ring fails. If a station does not receive the incoming bitstream, it sends BEACON to report the possible error condition to the downstream stations and the active monitor. The NAUN address is included in the BEACON to assist in the determination of the actual fault.

Priority The Access Control byte contains two three-bit priority fields. These fields allow the use of a priority scheme for the access to the ring. The three bits allow for eight priority levels. The lower four (B' 000' – B' 011') are used for user transmissions. MAC frames are transmitted either at the lowest priority (B' 000') or at the highest user priority (B' 011'), depending on the type. Of the four higher priority levels B' 100' is used for bridges and B' 111' for special station management. The other two are reserved.

When a station wants to transmit a frame at a certain priority, it may do so using a token of lower or equal priority. The current priority is indicated in the Priority Mode (Fig. 3.14). If such a token is not available, the station may make a reservation for its priority by indicating the requested priority in the Priority Reservation field in any passing frame for which the Priority Mode is lower than the one requested and no higher priority is already reserved. If a transmitting station removes a frame from the ring, it must check the Priority Reservation field and issue a priority token accordingly. This will give control to the first station requesting the higher priority. When that station is finished, it will issue a token with the same priority. Assuming that no further priority transmissions are pending in other stations, the token returns to the station that initially issued this priority. This station will now issue a new token *at the priority from which it was preempted*. This mechanism guarantees that even the lowest priority will eventually get its turn.

Logical Link Control

Logical Link Control as used in the IBM Token Ring is described in ISO DIS 8802.5 [16]. Basically it is similar to the HDLC Balanced Mode of operation (connected-oriented), but in addition it can be used for connectionless transmission. The two versions are described below. Although LLC is similar to HDLC (and thus to SDLC), it has some peculiar aspects. The link defined in SDLC allows only point-to-point or point-to-multipoint operation. Therefore, the SDLC frame has only one address field, which always indicates the address of the Secondary station (or the one with that role).

On the ring, matters are somewhat different. There are many stations which may communicate directly. This can be viewed as many point-to-point communications sharing the same communications medium. These communications use the MAC addresses, the addresses that the stations (or *adapters*) have on the ring. Because of the any-to-any connectivity, the MAC frame carries source *and* destination addresses. At the LLC level, it is possible to have multiple 'users' of Logical Link Control in one MAC station. Each of these users may access the services of the MAC-layer through a Service Access Point, or SAP, with its own address. So, it is also necessary for the LLC frame to carry source and the destination (SAP) addresses. In an SNA environment the user would normally be only one instance of Path Control in a node. In this case the default SAP address X' 04' is used.

In a connection-oriented environment each SAP may be involved in several communications, and therefore a Link Station Address is set up within the SAP when a communication is established. This station address is not carried in the LLC frame, since it is a local matter, used to distinguish between the various link connections. It is the equivalent of the OSI connection endpoint identifier [41].

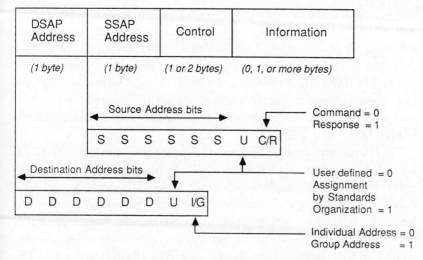

Fig. 3.15 Logical Link Control: frame format

The frame structure for LLC (which is carried in the information part of the MAC frame) is shown in Fig. 3.15. It was mentioned that delimiters or flags are not necessary at this level, so the first bytes are the two address fields, the Destination Service Access Point (DSAP) Address Field and the Source Service Access Point (SSAP) Address Field. Each of these fields is one byte long. In the DSAP address the first bit to be transmitted (least significant) is used to indicate whether the address is an individual address or a group address (similar to the MAC addresses). If, for example, there are several Path Control instances in a node, they can be addressed as a group using DSAP address X′ 05′ .

The SSAP address can never be a group address. However, the same bit is used here to indicate whether the frame is a command or a response frame. Remember that in SDLC, in the Balanced Mode, the address was used to distinguish between commands and responses.

The next field in the LLC frame is the Control field. This field is exactly the same as defined for the extended format in SDLC (Fig. 3.3). The sequences counters in this format are seven bits wide, which means that 127 unacknowledged frames may be outstanding at any time.

LLC Operation   As was indicated above, LLC can be operated in two modes, the connectionless mode and the connection-oriented mode. In the connectionless mode data can be sent to another station without a connection being set up. All that has to be done is to supply the destination and source addresses. However, because there is no connec tion, there is no relationship between one data message and the ones following (or preceding) it. There is also no guarantee for delivery of the data (nor an acknowledgement) and it is not possible to exercise flow control. In ISO 8802.2 this mode is called Type-1 Operation. The only LLC frames supported are three frames of the Unnumbered format (with an 8-bit control field): Unnumbered Information (UI), Exchange Identification (XID) and TEST.

The connection-oriented operation (Type-2 Operation) uses the SDLC Extended Asynchronous Balanced Mode. In this mode the link connection is established through the exchange of SABME (Set Asynchronous Balanced Mode Extended) and UA frames. Information is carried in the Information (I) frame during the life of the connection. For the control of the flow on the connection the Supervisory type frames RR (Receive Ready), RNR (Receive Not Ready) and REJ (Reject) are used. The connection is released with the DISC (Disconnect) and UA (Unnumbered Acknowledgement) frames. Other unnumbered frames are Exchange Identification (XID), Frame Reject (FRMR) and Disconnected Mode (DM). The reader is referred to Section 3.4 for a description of these frames.

4 Path Control

4.1 Introduction

Path Control is the SNA function that creates a logical channel through the network using the physical connections available. It is therefore the task of Path Control to deliver a message to its destination, given the address of that destination. In an SNA network, the addressing is based on the concept of the Network Addressable Unit (NAU). Each of these Network Addressable Units gets a Network Address assigned. This Network Address is used by Path Control in establishing connections and routes. Note that these addresses are internal to the SNA network, since in addition each Network Addressable Unit has logical *names* assigned, for use by the network operator and the end-users of the network. Below, we first discuss the addressing structure used by SNA. The remainder of this chapter discusses the specific Path Control functions.

4.2 Addressing in an SNA network

An SNA network consists of two main types of node: Subarea Nodes and Peripheral Nodes (Fig. 4.1). The 'backbone' of this network is formed by the interconnected subarea nodes. We will call this network the *major* network in the following text. Except for PU 2.1, peripheral nodes must attach directly to one and only one subarea node. Physical Units 2.1 may attach to more than one subarea or they may attach on a peer-to-peer basis (without a major network). The major network can have a mesh-like topology, while inside the subarea (the *peripheral* network) the topology is usually star-shaped.

Based on this view of the SNA network, we will first discuss Path Control as it is defined for the major network. The peripheral network will be discussed in Section 4.4. The addressing aspects of PU 2.1 are discussed in Section 4.5. Other aspects of PU 2.1 are covered in Chapter 11 in the context of APPN.

Every NAU in an SNA network is assigned a *network address*. It is divided into two parts: a *subarea* address and an *element* address. The element address is unique for each Network Addressable Unit in the subarea. Between subareas, it is sufficient to use the subarea part of the address for the routing.

The addresses are carried in the *Transmission Header*. This Transmission Header may come in different formats, and it depends on the specific format which type of address is used. In the following discussion we concentrate on the TH-format (FID-4), used for the full-function Path Control, i.e. since SNA-4 in 1979. It accommodates addresses of which the subarea part can be thirty-two bits wide and the element part sixteen bits. Not all of this capacity is used however. Originally, only parts of both fields were used, to make a total address of sixteen bits. This is the equivalent of the address field in the FID-1 header. This 'old' SNA address had some flexibility, in that the subarea could be between one and eight bits and the element address between fifteen and eight, as long as the sum of the two was sixteen. Currently, the total network address can be twenty-three bits: an eight-bit subarea address and a fifteen-bit element address. (The support of the extended address field is known as *Extended Network Addressing*.) It is to be expected that, in future versions of SNA, the full capacity of the addresses will be used. It should be noted, however, that the implications of this are not architectural, but very much on the implementation side!

4.3 Path Control functions

The most important function of Path Control is the routing of messages through the major network. This is performed through three sub-layers:

a   *Virtual Route Control*. This layer creates subarea-to-subarea logical pipes on which the traffic from the sessions is multiplexed and on which flow control mechanisms are applied to protect the network.

b   *Explicit Route Control*. In this layer, physical paths through the network, i.e. sequences of subarea nodes and Transmission Groups, are defined.

c   *Transmission Group Control*. This layer makes a number of parallel links behave as if they were one link.

These functions were only included in SNA in later releases (SNA-4.2, refer to [1]). Earlier releases just had a simple routing function that used fixed routing directories with only one path between any two nodes.

In addition to the above functions, there are other functions that are related to the transmission function and therefore located in the Path Control Layer. They were already present in the first release of SNA.

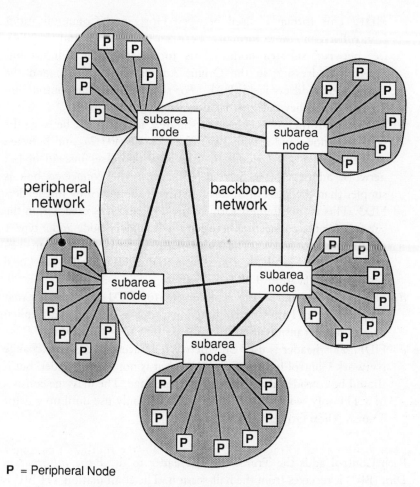

P = Peripheral Node

Fig. 4.1 Example of SNA network topology

These functions are the segmenting of messages and the blocking of messages.

Information needed to perform the Path Control function is carried in the header that is related to the Path Control Layer, the *Transmission Header* (TH). Five different formats of the Transmission Header are defined. Their usage depends on the type of Physical Unit (i.e. the type of function it can perform) on each side of the connection (see Section 2.2).

a FID1. This format is used between Hosts and Communications Controllers, or, more formally, between (PU 4 or 5) and (PU.T4), i.e. between subarea nodes. This format uses the full (16-bit) network addressing in the Origin Address Field (OAF) and the Destination Address Field (DAF). For the full Path Control function (SNA-4.2 and beyond) this header is replaced by FID4.

b FID2. This format is used inside a subarea, for the traffic between the boundary node and a type-2 peripheral node (PU 2), and between two adjacent PU 2.1 nodes. It uses local addresses instead of full network addresses (see Section 4.4). Since the connected box is simpler than the PU 4 or 5, less function is supported by the header.

c FID3. This is the simplest form of the TH, and it is used within the subarea for the connection between the boundary node and a type-1 peripheral node (PU 1). The address carried in this header is an even simpler form of local addressing than that in FID2, called the Local Session Identification (LSID).

d FID4. This format is the replacement for FID1 in networks that support the full Path Control functions, such as Virtual and Explicit Routes and Transmission Groups (i.e. the SNA-4 functions).

e FIDF. This header is used only between adjacent nodes to exchange Network Control Information. As such it is not a real 'header' but it should be considered a 'Path Control'-message. The message consists of a TH only, with no imbedded BIU. The only use until now is for Transmission Group Control.

Path Control adds the Transmission Header to the *Basic Information Unit* (BIU) it receives from the half-session. The combination TH.BIU is called a *Path Information Unit* (PIU). When a PIU is passed to Data Link Control it is called *Basic Transmission Unit* (BTU). One BTU may contain more than one PIU (see below under 'Blocking').

Transmission Group Control

The bottom (sub-)layer in Path Control is Transmission Group Control. It combines one or more parallel links (i.e. SDLC stations in the Link Layer) and makes them appear to the higher layers as one link. The main advantage of this is the increased capacity between two nodes while the first in/first out (FIFO) nature of one link is now guaranteed for the Transmission Group as a whole. In order to achieve this, PIUs are placed in a queue, the *PIU Outbound Queue*, when they must be transmitted.

Any SDLC station that is part of the Transmission Group takes PIUs out of this queue when it can transmit. The moment a PIU is taken out of the queue, a sequence number is assigned to it, the *Transmission Group Sequence Number*. The PIU is treated by the SDLC station as a normal message; the SDLC station is not aware that it is part of a multi-link Transmission Group. When the PIU is received at the other side of the link, its sequence number is compared with the expected number. If they are equal, the PIU is passed through, because it was expected. If the sequence number is higher than the expected number, the PIU is apparently ahead of others and should wait until the others arrive. It is therefore placed in the *Transmission Group Resequence Queue*. Whenever a PIU is passed through, the Resequence Queue is scanned for PIUs that can now also be passed through.

Expect	Receive	Action
2	2	pass through no. 2
3	5	queue
3	3	pass through no. 3
4	6	queue
4	4	pass through no. 4, 5, 6
7	7	pass through no. 7

When a PIU is received with a sequence number lower than expected, it is discarded because it must be a duplicate. Duplicates may be created when it is necessary to retransmit frames due to transmission errors, etc. When such an error occurs, the link should try to recover from it by retransmitting the frame. There is, however, a risk that the error is data-dependent and therefore recurring. That could cause a long build-up in the Resequence Queue if the other links were to continue their transmissions. In order to avoid such a build-up problem, a frame is always scheduled for retransmission on the next link. The dependence on a particular sensitivity of one link is then removed. However, a copy of the frame is retained for retransmission on the original link. This is necessary to obtain information about the behaviour of the link. The hand-over process is repeated if the frame also encounters a transmission error on the new link, i.e. the frame is handed over from link to link until it is successfully transmitted *or* it is scheduled for retransmission on all links in the Transmission Group. A *hand-over count* is maintained to detect the latter situation.

The result of this procedure will be that, after a frame is successfully received, one or more duplicates may arrive when their re-tries are eventually successful. Because of the low sequence number, they can be discarded as duplicates. A side effect of this procedure is that the Transmission Group Sequence Number cannot be used as a wrap-around counter like the HDLC Send/Receive counters on each link. It would be impossible to decide whether a frame was ahead or delayed. The Transmission Group architecture specifies, therefore, that all links in the Transmission Group must be quiesced when the maximum count is reached. The receiving Transmission Group Control signals, through a special (FID-F) PIU, the *Sequence Number Wrap Acknowledgement*, that it has delivered in sequence the PIU with sequence number 4095. When this acknowledgement is received and all links are free, one PIU will be sent with Transmission Group Sequence Number 0. Transmission Group Control then waits again until all links are free. Now, no further duplicates of sequence number 0 can be generated and the sending of frames may continue. Note that it is necessary to wait for the links to become free again after the PIU with sequence number 0 is scheduled. If PIUs with sequence numbers 1, 2, etc., were also sent right away, they might arrive before number 0 and then be discarded as duplicates from the previous group. The process of waiting for the links to become available is called the *TG Sweep* action. The sweep action can also be initiated earlier, i.e. before the TG sequence number reaches 4095, for specific control messages that have to do with the control of the Explicit and Virtual Routes and must stay ahead of any messages that are scheduled later. Discussion of these is beyond the scope of this book.

Blocking A special function of Transmission Group Control is the blocking of several PIUs into one Basic Transmission Unit (BTU), to be transmitted to the next node. Blocking is only defined for Transmission Groups that have only one Data Link. The grouping of several (small) messages into one larger message can be done in order to use the link more efficiently, or to avoid unnecessary interrupts in a host machine. Depending on the channel architecture, each BTU could require the processing of an interrupt. IBM's own S/370 channel architecture allows the use of Channel Control Word (CCW) chaining. This has the same effect as blocking, i.e. only one interrupt for a series of BTUs.

The blocking mechanism itself is very simple: the PIUs are just concatenated to form the BTU. In its Transmission Header, each PIU contains a Data Count Field with the length of the PIU. When a BTU is received, Transmission Group Control compares the count field in the first or only Transmission Header with the total BTU length. If the two are equal, there is only one PIU, i.e. no blocking was performed. Otherwise, there are more PIUs in the BTU and de-blocking must be done using the count fields.

As we explained before, an SNA network can be viewed as an interconnected network of subarea nodes (Physical Units type 4 or 5) and the local access networks to each subarea node. These local access networks are all star-shaped networks, terminals and cluster controllers directly attached to the subarea nodes. This means that the routing function inside the subarea is a simple process. It is based on the local addresses and consists of selecting the proper link to the Physical Unit in which the destination NAU is located. There are no alternatives to select from.

In the major network, arrangements are different. Since the nodes (in the following discussion, we will use the word 'node' as a synonym for 'subarea node') can be interconnected in several ways in a mesh-shape network, procedures must be defined to find a suitable path through the network for each message. In SNA, the choice has been made for Explicit Routing, i.e. based on the topology of the network, a number of routes between a source and a destination node is predefined. All traffic that originates or terminates in those nodes must use one of these defined paths [2, 3, 17].

Between any two nodes, SNA defines up to eight Explicit Routes. Each Explicit Route consists of a *forward path* and a *reverse path*, and is identified by the quadruple (SA1, SA2, ERN, RERN). SA1 and SA2 are the endpoint subareas, ERN is the number of the forward path (SA1 to SA2, Explicit Route Number) and RERN is the number of the reverse path (SA2 to SA1, Reverse Explicit Route Number). The identification used suggests that, since the forward path and the reverse path may carry different numbers, they might also be different otherwise, i.e. be disjoint. This is, however, not the case. One path is a sequence of (subarea) nodes and Transmission Groups and the reverse path must contain the same nodes and Transmission Groups, but traversed in the opposite direction.

One reason for still allowing the different numbers is in the routing algorithms. The routing decisions, i.e. the selection of the next Transmission Group on which to send the PIU, use only the Destination Subarea Address and the Explicit Route Number, ignoring the Origin Subarea Address. This places a restriction on the assignment of the Explicit Route Numbers. Two paths that have the same Explicit Route Number and go to the same destination node must, if they intersect somewhere, be the same from there on. This is illustrated in Fig. 4.2.

If both indicated paths with destination F also have the same Explicit Route Number, node C would be unable to make the decision whether to transmit a PIU next to node D or to node E. This restriction complicates the Explicit Route Number assignment problem considerably. Allowing different numbers alleviates it a little. In a complex network, the assignment of Explicit Route Numbers may still be a very complex task, for which assistance is required[18].

Virtual Route Control

The concept of a Virtual Route provides the network with a mechanism for end-to-end control between subarea nodes. This implies, first, the Virtual Route Sequence numbering, to assure the integrity of the flow on the Virtual Route, and secondly the Virtual Route Flow Control. This Virtual Route Flow Control is used to dynamically adjust the two sides of the Virtual Route, while all nodes in the Explicit Route that supports the Virtual Route can request a reduction in the PIU flow if circumstances, such as congestion, require it. This mechanism will be discussed below. A Virtual Route is identified by the subarea addresses of the two end-nodes, a *Virtual Route Number* (VRN) and a *Transmission Priority Field* (TPF). There are three Transmission Priorities defined, high, medium and low. These priorities are used by Transmission Group Control in deciding which PIU to de-queue first from the PIU queue. An 'ageing' algorithm will raise the priority of low-priority messages whenever they are in the queue too long.

The combination of Virtual Route Number and Transmission Priority is also called the *Class of Service* (thus giving a maximum of 48 classes of service between any two subarea nodes). It permits the request of a particular 'service class' such as 'interactive', 'batch' or 'secure' by the session partners, without any knowledge of the underlying network. The allocation of a specific Explicit Route that can support the requested service to the Virtual Route is done by the Virtual Route Control, transparent to the session partners.

On the other hand, the same mechanism also relieves the session partners from any responsibilities for the network operation; more specifically, they need not worry about what amount of traffic the network can accept without becoming congested. They may try to communicate at the 'pace' they have agreed during session set-up. Virtual Route Control will make sure that this does not conflict with the network capabilities by reducing the overall rate, if necessary. This reduction will, however, take place for all sessions using the particular Virtual Route.

The scheme defined in SNA for this end-to-end flow control is based on the concept of allowing less traffic into the network at the point of entry, when congestion begins to manifest itself. This manifestation is defined as 'minor' and 'severe' congestion, with further definition of the exact meaning of these terms left to the implementations. A small network

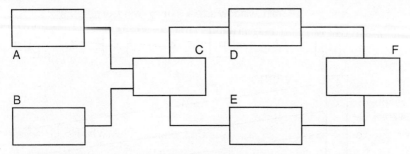

Fig. 4.2 Example of intersecting Explicit Routes. One Explicit Route is
A—C—D—F, the other is A—C—E—F

node machine with limited storage capabilities may have quite a different
view on 'minor' and 'severe' than a large node. They will both, however,
use the same mechanism to report a condition as they experience it. For
this purpose, a *pacing* mechanism is used that is similar to the session
level pacing that will be described in Chapter 5. The difference is that the
mechanism at the session level is fixed when the session is established, but
the Virtual Route mechanism is dynamically adjustable within certain
limits. These limits are set through a minimum value of the pacing
window and a maximum value. The minimum value is set, based on flow
control studies [19], to the number of transmission groups that make up
the Explicit Route to which the Virtual Route is assigned. This number is
therefore reported back to Virtual Route Control during the activation of
the route. The maximum size of the window is defined as three times the
minimum.

The source node can send a number of PIUs (Path Information Units,
the basic message transfer unit at the Path Control level) equal to the
current size of the window, but then it must stop and wait for a signal
from the destination node that it may continue. This signal is called the
Virtual Route Pacing Response (Fig. 4.3). The first PIU transmitted in
the window carries a *Virtual Route Pacing Request* that invites the
destination node to send a VR Pacing Response. The destination may
send the response immediately, but it may also delay sending for some
time if it is very busy.

If the response arrives at the source node before the window is
completed, the sender continues with another window after the current
one. If the response arrives after the window has been completed and the
sender thus has to *wait* for the response, the window size may be
increased by one, unless the maximum has been reached already, or
certain other conditions prevent an increase (see below). In that situation, the last PIU in the window would have carried another indicator,

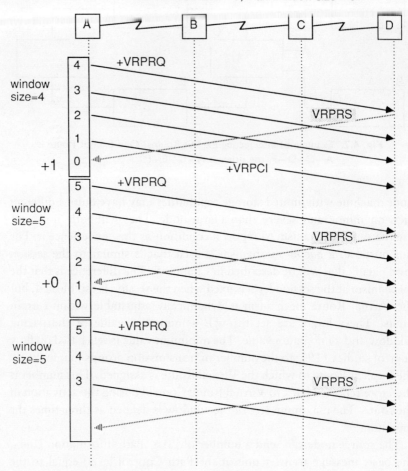

Fig. 4.3 Virtual Route flow control: no congestion

the *Virtual Route Pacing Count Indicator*, telling the destination node that the Pacing Response was not received in time and the sender could not continue at maximum rate. So, would it please try to send the response earlier, if at all possible.

In this way, the window will gradually increase (congestion excluded for the time being) until the maximum is reached, or until the pacing response is received inside the window. It does not make sense to increase the window any further, since the sender can already transmit at its maximum speed.

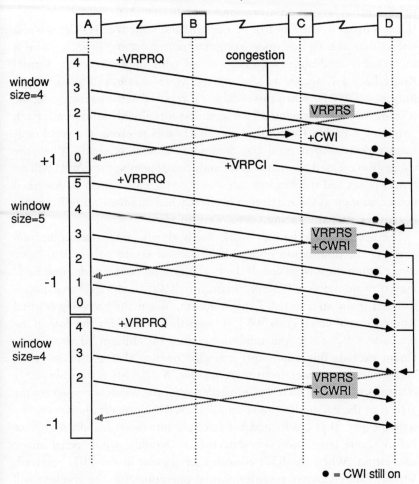

min. window size = 3; max. window size = 9

Fig. 4.4 Virtual Route flow control: minor congestion

Now what happens if somewhere along the Explicit Route congestion occurs? Let us first assume that a node is getting into what is called 'minor' congestion (Fig. 4.4). The congested node will turn on an indicator (the *Change Window Indicator*—CWI) in the PIUs that pass through it, telling the destination nodes that there is congestion along the route. Note that all nodes along the Explicit Route may turn on this indicator (but none may turn if off) so the destination cannot tell which node is having problems. It should also be noted that, since the congested node turns on the indicator in all PIUs flowing on Explicit Routes that are affected by the congestion, the following description applies equally to all Virtual Routes that are supported by the those Explicit Routes. When Virtual Route Control in a destination node receives the CWI, it knows that at least one node along the route is having problems and it reports this condition back to the origin node the next time a Virtual Route Pacing Response is sent, by setting the *Change Window Reply Indicator* (CWRI). When this indicator is received at the source node, the window size is decremented by one (unless it is already minimum). Each time now a Pacing Response with CWRI on is received, the window is further decremented until the minimum value is reached. When the congestion is eased away, the CWI and, consequently, the CWRI will no longer be set and the window can slowly be increased again as described before, as long as the maximum is not reached and the Pacing Response is arriving after the Pacing Count went to zero.

The described mechanism works fairly slowly, since the notification goes via the destination node. In the case of severe congestion, more direct action must be taken. If the condition occurs in a node, that node may turn on a *Reset Window Indicator* (RWI) in any PIU that passes through it on an affected Explicit Route. When the receiving Virtual Route Control detects this RWI, it resets the window for the flow in the *opposite direction* to the minimum value. In addition, if the Pacing Count exceeds this minimum, it is also reset to this minimum value, and sending continues from there on (Fig. 4.5). This action obviously overrules any other increases or decreases of the window, based on the arrival of the Pacing Response and the CWRI. Normally, however, one would expect that CWRI had been present for some time already, since before severe congestion was detected one would have detected minor congestion. When the RWI is no longer present in the PIUs received, Virtual Route Control resumes normal operation, i.e. the window will be incremented and decremented as indicated by the Pacing Response arrival and the presence of the CWRI.

Both flow control mechanisms described thus far have end-to-end significance. Let us repeat again that the CWI is set to reduce the flow in the same direction as it is carried—it is reported back to the source through the CWRI. The RWI, which is more immediate, is reducing the flow in the direction opposite to the one on which it is carried. If both methods fail to ease the congestion problem, the node has a final resort—bringing down the traffic on the incoming links through the SDLC command Receive Not Ready. In that case, the node should report this to the SSCP via the *Enter Slowdown* Request Unit, sent on the PU-SSCP session.

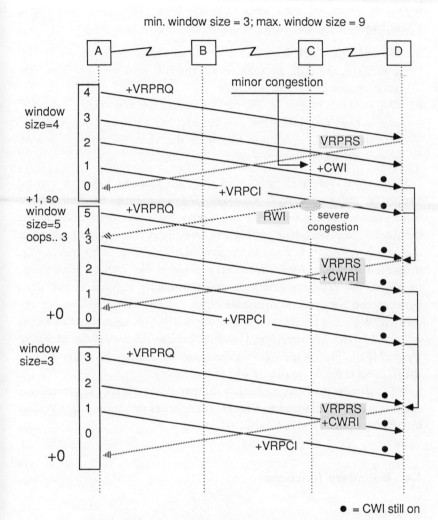

Fig. 4.5 Virtual Route flow control: severe congestion

It may be necessary sometimes to split a long BIU into smaller parts. There can be several reasons to do so:

a The individual BIU length is large compared to the mean error-free interval on the link. By segmenting the BIU into smaller parts, the retransmission rate can be lower.
b The available buffers on the particular link are too small.
c The overall response time can be improved if transmission never exceeds a certain maximum length. In that case, the transmission of several BIUs can be interleaved.

Segmenting is defined in SNA in the Path Control Layer. It can be applied at different 'places', however. Segmenting can be done by the subarea node, by the Boundary function or by a peripheral node across the Route Extension. Reassembly can be done in the subarea node or in the peripheral node, but *not* in the Boundary function. This means that the necessary coordination must take place in the Path Control Layer to obtain the proper segmenting and reassembly in such a way that, between the Network Addressable Units, always complete (i.e. unsegmented) BIUs are transported. Whether a BIU was segmented or not is indicated in the Transmission Header, through the use of the *Mapping Field* (MPF). This mapping field has two indicators, the *Begin of BIU* (BBIU) and the *End of BIU* (EBIU) indicators.

When a message is segmented, a Transmission Header is created for each segment. The Transmission Header carries the appropriate setting for the Mapping Field, as indicated in Fig. 4.6.

4.4 Boundary functions

Local addressing

Since an NAU is uniquely defined by its element address inside the subarea, routing inside the subarea can be done on the basis of these element addresses. The NAUs in the subarea are contained in Physical Units type 1 or 2 and these boxes are relatively simple. In particular, one would like to be able to manufacture them without having to be confronted with the need for logic to recognize different address lengths (as for pre-SNA-4 major network) or the two-byte element addresses of the SNA-4 and later networks. It would furthermore be nice if these boxes could get the network addresses assigned to their NAUs during the

Mapping Field

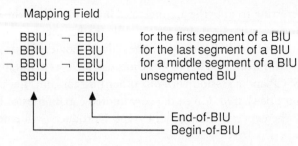

BBIU	¬ EBIU	for the first segment of a BIU
¬ BBIU	EBIU	for the last segment of a BIU
¬ BBIU	¬ EBIU	for a middle segment of a BIU
BBIU	EBIU	unsegmented BIU

End-of-BIU
Begin-of-BIU

Fig. 4.6 Use of the Mapping Field for Segmenting

manufacturing process without regard to the address they will eventually get in the network. Then, it need not be necessary to include facilities for dynamic address adjustment, which again makes the box simpler and thus cheaper.

For this reason SNA uses *local addressing* in the peripheral network. Even though every Logical Unit does get a full network address assigned, which is unique across the network, it is, inside the peripheral network (or even inside the node), only known by its local address. The mapping between the addresses is performed by the Boundary Function. Below we discuss the concept of local addresses as it was defined for Physical Units type 1 and type 2. In Chapter 11 where SNA/Low Entry Networking is discussed, we will describe how these local addresses, originally defined for Physical Unit type 2, might be used to achieve a more flexible topology and routing scheme.

Physical Units type 1   For Physical Units type 1 (terminal node), the simplest form of addressing has been chosen: *Local Session Identification* (LSID). In fact this is not just an address, but it is the combination of two addresses: the Origin Address and the Destination Address. The translation of full network addresses to these LSIDs, and vice versa, is performed in the subarea boundary node. The LSID is 8 bits long and has the following layout:

bit 0   Message is coming from or going to the SSCP (bit is off) or the Logical Unit's session partner elsewhere in the network (bit is on).

bit 1   Message is going to or coming from the Physical Unit (bit is off) or a Logical Unit (bit is on) in this box.

bit 2–7   If the message is related to a Logical Unit (bit 1 is on) then these bits identify the particular Logical Unit.

It is interesting to note the architectural limits placed on the number of Logical Units in a Physical Unit type 1 and whether they can be shared by this definition of the LSID: there can be only 64 Logical Units in a type 1 Physical Unit. Each of these Logical Units can have its mandatory session with the SSCP and a session with *one* other Logical Unit, i.e. the Logical Units cannot be shared. Given the very limited capabilities of PU type 1, it is not to be expected that new PU type 1 products will emerge.

Physical Units type 2   For the Physical Units type 2 (cluster controller node), a form of local addressing is defined, which is 8 bits long. These local addresses are *local to* the Physical Unit type 2, i.e. to the particular box. A Logical Unit in the PU type 2 can now be identified in any one of three ways:

a   Through the use of the full network address. This is done outside the subarea. Inside the subarea, the other two ways (*b* and *c*) can be used.
b   Through the use of the full network address of the Physical Unit (which identifies the box) and the local address of the Logical Unit (which is unique in that box).
c   The (network) address of the link through which the box is connected to the subarea node, and the SDLC station address on that link. This again identifies the box. Inside the box, the LU is identified through its local address.

The definition of this local address also places architectural restrictions on the number of Logical Units in a PU type 2 node. Since the local addresses are eight bits long, a PU type 2 can contain 256 Network Addressable Units. Address X′ 00′ is reserved for the Physical Unit; the remaining 255 addresses could be used for Logical Units. The network addresses of the NAUs in the network that are in session with the NAUs in the cluster, must also be mapped into an 8-bit address. This mapping is performed in the PU type 4 or 5 to which the cluster attaches, the boundary node. Again, the address X′ 00′ is reserved, now for the SSCP. The remaining addresses can be used for the Logical Units. This implies that each LU in a cluster could conceivably have sessions with 225 LUs elsewhere in the network. Implementations, however, did not allow shared LUs in cluster controllers. With the definition of PU type 2.1 this restriction has been removed. LUs in these Physical Units may have sessions with more than one partner LU. They may even participate in parallel sessions, which is an important aspect of APPC.

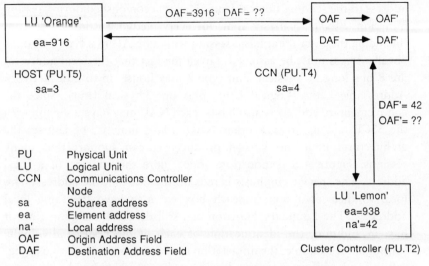

Fig. 4.7 Local Addressing in a Physical Unit type 2

The diagram labels:

LU 'Orange'
ea=916

HOST (PU.T5)
sa=3

OAF=3916 DAF= ??

OAF ──▶ OAF'
DAF ──▶ DAF'

CCN (PU.T4)
sa=4

DAF'= 42
OAF'= ??

PU   Physical Unit
LU   Logical Unit
CCN   Communications Controller
        Node
sa   Subarea address
ea   Element address
na'   Local address
OAF   Origin Address Field
DAF   Destination Address Field

LU 'Lemon'
ea=938
na'=42

Cluster Controller (PU.T2)

The Boundary

The use of the local addresses makes peripheral nodes independent of their actual place in a network. This knowledge is kept by the attaching subarea node, the boundary node. Here, we find the tables to translate the full network address into the local address and vice versa. For example, consider a message sent from a Logical Unit *Orange* in a Host node (type 5) to a Logical Unit *Lemon* in a Cluster Controller (type 2).

Since *Orange* has element address 916 in subarea 3, its full network address is 3916. Similarly, the network address of *Lemon* is 4938 (see Fig. 4.7). When the message flows from the Host to the Communications Controller, the header carries the full network address with an Origin Address Field (OAF) ' 3916'. Since the destination is outside the current subarea, the Destination Address Field (DAF) is ' 4938'. When the message arrives in the Communications Controller, the Boundary function translates the network addresses into the local addresses for the Logical Unit. For the Destination Address, this is no problem: it is the Logical Unit itself, with local address ' 42'. But what are we going to do for the Origin Address Field? We can fit only an 8-bit address, whereas Orange's address is the full network address, 16 or 23 bits long. The solution here is that the Boundary function will *assign* an 8-bit local address to the sending Logical Unit. This is accomplished during session initiation (BIND). It means that, for every Network Addressable Unit (including the SSCP) that has a session with an NAU in a type 2 node, a 'local' address must be assigned. Given the fact that the local addresses are 8 bits long, a Physical Unit type 2 may house up to 256 Network Addressable Units (Logical Units plus one Physical Unit). Since the complementary address is also 8 bits, each NAU may have a session with the SSCP and up to 255 other NAUs. This limit is, of course, the architectural limit: no known product yet can support that many sessions. Figure 4.8 demonstrates once more the concept of a local address. The specific emphasis here is on the fact that the addresses are local to their own box: in each box we may have the same local addresses. The Boundary Function can still do the translation since it has, in addition, the identification of each of the nodes individually (through, for example, the link-station combination). As is shown in Fig. 4.8, a local address must also be assigned to the NAU with which the Logical Unit is in session. Although in the case of the figure, both LUs are in session with the same LU in the Host, this LU has been assigned a different local address for each of the sessions. Whether this is actually done or not depends on the implementation.

4.5 Physical Unit 2.1 addressing

In the preceding section we discussed the addressing in the peripheral network, using the local addresses contained in the FID-2 header. We also discussed the role of the Boundary function in the mapping between the full network addresses and the local addresses. The full network addresses are assigned to the Physical and Logical Units when the network is defined; the local addresses are usually assigned when a particular box is manufactured (or configured). This procedure forces a certain inflexibility on the network. In Chapter 11 we will discuss these problems in more general context. For now it suffices to note that a need for SNA boxes emerged, which had at least the PU 2 functionality, but were more flexible from an addressing point of view. Moreover, they should be able to operate without the need of attachment to the network manager, the SSCP. In other words, these boxes should be able to connect on a point-point basis.

The solution to this problem is Physical Unit 2.1. It is an extension of some aspects of Physical Unit 2 and it contains a Control Point, which may locally act as an the SSCP. In the present chapter we are concerned with addressing and we will look at the PU 2.1 addressing in more detail

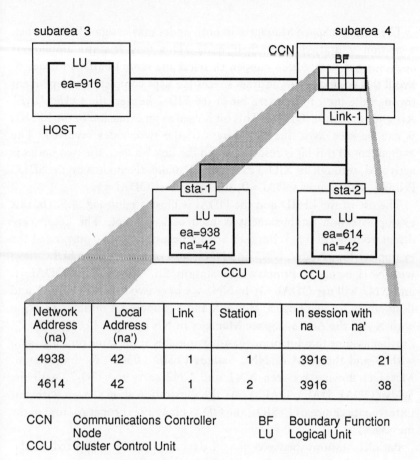

Network Address (na)	Local Address (na')	Link	Station	In session with na	na'
4938	42	1	1	3916	21
4614	42	1	2	3916	38

CCN   Communications Controller   BF   Boundary Function
          Node   LU   Logical Unit
CCU   Cluster Control Unit

Fig. 4.8 Use of local addresses

now. As was said before, it is based on the two-byte local addresses in the FID-2 header. However, these addresses are no longer directly related to Logical Units. For each side of a link attaching two PU 2.1 nodes, a separate address space, both for the local and the remote addresses, is created. The combination of a local address with a remote address (OAF'-DAF' pair) is called the *Local-Form Session Identifier* (LFSID). When a new session must be established, an LFSID is assigned by the Address Space Manager (ASM) in the Physical Unit, where the session request originates.

The Address Space Managers in both nodes may assign LFSIDs, when a session is started from their node. This may lead to ambiguous addressing if both ASMs happen to select the same LFSID. In order to avoid this conflict, both address spaces are kept completely independent through the use of one extra bit in the FID-2 header, the *OAF'-DAF' Assignor Indicator* (ODAI). This bit is used as an extension to the LFSID. It can be seen as a one-bit address of the two nodes involved. The assignment of this bit is resolved when the link between the two nodes is activated, through an XID-3 exchange. Usually, the node with the SDLC Primary station uses ODAI = 0, the other uses ODAI = 1.

The use of the LFSID and the ODAI is illustrated in Fig. 4.9. (In this example session establishment is used as a concept. The details are discussed in Section 5.3, but they are not necessary for the purpose of the example.) Two Nodes, NN1 and NN2, are connected via an SDLC link, with NN1 being the Primary Link station. So, NN1 will use ODAI = 0 and NN2 will use ODAI = 1. In NN1 we have two Logical Units, A and B, in NN2 also two Logical Units, X and Y. Suppose A initiates a session with X and the Address Space Manager in NN1 assigns LFSID '0103'. Further assume that for some reason Y initiates at the same time a session with B and the ASM in NN2 assigns LFSID '0301' to that session. Messages flowing between NN1 and NN2 carry the FID-2, with the fields ⟨ODAI, DAF', OAF'⟩. As the illustration shows, even with this unfortunate choice of LFSIDs, the ODAI bit assures proper routing of the messages.

Parallel sessions between two LUs can also be supported easily, because both sides can, when they initiate a session, assign an independent LFSID, much simpler than the 'standard' parallel session solution (Section 2.1). The OAF'-part and DAF'-part in the LFSID are no longer directly associated with Logical Units as their local addresses. It is much better to view the LFSID as an identification of a particular session between two LUs, or to view it as a 'logical channel' identification on the link. The latter view makes it easier to understand the concept of 'Session ID swapping' used in large networks built of many PU 2.1s, Advanced Peer-to-Peer Networking (APPN). This is further discussed in Chapter 11.

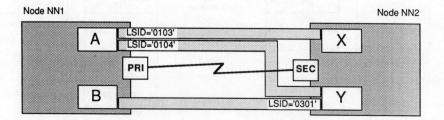

direction	ODAI	DAF'	OAF'	from	to
⟶	0	03	01	A	X
⟶	1	03	01	B	Y
⟵	0	01	03	X	A
⟵	1	01	03	Y	B
⟶	0	04	01	A	Y
⟵	0	01	04	Y	A

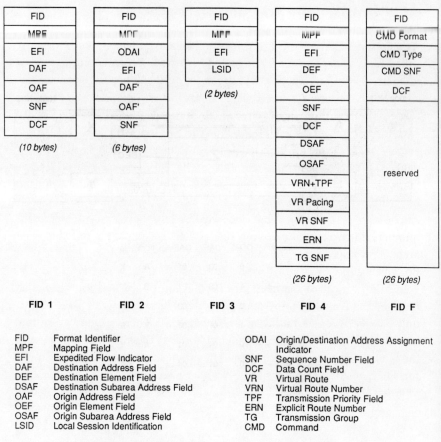

Fig. 4.10 Contents of the Transmission Header

FID 1   FID 2   FID 3   FID 4   FID F

FID	Format Identifier	ODAI	Origin/Destination Address Assignment Indicator
MPF	Mapping Field		
EFI	Expedited Flow Indicator	SNF	Sequence Number Field
DAF	Destination Address Field	DCF	Data Count Field
DEF	Destination Element Field	VR	Virtual Route
DSAF	Destination Subarea Address Field	VRN	Virtual Route Number
OAF	Origin Address Field	TPF	Transmission Priority Field
OEF	Origin Element Field	ERN	Explicit Route Number
OSAF	Origin Subarea Address Field	TG	Transmission Group
LSID	Local Session Identification	CMD	Command

4.6 Formats of the Transmission Header

As mentioned earlier, the Transmission Header is defined in five formats, called FID-types (*Format Identifier*). Their usage depends on the type of node between which the PIU flows. Figure 4.10 shows the formats as far as the logical content is concerned. For the actual layout of the fields the reader is referred to, for example, [12]. From Fig. 4.10 the effect of the function subsetting for each node-type can be seen. All SNA-4 functions, such as Virtual and Explicit Routes and Transmission Groups, are only defined between subareas through the FID4 Transmission Header. Similarly, the blocking function can architecturally only be used in the inter-subarea traffic since FID2 and FID3 do not carry the Data Count. It can be seen, furthermore, that since the FID3 does not carry the sequence number, no correlation between requests and responses is possible. The architecture thus limits the number of messages outstanding between the Boundary function and a peripheral node (PU type 1) to one.

In FID-F, most of the fields of FID-4 are not used and are defined as reserved. This includes the address fields. The reason is that FID-F can only flow between two adjacent subarea nodes. There are however three new fields for this TH, the Command Format, the Command Type and the Command Sequence Number. The only use for this TH until now is for TG Sequence Number Wrap Acknowledgement.

5 Transmission Control

5.1 Introduction

This section discusses the layer between Path Control and Data Flow Control. We might say that the function of this Transmission Control layer is: to couple the two sides of a session together and to make sure that the transmission within the session is orderly (from a *transmission point of view* and not from a *logical* one). For that reason, Transmission Control has the functions to establish sessions, to operate and monitor them (e.g. checking of the sequence numbers), and to perform error recovery if necessary.

Transmission Control as a layer is composed of a (distributed) set of *Transmission Control Elements* (TCEs), one on each side of a session (they are part of the half-session). In the case of shared Logical Units (i.e. LUs that are in session with several other LUs), one TCE is present in *each* half-session. The TCEs are characterized by the *Session Identifier* (SID), which is the pair of addresses of the two NAUs in the session. In this way, the TCEs assigned to one LU can still be distinguished. This is used, for example by Path Control (Section 4.3), in routing messages to an LU: after the LU has been identified through the Destination Address, the appropriate TCE can be selected through the Origin Address Field.

Each Transmission Control Element has basically two components: the *Connection Point Manager* (CPMGR) and the *Session Control* (SC). These components will each be discussed in the following sections.

5.2 Connection Point Manager

The Connection Point Manager is the 'heart' of the session. It functions as an interface to Path Control for all components that may create Request/Response Units:

Inside Transmission Control: ● Session Control
● Network Control (Physical Units only)

In the higher layers: • Data Flow Control
                        • Function Management

For this function the CPMGR performs a routing function towards these components. Since sessions may use cryptography to protect certain or all messages, the CPMGR also performs encryption/decryption of those messages. The encryption mechanism is described in detail in Section 5.4.

Request/Response Header

The information that must be passed between the two Connection Point Managers is placed in the Request/Response Header (RH). This header is built by the CPMGR when a message is transmitted and it is checked for consistency and correctness when a message is received.

The Request/Response Header is always a 3-byte header, independent of the protocols agreed between the session partners, i.e. the profiles. The first bit indicates whether it is a Request Header or a Response Header; the next two bits the RU *category*, i.e. to which component the RU 'belongs'. As explained above, this can be Function Management, Data Flow Control, Session Control or Network Control. The other bits are used as indicators for the various protocols. Normally, they have the same meaning in both the request and the response. If the information applies to a request only, then the bits in the response are set to a predefined value or they are defined as 'reserved'. This depends on the particular protocol involved. The various indicators are discussed below for the protocols relevant to the CPMGR and in Chapter 6 for those related to Data Flow Control (DFC).

Two indicators are not related to either the CPMGR or DFC, but to Function Management, the *Format Indicator* (FI), which is discussed in Section 7.2, and the *Code Selection Indicator* (CSI), which can be used to select an alternate code set.

Expedited delivery of messages   For several reasons, it can be necessary to let messages bypass the 'normal' flow of data. This can be the case when session management or recovery messages must be passed: they should not influence the data flow sequence numbering. A typical example is the recovery of the data flow. In that case, the recovery messages cannot use the normal flow because that is the one that must be recovered.

For this purpose, the *Expedited Flow* was introduced in the architecture. An *Expedited Flow Indicator* (EFI) is carried in the Transmission

Header. When the EFI is on, the CPMGR will not queue the message even if queuing is necessary for normal messages. The reason that the EFI is in the Transmission Header and *not* in the Request/Response Header has probably to do with the fact that initially a kind of priority in the Path Control network was envisaged for the Expedited Flow. The current definition does not use this in Path Control since Expedited messages still flow in the session and therefore on the same Virtual Route. Logically, the EFI should now be in the Request Header.

Response types   The sender of a Request Unit can specify what type of response he wants to have. The possibilities are

a   no response at all (RQN);
b   response only in case of an error (Exception Response, RQE);
c   always a response (Definite Response, RQD).

The response type requested is indicated in the Request Header, using three indicators (Fig. 5.1): DR1I and DR2I (Definite Response Type 1 and 2 Indicators) and ERI (Exception Response Indicator). In the case of a Response Header, the ERI is called the RTI (Response Type Indicator). If it is on in a response, this indicator means that the response is actually an Exception Response (independent of whether a Definite Response or an Exception Response was requested). The meaning of the DR1I and DR2I indicators is not defined in the architecture: it is left to the sender of the request to attach a special meaning to either one.[*] When the RTI indicates that a response is an Exception Response, the response cannot merely be the RH, but it must include Sense information and, depending on the type of RU, some bytes of the original RU.

When Sense data is included, the Sense Data Included Indicator (SDI), is also set. This is mandatory in Exception Responses, but in some cases it can also be turned on in a request. An example is the case where the Connection Point Manager detects a sequence number error on a received BIU. The CPMGR will then include sense information to indicate the error and turn on the SDI. The request is now called an *Exception Request* (EXR). This Exception Request is not immediately returned to the sender, *but delivered to the addressee*, e.g. Data Flow Control. The reason is that the Request Header may contain protocol information still relevant to the addressee. (It is a basic philosophy in SNA that communication is between equivalent layers, if at all possible.

---

[*]This applies to the 'end-user generated' requests only. Whenever an architectured component sends an RU, e.g. Session Control, the architecture does specify what type of response must be requested.

DR 1 DR2 ER

0	0	0	(RQN)	No response required
x	y	0	(RQD)	Definite response
x	y	1	(RQE)	Exception response (x and/or y must be 1)

Fig. 5.1 Types of response that can be requested

It does not apply if, for example, an RU cannot be delivered because the addressee is unknown, but in the case of a CPMGR-detected sequence error it still does.) The addressee can then decide what it wants to do with the request. It may send a negative response based on the Exception Request, or another response based on its own information.

A positive response carries additional data only in special cases. An example is the response to the STSN (Set and Test Sequence Numbers) Request from Session Control.

Pacing The pacing mechanism in SNA controls data *flowrate*. (It should not be confused with the Data Flow Control Layer, which is a logical flow protocol.) Pacing has to do with the rate at which requests can flow between the session partners, without them overrunning each other and/or claiming too many network resources.

The basic mechanism is the same as for the Virtual Route, but now it works with a *fixed* window and on a per session basis. One end of the conversation can send an agreed number of requests (say *n*) and must then wait for permission from the other side before the next group of *n* requests can be sent. The first request in the group must have the *Pacing Request Indicator* on in the Request Header. The response uses the same indicator, which is then called *Pacing Response Indicator*. Although the Pacing Request Indicator must always be on in the *first* request of the group, the receiver may use any response available to turn on the Pacing Response Indicator when it wants to signal that the next group of requests may be sent. This could cause a problem when there is no such response available when the Pacing Response must be sent, e.g. a long series of requests that ask for Exception Responses only. In that case, the CPMGR will create a special response called the *Isolated Pacing Response* (IPR). This response consists of an RH only, with all bits set to zero, except the ones for Response type, Pacing Response and Chaining.

Pacing is defined in SNA in one or two stages in each (normal) flow direction:

a From the Primary to the Secondary in one stage.
b From the Primary to the Secondary in two stages:
  i from the Primary Logical Unit to the Boundary function and
  ii from the Boundary to the Secondary Logical Unit.
c From the Secondary to the Primary in one stage.
d From the Secondary to the Primary in two stages:
  i from the Secondary Logical Unit to the Boundary and
  ii from the Boundary to the Primary Logical Unit.

When Pacing is used in a session, it can be used for both directions independently. The value of n can be different for each of them.

A typical example is a session between a Logical Unit in a Host and a Logical Unit in a Terminal Node. Since the FID3 header to the Terminal Node does not support sequence numbers, the pacing count from boundary to terminal node will be set to 1. The count from the primary LU to the boundary can, however, be higher, e.g. 4 or 5. This ensures that there is always a BIU available in the boundary, when the terminal can use the next one, i.e. sends a Pacing Response to the boundary.

Note that the use of pacing may interfere with the use of the Request/Response control modes (discussed in Section 6.2). It is the task of the system designer to ensure that all these protocols cooperate harmoniously.

The performance of a particular system may depend heavily on the choice of the pacing parameters. Only through research and modelling can one find what the effects in a particular environment are (see, for example, [19]).

Sequence numbers and IDs When requests are sent in a session and responses are expected, either normal or exception, the sender must correlate the responses to the related request. For that purpose, the requests carry a sequence number or an Identifier (ID). The sequence number is also used by the CPMGR to ensure that the flow is sequential: the received sequence numbers must increase monotonically.

On the normal flow, one can use either IDs or sequence numbers (this is selected when the session is started—BIND). When sequence numbers are used, they are assigned by the sending Data Flow Control and checked by the receiving CPMGR. In case the CPMGR finds an error, the Sense Data Included Indicator is set and the RU replaced with sense information that identifies the error. The request is then passed on to the addressee. When a negative response which indicates a sequence number error is received, recovery action is started by Session Control using the *Set and Test Sequence Number RU.*

On the Expedited Flow, IDs are always used. These are (more or less) arbitrary numbers, which need not be sequential. This is sufficient since the Expedited Flow uses Immediate Request Mode (see Section 6.2) and Definite Responses only, which means that only one Request can be outstanding at any time. For Session Control and Network Control, the IDs are assigned by the CMPGR. For Expedited Data Flow Control and Function Management Requests, the IDs are assigned by Data Flow Control.

5.3 Session Control

Session Control is the function that can

a   activate and deactivate sessions;
b   open and close the flow gate for the normal flow in an active session;
c   perform session error recovery (particularly sequence number recovery).

These functions will now be discussed in more detail. Since most of these Session Control activities are not directly related to specific RUs in the session, the exchange of information between Session Control in the two half-sessions cannot use the Request/Response Headers. For that reason a number of Session Control Request Units are defined in the architecture.

Session activation

A session is the basic SNA concept to establish a logical relation between Network Addressable Units. Since there are several types of NAU, there are also several types of session possible:

a   SSCP-SSCP   These sessions are used for the communication between control domains in a multi-domain network. They must be activated to make any cross-domain activities possible.
b   SSCP-PU   These sessions must exist between the SSCP and *all* Physical Units in its Control Domain. They must be activated before any other activity with the nodes controlled by the PUs is possible. The sessions are used to exchange network control information between the SSCP and the PU.
c   SSCP-LU   These sessions are established between the SSCP and all Logical Units in its Control Domain. They must be activated before the LUs can get involved in any other activity.

(a)

	1	2	3	4	5	7	17
Pacing		•	•	•	•	•	•
SQNs used on Normal Flow	•	•	•	•	•	•	•
IDs used on Normal Flow			•				
CLEAR	•			•		•	
SDT	•			•			
RQR				•			
STSN					•		
CRV					•		•
max. RU size Normal Flow 256							
no max. RU size Normal Flow			•				
Usage Options							
Pacing Counts	•					•	•
max. RU size Normal Flow							
Applies to Session:							
SSCP <--> SSCP					•		
SSCP <--> PU							
SSCP <--> LU						•	•
LU <--> LU	•	•	•	•		•	

(b)

	0	2	3	4	5	6	7	17	18	19
Chaining		•	•	•	•	•	•		•	•
Req. Mode (P/S)	I,I	*,D	*,-	*,-	D,D	D,D	*,-	D,D	*,-	*,-
Resp. Mode (P/S)	I,I	*,-	I,I	I,I	*,D	D,D	I,I	D,D	I,I	I,I
DFC Requests:										
CANCEL			•	•			•		•	
SIGNAL			•	•			•		•	
LUSTAT	SLU		SLU	•		SLU	•		•	•
QEC/QC/RELQ				•					•	
SHUTD/SHUTC				•					•	
RSHUTD				•					•	
CHASE				•					•	
QEC/QC				•					•	
BID/RTR				•			•		•	•
SBI/BIS				•			•		•	•
Brackets (P/SLU)		B,F								
Send/RCV Mode	Ctn	FDX	F/F	F/F	FDX	FDX	F/F	FDX	F/F	=/F
SSCP <--> SSCP	•	•			•		•	•		
SSCP <--> PU	•	•			•	•				
SSCP <--> LU				•		•				•
LU <--> LU			•	•					•	

I = Immediate Control Mode
D = Delayed Control Mode
B,F = if Brackets are used:
  PLU is Bidder,
  SLU is First Speaker

Ctn = Half Duplex Contention
F/F = Half Duplex Flip/Flop
FDX = Full Duplex

Fig. 5.2 Summary of profiles:
(a) Transmission Services Profiles
(b) Function Management Profiles

d LU-LU   These are the sessions that are fulfilling the purpose of the network; through them the actual transfer of data between end users can take place.

e PU-PU   Between Physical Units no specific sessions are defined. There is, however, communication possible between PUs that are adjacent, in order to exchange Network Control information. Request Units that are supported are Network Control (NC) RUs, for the management of the Explicit Routes.

The way in which sessions are established depends on the type of session. The SSCP-SSCP sessions will be discussed in detail in Section 7.3. In the remainder of this section, we discuss the start-up of the session that is the most relevant from an end-user's point of view, the LU-LU session. The SSCP-PU and the SSCP-LU sessions are discussed briefly after that, since there is not much difference.

LU-LU session activation   A session between two Logical Units is established when Session Control in one LU (the *Primary*) sends the BIND Request Unit to Session Control in the other LU (the *secondary*) and receives a positive response. Session Control does this at the request of some management function, usually the Logical Unit Services in the LU. This is described in more detail in Section 7.3. Session Control needs to know what the characteristics of the other LU are, so it can build the BIND Request Unit with that information. This is usually communicated from the SSCP in a special Request Unit. The most important information that the BIND contains are proposals for the protocols to be used in the new session. These protocols are specified through the *profiles* for Transmission Control and Data Flow Control. In Fig. 5.2 a summary of these profiles is given. Another example of the information sent to the Primary Logical Unit (PLU) by the SSCP is the key that will be used for the encryption of messages (if cryptography is to be used on the session).

The BIND RU is sent to the destination Session Control, but there a small problem arises. Since the session is not yet established, Path Control cannot deliver the message to the proper half-session. The RU is therefore delivered to a component called *Common Session Control*, which is part of the Physical Unit Services. Common Session Control checks to see whether the destination LU is already in session with the SSCP, since otherwise an LU-LU session would not be allowed, and whether the RU is a BIND. If these conditions are met, a new half-session is created and the BIND RU passed to it.

In the preceding discussion, we have simplified the procedure grossly, in order to concentrate on the important aspects of the establishment of a

75

session. Other aspects, such as the involvement of the Boundary function where the mapping tables for the local addresses must be set up, etc., had to be left out. The reader is referred to the official documentation [5] for these details.

SSCP-PU and SSCP-LU session activation The sessions between the System Services Control Point and the Physical and Logical Units are established in much the same way as the LU-LU sessions. At the level of Session Control, the only difference is that the Primary (in this case, always the SSCP) does not send a BIND RU, but an *Activate Physical Unit* (ACTPU) for the SSCP-PU session or an *Activate Logical Unit* (ACTLU) for the SSCP-LU session. These Request Units are much simpler than the BIND since the sessions with the SSCP do not require complicated protocol agreements. Usually, very few messages will flow on these sessions, if all goes well.

One special characteristic of the ACTPU is that it can be used to specify an Error Recovery (ERP) activation. This is used when a session with a PU has been broken, e.g. after an SSCP failure. When the SSCP comes back to life, it can do an ERP ACTPU in order not to destroy the active state, tables, etc., of the Physical Unit.

Data Traffic activation

When a session is established through the BIND, it is not necessarily immediately available for message exchange. This depends on the profile chosen for Transmission Control. If the profile specifies that the *Start Data Traffic* (SDT) RU will be used, this (Session Control) RU must be sent after BIND to actually open the data flow. The reason for separating this from the BIND is in the recovery possibilities. If a problem occurs on the Normal Flow, it can be recovered using Session Control RUs such as *Set and Test Sequence Number* (STSN). CLEAR is used first to reset the flow and 'clear' it. After CLEAR has been sent, the normal flow can no longer be used, until after the recovery is complete. The SDT RU is used to signal to the secondary LU that the recovery is successful and that the normal flow is open again.

If the profile specifies that SDT will not be used on the session, no recovery is possible, since the flow cannot be reopened after successful recovery.

In the profile summary in Fig. 5.2 it can be seen that LU 6.2 does not use SDT (nor sequence number recovery through STSN).

When a session needs to be terminated, the logical relation between two NAUs must be broken. From a Session Control point of view, it means that resources allocated to the two half-sessions can be freed. Session Control assumes that the conversation as such has come to an end already, such that no more messages or responses are underway. This is handled at the next higher level, Data Flow Control (refer to the next section). When Session Control in the primary NAU is requested to terminate the session, it may—depending on the profiles—first send a CLEAR RU to reset the data traffic state such that no more messages can be sent and then it sends UNBIND. This Request Unit tells the Secondary to free all the resources and terminate the relation. How this is actually done depends on the particular implementation, of course. The positive response to the UNBIND is the very last BIU that flows on the session.

The involvement of higher layers, such as Data Flow Control and Session Services, to prepare for an orderly session termination and to inform the SSCP about the end of the session are discussed in later sections.

5.4 Cryptography support

In certain situations it may be necessary to protect the messages that flow on a session against interference from outside. This can be either *active monitoring*, where somebody actually changes messages, or *passive monitoring*, where somebody gets access to the message content by copying it. In SNA the protection is provided in Transmission Control through encryption of the Request Units. The actual encryption is performed by the Connection Point Manager. The mechanism used is the standard DES algorithm with block chaining. (The reader is referred to the general literature, e.g. [11] for an explanation of the DES algorithm.)

When the session is established, it is agreed via the BIND options whether encryption will be used. This encryption can be *mandatory* (all messages must be encrypted) or *optional* (only selected messages will be encrypted). With optional encryption, the *Enciphered Data Indicator* (EDI) in the Request Header indicates whether a specific message is actually enciphered.

The SNA encryption mechanism is illustrated in Fig. 5.3. For each session a 64-bit key, the *session key*, is selected, as well as a so-called *session seed*, a random 64-bit number. The first eight bytes of the message are exclusively OR-ed with the session seed and the result is encrypted with the session key, using the DES algorithm. The encryption result is placed in the output buffer for transmission and it is also used instead of the seed value to exclusively OR the next eight bytes before these are encrypted and so on. Since the message may not consist of a multiple of eight bytes, it may be necessary to 'pad' the end of the message to get to this multiple. The *Padded Data Indicator* (PDI) in the Request Header indicates whether the message was padded. The last byte of the message contains the number of padding bytes (1–7), including itself.

An important problem in all encryption systems is the management of the encryption keys. These must be exposed as little as possible, even towards session partners. In SNA, each Logical Unit that may use encryption is assigned a Device Key. This Device Key is securely stored in the Logical Unit. In the SSCP the key is also stored, but in an encrypted form, using an SSCP master key. (How the keys are physically stored is implementation-dependent. IBM provides special hardware for the storage of these keys, that cannot be read out without use of the master key.)

Now, when a session must be established between LU-A (primary) and LU-B, the SSCP selects a random key which will be used as the session key for this session only. The session key is encrypted using LU-A's device key and also using LU-B's key. Both encrypted versions of the key are sent to LU-A in the CINIT, together with other protocol information that is necessary for the BIND (Fig. 5.4).

LU-A uses its device key to decrypt the field which contains the session key encrypted with its own device key. This yields the session key. The other field contains the key as it was encrypted using LU-B's key and LU-A can do little with it . It copies the field unchanged into the BIND and sends it to LU-B, which can decrypt it using its own device key. The device keys are only used for this distribution of the session key, so the exposure is minimal. Even LU-A has only 64 bits of plain (the session key) and enciphered data with LU-B's key. Assuming that the DES algorithm could be broken, then 64 bits of plain and enciphered text would certainly not be sufficient!

Both LUs now have the session key, but how do they know that they actually have the *same* key? Something might have gone wrong with the device keys... LU-B therefore selects a 64-bit random number (the Session Seed) which is sent in the BIND response, encrypted with the session key. LU-A decrypts it and inverts the first 4 bytes, which yields the so-called Test Value. This Test Value is again encrypted using the session key. The result is sent to LU-B in the Cryptography Verification

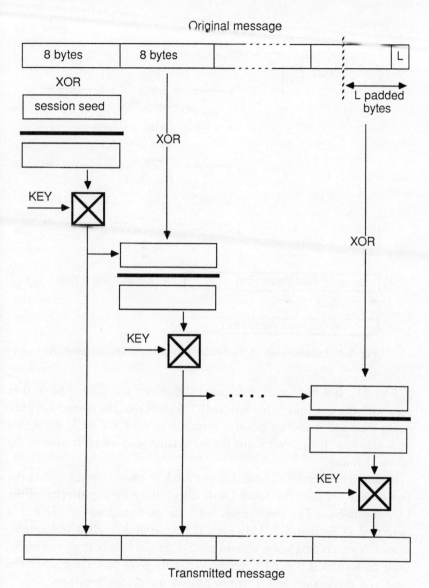

Original message

8 bytes | 8 bytes | | | L

XOR

session seed

L padded bytes

XOR

KEY

XOR

KEY

. . . .

KEY

Transmitted message

Fig. 5.3 The SNA encryption mechanism with block-chaining

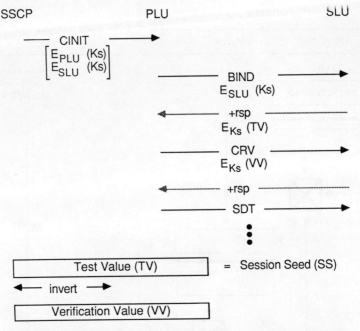

Fig. 5.4 Establishment of the Session Key (Ks) and Session Seed (SS)

(CRV) RU. If B finds after decryption the correct test value (the session seed with the first four bytes inverted), it knows that the correct keys are being used and it sends a positive response to the CRV to A. Both LUs now also have the correct value for the session seed which is used in the block chaining.

It should be mentioned here that this mechanism only synchronizes the session key between the two LUs. It does not verify the identity of the LUs themselves. The mechanism used for that purpose by LU 6.2 is described in Section 8.2. However, if the network itself is not secure, session-level cryptography should always be used since it gives continuous protection. LU 6.2 LU verification only gives protection when the session is established and does not protect from later 'break-ins'.

6 Data Flow Control

6.1 Introduction

In this section, we will focus on the functions of the Data Flow Control Layer. Once more, it must be pointed out that this layer should not be confused with the data *flowrate* control function. That particular function is performed by the pacing mechanism in the Connection Point Manager. The discussion of DFC can be split in two parts:

a The protocols that are related to the Request Units directly. These protocols are enforced through the use of indicators in the Request/Response Headers, i.e. they are strictly RU-related. The major protocols are Request/Response Control Mode, Chaining, Send/Receive Mode, and Brackets.

b The DFC functions that are not strictly RU-related, but more with the general control of each of the (normal) data flows. These functions utilize their own set of Request Units.

Sometimes a combination of the two is used: for example, when an RU-related protocol must be initiated via a specific request. An example is the BID RU, used with the bracket protocol.

6.2 Flow protocols

The Flow Control protocols which are RU-related provide for a hierarchical set of facilities to relate groups of requests and responses together.

At the lowest level, the Request/Response Control Mode protocol sets rules for the relation between the requests and their responses. At the next level, the Chaining protocol allows one to combine a group of RUs flowing in one direction into a 'chain'. Next, the Send/Receive Mode protocol governs the exchange of chains between two half-sessions. Finally, a whole series of such bidirectional exchanges may be grouped together into a so-called 'bracket' (or 'transaction') by the bracket protocol.

The Request/Response Control Mode protocol sets rules for the relation between a Request and its Response. It is closely related to the Response types that can be requested through the Request Header. In summary, they are

- RQN do not send a response
- RQE send a response only in the case of an exception
- RQD always send a response

The following Control Modes exist:

- Request Control Mode
  — Immediate Request Mode
  — Delayed Request Mode
- Response Control Mode
  — Immediate Response Mode
  — Delayed Response Mode

When the *Immediate Request Mode* is used on a flow, the sender may send several Requests that ask for Exception Response (RQE) only. The sender may, however, send only one request that asks for a Definite Response (RQD). After that, no more requests (of any type) may be sent on that flow until the requested response is received. On should realize that this is not synchronized with the Pacing Mechanism at the next lower level (CPMGR): when a series of requests (all RQE) is being sent, the actual transmission may temporarily be halted because of the pacing. In that case, the Isolated Pacing Response can be used to resume the transmission. This is illustrated in a (hypothetical) sequence in Fig. 6.1.

When the *Delayed Request Mode* is used on a flow, as many requests (of any type) can be sent on that flow as the sender wants, without waiting for a response. It involves more logic in the sending Logical Unit to correlate a received response to all outstanding requests, particularly when the Delayed Response Mode is used as well (see below).

The *Immediate Response Mode* forces the half-session to return responses (if there are any) in the same sequence as the requests were received in. This can be used to get an acknowledgement for a series of requests for which Exception Response only (RQE) was asked. In such a case, the last request of the series would request a Definite Response (RQD). When that response is finally received, the sender knows that no more Exception Responses to previous requests can come in, since they must have been received before the Definite Response.

In the *Delayed Response Mode*, a half-session may return responses in

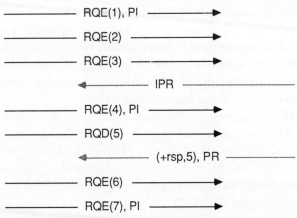

Fig. 6.1 Effect of Pacing and Immediate Request Mode. The flow of data can be temporarily stopped when either an expected Pacing Response or an expected positive response has not yet arrived. The two are not synchronized. (In the example, one-stage pacing with n = 3 is used)
[PI = Pacing Indicator, PR = Pacing Response, IPR = Isolated Pacing Response]

any order, independent of the order in which the requests were originally received. Obviously, this Response Mode could cause problems when Requests for Exception Response are used in the flow: there would never be any guarantee that no odd negative response might still come in. There is one exception to this rule—the response to the Data Flow Control Request Unit CHASE.

The CHASE Request is used by an NAU to verify that all responses that could be on their way, are received. The RU is sent on the normal flow and must be kept in sequence with other requests, even when the Delayed Response Mode is used. Thus, when an NAU sends a series of requests that specify Exception Response, the CHASE RU can be used to verify that the series was received correctly. When the response to the CHASE is returned, no other (exception) responses can be on their way, independent of the Response Mode.

Chaining

The chaining protocol is used to group related Request Units as one entity, the *chain*. This chain is then by definition the basic unit of recovery in the session. It is also the basic unit of 'concern' in some of the other protocols: Send/Receive Mode and Brackets. An example of the use of chains is the printing of output: each line of output is sent as a separate RU, but all RUs for one page belong together, so they are chained. Now, when a problem occurs (e.g. the paper breaks), the whole chain is recovered; that is, after the problem is repaired printing starts with the first RU of the chain at the beginning of the page.

The use of the chaining mechanism is indicated in the Request Header. Similar to the Mapping Field in the Transmission Header, there are two indicators, BC (Begin of Chain) and EC (End of Chain). When both indicators are on, the RU in question is a Single-RU Chain.

There are special rules relating to the type of response that may be requested for a chain (Fig. 6.2):

a   All requests may be marked No Response (RQN). In this case, no response will be generated for any RU in the chain and the chain itself is called a *No-Response Chain*.
b   All requests may be marked *Exception Response only* (RQE). In this case, a response will only be generated for an RU in which an error condition exists. The remainder of the chain will then be purged (without further responses being generated). When no error at all is detected, no response will be generated. This type of chain is called the *Exception Response Chain*.
c   All requests in the chain, except the last one, may be marked 'Exception Response only' (RQE) and the last one 'Definite Response' (RQD). In this case, an Exception Response is returned when an error is detected in an RU (and the rest of the chain is then purged). When no error is detected, a positive response is generated for the last RU in the chain. This chain is called a *Definite Response Chain*. It is the most common type of chain and normally used in conjunction with the Immediate Request Mode protocol: the response to the last RU is then the acknowledgement of the total chain.

Note that it is not allowed to request a Definite Response for any RU but the last in a chain.

The CANCEL RU is used in the Chaining protocol to terminate a failing chain. When an NAU generates a negative response to a request in a chain, it will enter a 'purge' state and discard all other RUs that come in until the End of Chain indication is received. This EC indicator may be set in a normal Request Header, but it can also be set in the Request Header that accompanies a CANCEL command. The effect of the CANCEL is that that part of the chain that was received *before* the error

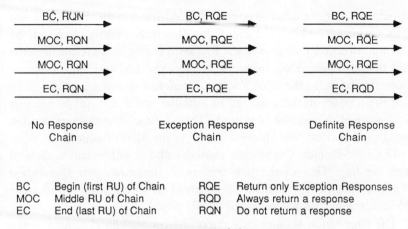

BC, RQN	BC, RQE	BC, RQE
MOC, RQN	MOC, RQE	MOC, RQE
MOC, RQN	MOC, RQE	MOC, RQE
EC, RQN	EC, RQE	EC, RQD

| No Response Chain | Exception Response Chain | Definite Response Chain |

BC	Begin (first RU) of Chain	RQE	Return only Exception Responses
MOC	Middle RU of Chain	RQD	Always return a response
EC	End (last RU) of Chain	RQN	Do not return a response

Fig. 6.2 Three types of chain response

occurred is also purged. An example of the use of CANCEL is given in Fig. 6.4.

Send/Receive Modes

Although the session between two Network Addressable Units is basically a Full-Duplex channel, it may be necessary to limit the operation of the session to Half-Duplex. An example can be a Logical Unit serving a terminal end-user and having only one buffer, which must be used for both send *and* receive operations. If it were involved in a Full-Duplex session, a message might arrive while the terminal operator was keying in a message. Then the message would overlay the contents of the buffer and the operator would have to re-type everything again. (With the risk that it was going to be overlaid again!)

The limited procedure is the Half-Duplex procedure, which can be selected for the session when the session is started (through the BIND Request Unit). SNA provides for two types of Half-Duplex operation: Half-Duplex Flip/Flop and Half-Duplex Contention.

In the Half-Duplex Flip/Flop mode, one of the Logical Units is in the Send state, the other in Receive state. It is the responsibility of the Sender to indicate that the other may go into Send state, while the Sender will then go into Receive state (Fig. 6.3). This indication is given via the Change Direction Indicator in the Request Header. Since it indicates the end of the transmission from the Sender, the End-of-Chain indicator must also be on in the same Request Header, if chains are used.

It is necessary in this protocol to initialize which LU will be the first sender when the session is started. This is done at initialization time, using the Function Management profile in the BIND Request.

The Half-Duplex Contention protocol allows either half-session to start sending. One of the half-sessions is designated the *Contention Winner*, the other the *Contention Loser*. (This specification is also made through the FM profile at session BIND time.)

The Contention Winner may reject any (normal flow) request that it receives while in the Send state (Fig. 6.4). The Loser must queue any request it receives while it is in the Send state. It terminates its current chain, either through End-of-Chain or via the CANCEL Request Unit when it receives the reject response. Next, it de-queues any requests that were queued while it was in the Send state. At the end of the chain, both half-sessions return to the contention state. The winner may avoid this after it has detected the contention, by using the Change Direction Indicator on the last RU in its chain, which allows the Loser to send. This is particularly useful within a bracket (see below). If CD is not on in the last RU of the chain, both sides return to the contention state.

Brackets

As indicated in the introduction to this chapter, the highest level of ordering normal flow requests in a session is the Bracket protocol. With this protocol, it is possible to group a series of exchanges of RUs (or chains) in both directions. This capability is needed when each half-session may initiate a new transaction. A simple example is the case of a remote station that has both a card reader and an operator keyboard attached to the secondary Logical Unit. If the primary LU would send a request to the secondary to read a card and at the same time the operator would key in some request, the primary would interpret the operator-keyed message as the result of the read operation (Fig. 6.5).

The Bracket protocol makes it mandatory for each half-session to use the *Begin Bracket Indicator* on the first request of a new 'transaction'. Once a bracket is started, both half-sessions may only send requests and responses that belong to that bracket. A bracket is terminated by the *End Bracket Indicator* (EBI, pre-LU 6.2) or the *Conditional End-of-Bracket*

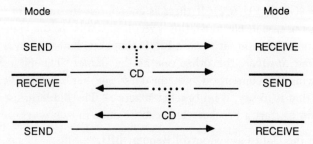

Fig. 6.3 Examples of Half-Duplex Flip/Flop

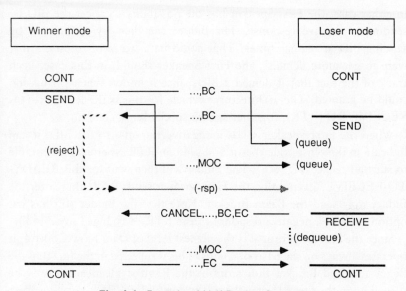

Fig. 6.4 Example of Half-Duplex Contention

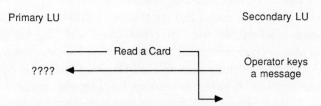

Fig. 6.5 Ships that pass in the night

Indicator (CEBI, LU 6.2). If there is contention to start a bracket (as would be the case in Fig. 6.6), this is resolved similar to the Half-Duplex Contention resolution: at session BIND time, one half-session is defined as the *First Speaker*, the other one as the *Bidder*. The First Speaker always wins the contention, i.e. the First Speaker can always start a bracket (that is to say, if no bracket is active). The Bidder must request permission to start a bracket. This can be done in two ways:

a Using the Data Flow Control Request BID.

b Just sending an RU with the Begin Bracket (BB) Indicator on. This is called an 'implied BID', and it is used mostly when the probability of rejection is low. The Bidder must be prepared, however, to have its request rejected, i.e. that it must resend the chain.

In either case, the First Speaker has the possibility to reject the BID by sending a negative response. The Bidder can then try again later by sending BID at regular times. That could be a waste of resources if it were to get more denials. The First Speaker should, in this case, keep track of the fact that it denied a BID, since it knows when permission could be granted. The architectural vehicle for this is the READY-TO-RECEIVE RU (RTR), together with a special sense code.

When the First Speaker sends a negative response to the BID, it can indicate in the sense code that it will send an RTR when it is acceptable to start a bracket (Fig. 6.6). The Bidder will then wait for this READY-TO-RECEIVE. Eventually, the First Speaker sends RTR, thereafter the Bidder may send the Begin Bracket. Note that the Bidder still has the option to send a negative response to the RTR ('I changed my mind').

Since the bracket protocol is the highest level of Data Flow Control, it operates always on the basis of chains. This is reflected in the fact that the Begin and End Bracket Indicators in the Request Header can only be turned on in the *first* RU of a chain (the one with the BC), but take effect only at the time the last one in the chain is processed. The LU 6.2 CEBI can only be used on the *last* RU of a chain (refer to Section 8.2). At what moment exactly all the bracket-state changes take place depends on several factors, such as the type of response requested and the Bracket Initiation and/or Termination rule selected.

From the discussion in this and the previous section, it should be clear that, when brackets are used in conjunction with the Half-Duplex Flip/Flop Mode, synchronization between the two half-sessions would be required. Actually in this situation Half-Duplex Flip/Flop is only used *inside* the bracket. Between successive brackets the mode is HDX-Contention, the Contention Winner also being the First Speaker. This is the protocol used by LU 6.2.

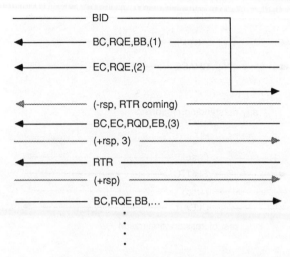

Fig. 6.6 Use of BID and Ready-to-Receive

6.3 Data Flow Control Request Units

As discussed in the introduction to this chapter, the Data Flow Control functions in the LUs may also communicate through the use of their own Request Units. This is the case when the communication is not directly related to a particular Function Management RU, but to the state of the session. Some of these DFC Request Units will be discussed below. For the others, the reader is referred to [5 and 12]. It should be noted that LU 6.2 does not use most of the Data Flow Control RUs. This can be seen from Fig. 5.2 and Fig. 8.1.

Quiesce When one half-session wants the other to temporarily stop sending RUs, it can use the QUIESCE AT END OF CHAIN (QEC) command. The receiving half-session is allowed to complete the current chain and then send the reply QUIESCE COMPLETE. Thereafter, it can no longer send on the *normal* flow, although it can still receive on that flow. When the other half-session wants to open the flow again, it sends RELEASE QUIESCE.

Note that all these commands, although they affect the normal flow, are carried in the expedited flow.

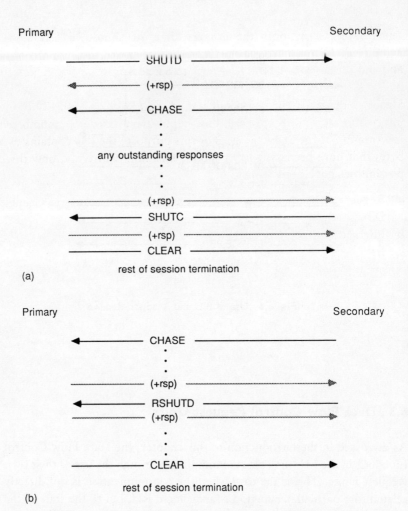

Fig. 6.7 Possible end-of-session sequences: (*a*) Primary initiated and (*b*) Secondary initiated

Shutdown The series of SHUTDOWN commands

- SHUTDOWN (SHUTD)
- SHUTDOWN COMPLETE (SHUTC)
- REQUEST SHUTDOWN (RSHUTD)

is used to prepare for session termination. When the primary NAU wants to terminate the session, it can send SHUTD to the secondary NAU (Fig. 6.7). The secondary does the necessary end-of-session processing (e.g. sending CHASE to return any outstanding responses) and then sends SHUTC to notify the primary that the shutdown action was completed. The primary can then complete its end of session processing and end the session (UNBIND—refer to Section 5.3).

Signal The SIGNAL RU can be used as a means of transmitting information on the expedited flow (equivalent to the Unnumbered Information at the SDLC level). For this purpose, the RU contains two bytes that have been assigned a specific meaning. Currently, only three possibilities have been defined:

a   Request to Send (used in Half-Duplex session to request a Change Direction).
b   Intervention required.
c   User code (i.e. there are two additional bytes that have a user defined meaning).

7 NAU services

The description in this section is based on the pre-LU 6.2 version of SNA. With LU 6.2 a number of things have been defined differently, which makes an integrated discussion difficult. LU 6.2 is therefore treated completely separately in Section 8.2.

7.1 Introduction

The highest layer in SNA is the Function Management or, formally, the Network Addressable Unit (NAU) Services Layer. Actually, this layer consists of two layers: Function Management Data (FMD) Services and NAU Services Managers.

The FMD Services perform a routing for the FMD Request Units to the appropriate NAU Services Manager that can provide the requested function. The FMD Services can be different for each half-session in which a Network Addressable Unit is engaged, whereas the NAU Services Managers are responsible for the operation of the NAU as a whole. In other words, one could say that the NAU Services Managers Layer contains all functions available to an NAU and the FMD Services Layer subsets those for a particular half-session.

The NAU Services can broadly be classified in two areas:

a End-user Services used in LU-LU sessions. They interface end-users to each other.
b Network Services used in sessions between SSCPs and between an SSCP and the PUs and LUs. These Network Services are distributed among the SSCPs and the PUs and LUs. In the Logical Unit, for instance, they interface the end-user to the functions that control the network operation.

7.2 End-user Services

In the End-user Services, we find all those functions that are aimed at assisting the end-users in the manipulation of data. This may restrict itself to the presentation or layout of the data, which is normally found when application program end-users communicate with terminal-type end-users, e.g. a display station, but also a remote printer, etc. In that case, the End-user Services are called *Session Presentation Services*. In other cases, the role of the End-user Services may be more complicated, allowing communication between different application programs, including the use of committed checkpoints, etc. The End-user Services are then called *Application-to-Application Services*.

The main vehicles with which the presentation of data can be controlled in an SNA network are the *Function Management Header* (FMH) and the *String Control Byte* (SCB).

Function Management Headers

The Function Management Headers can be used to specify the use of special codes for the presentation of the data. They can also be used to select a particular destination for the device, i.e. the particular end-user if the Logical Unit serves more than one end-user.

FM Header-1 is defined to control a multi-device terminal. An example is a workstation for Remote Job Entry Applications, where several devices are served by one Logical Unit, or a station for word processing. The FMH-1 specifies such things as to which medium the data is going, where the medium can be a specific device, a data set on a device or a data stream. When multiple destinations are possible in an NAU, a destination cannot only be selected with FMH-1, but also suspended to allow temporary selection of another destination, resumed and terminated. A destination stacking mechanism is therefore defined in the FMD Services that interpret the FMH-1. It should be noted that it is agreed, via the BIND Presentation Services Profile when the session is established, whether Function Management Headers will be used. But even when it is agreed that they can be used in the session, this does not mean that they will be present in every Request Unit. In a chain, for example, only the first RU may carry an FM Header. The presence of the FMH is indicated with the Format Indicator in the Request Header (refer to Section 5.2). An example sequence of the use of FMH-1 for destination selection is given in Fig. 7.1. In this sequence the first RU in the first chain carries a type 1 Function Management Header, which selects a printer. All following RUs in this chain go to the same destination, i.e. the printer. The next chain does not carry an FMH-1, but since the printer is the *active* destination, this chain also goes to the printer. The third chain is a single-RU chain, with an FMH-1 that suspends the selection of the printer. In such an RU, no data is allowed. The next chain is again a single-RU chain, now with an FMH-1 that specifies Begin/End selection of the operator console, i.e. this chain, but only this chain, goes to the console. Finally, the next RU begins a new chain and its FMH-1 specifies that the printer selection must be resumed.

Another aspect of FMH-1 is that it can be used to indicate whether the data in the Request Unit is compressed or compacted. *Compression* means that repetitive characters in the data are recognized by the sender and replaced by a certain code. The receiver must analyze these codes and generate the required number of characters. *Compaction* is a technique in which characters that are very frequent are given a new code that is shorter than the normal 8 bits. In the SNA compaction, this new code is always 4 bits, with two of these characters packed in one byte. The control code that is used for both compression and compaction is the *String Control Byte* (SCB). The presence of SCBs in the data is indicated in the FMH-1. If they are present, of course all RUs following that FMH-1 must be completely described using SCBs (Fig. 7.2). If the sender wants to transmit data without compression or compaction to the same destination, it must insert another FMH-1 and use the Continue option for the destination selection.

Function Management Header-2 is used for operations on the data that are destination dependent. These include Data Management operations like the creation and deletion of data sets (files) and the manipulation of records in these data sets. Another example of the use of FMH-2 is the selection of special forms, number of copies, etc., on printer devices. Translate tables for compaction (see above) can also be sent with FMH-2 if they apply to one destination only. Where they apply to *all* destinations in a Logical Unit, Function Management Header-3 must be used instead.

Other Function Management Headers can be used for the communication between programmed processes that are end-users to the communicating Logical Units, such as two transaction processing subsystems that distribute the processing of a particular transaction. For this purpose, the Headers 4 through 8, 10 and 12 have been defined. A detailed discussion of their use is outside the scope of this book. For LU 6.2, only Function Management Headers 5, 7 and 12 (and a variation of FMH-10) are used. This is explained further in Section 8.2.

Another aspect of the presentation of data is the data stream that is used to carry the actual data and to control its presentation on a physical medium such as a printer or a display. In SNA, two data streams have

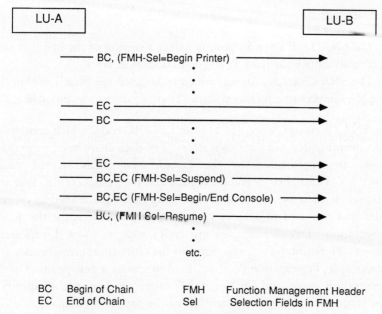

BC   Begin of Chain   FMH   Function Management Header
EC   End of Chain   Sel   Selection Fields in FMH

Fig. 7.1 Usage of Function Management Headers

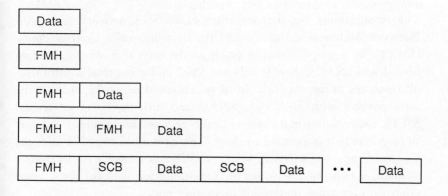

FMH   Function Management Header
SCB   String Control Byte

Fig. 7.2 Structure of the Request Unit: use of Function Management Headers and String Control Bytes

been defined:

a   The SNA 3270 Data Stream, which is a version of the one that was already in use for IBM 3270 (-like) display devices.

b   The SNA Character String, which is designed specifically within the SNA context to cover as wide a variety of devices as possible.

The SNA Character String (SCS) is an EBCDIC code, which consists of SCS control codes and data characters. The data characters, or *graphic codes*, are represented by the hexadecimal codes in the range $X'40' - X'FE'$. Their definition depends on the particular alphabet and national character set used. The remaining codes are defined as control codes that are used to achieve certain control functions for the actual presentation. Trivial examples are codes such as 'New Line/Carrier Return', 'Horizontal Tab', etc. Some of the more complicated codes are, for example, Presentation Position, used to specify a new position in the presentation space, and Set Vertical Format, which is used to specify a new layout in the vertical dimension of the presentation space, such as page length, top and bottom margins, etc. They may use more than 1 byte, to allow for parameters. Figure 7.3 gives a summary table of the currently defined control codes for SCS. For a detailed explanation of these codes, the reader is referred to the appropriate IBM literature [20].

7.3   Network Services

The responsibility for the operation of an SNA network rests with Network Addressable Units called the *System Service Control Points* (SSCPs). In a simple network (such as the ones that were defined in SNA-1 and SNA-2), there is only one SSCP and it has total control over all resources in the network. In more advanced networks, such as the ones possible with SNA/ACF (SNA-3 and up), there can be several SSCPs, each residing in a Physical Unit type 5 and responsible for the set of resources that is assigned to them. These resources together form the *Control Domain* of an SSCP. Since an SSCP is responsible for its control domain, it must have a means of communication with the resources it controls, even when they reside in another node.

SNA requires therefore that when an SSCP owns a resource, it must also own the *physical path* towards that resource. For that reason, the Physical Units type 4 (i.e. the normal subarea nodes) and the Transmission Groups can be owned by more than one SSCP—the *shared ownership* concept. It is illustrated in Fig. 7.4, where SSCP1 owns

Abbreviation	Code (EBCDIC)	SCS Control Function
BS	16	Backspace
BEL(STP)	2F	Bell (Stop)
CR	0D	Carriage Return
CU1	1B	Customer Use 1
CU3	3B	Customer Use 3
DC1	11	Device Control 1
DC2	12	Device Control 2
DC3	13	Device Control 3
DC4	3C	Device Control 4
ENP	14	Enable Presentation
EBS(NBS)	36	Expanded Backspace (Numeric Backspace)
ESP(NSP)	E1	Expanded Space (Numeric Space)
FF(PE)	0C	Form Feed (Page End)
GE	08...	Graphic Escape
HT	05	Horizontal Tab
IT	39	Indent Tab
IR	33	Index Return
INP	24	Inhibit Presentation
IFS	1C	Interchange File Separator
IGS	1D	Interchange Group Separator
IRS	1E	Interchange Record Separator
IUS	1F	Interchange Unit Separator
LF(INX)	25	Line Feed (Index)
NL(CRE)	15	New Line (Carrier Return)
NUL	00	Null
PP	34...	Presentation Position
POC	17...	Program Operator Communication
RPT	0A	Repeat
RFF(RPE)	3A	Required Form Feed (Required Page End)
RNL(RCR)	06	Required New Line (Required Carrier Return)
RSP	41	Required Space
SSR	0450	Secure String ID Reader
SLP	04C1	Select Left Platen
SME	046n	Select Magnetic Encoder
SRP	04C2	Select Right Platen
SA	28...	Set Attribute
SC1	2BD1 Cn	Set Chain Image
SGEA	2BC8	Set Graphic Error Action
SHF	2BC1	Set Horizontal Format
SLD	2BC6	Set Line Density
SPD	2BD2 29	Set Print Density
STT	2BD1 Cn	Set Translation Table
SVF	2BC2	Set Vertical Format
SI	0F	Shift In
SO	0E	Shift Out
SOF	2BC3	Start of Format
SBS	38	Subscript
SUB	3F	Substitute
SPS	09	Superscript
SW	2A	Switch
SHY	CA	Syllable Hyphen
TRN	35...	Transparent
UBS	1A	Unit Backspace
VCS	04...	Vertical Channel Select
VT	0B	Vertical Tab
WUS	23	Word Underscore

Note: Functions with ellipses extending their 1-byte code (i.e. those that have the expression '...' following them) have one or more parameters and are multiple-character code points

Fig. 7.3 SNA Character String Codes

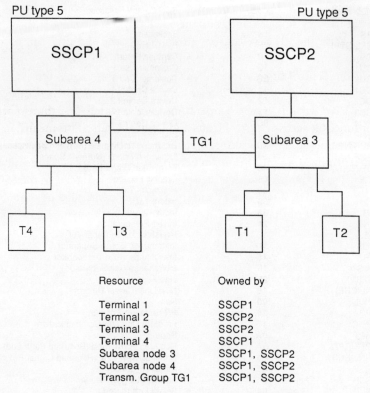

Resource	Owned by
Terminal 1	SSCP1
Terminal 2	SSCP2
Terminal 3	SSCP2
Terminal 4	SSCP1
Subarea node 3	SSCP1, SSCP2
Subarea node 4	SSCP1, SSCP2
Transm. Group TG1	SSCP1, SSCP2

Fig. 7.4 Sharing of resources by several SSCPs

Terminal T1 in Subarea 3, but SSCP2 owns Terminal T2 in the same subarea. The subarea node 3 must thus be shared. Since SSCP2 also owns Terminal T3 in Subarea 4, subarea node 4 is shared *and also* Transmission Group TG1 that connects the two subareas.

In order to be able to control the resources in its domain, the SSCP communicates with the 'local' authorities, the *Physical Unit Services* and the *Logical Unit Services*.

Physical Unit Services reside in every node in the network. They form the function responsible for the resources in that node. That is, when the SSCP wants action for or from a particular resource in that node (e.g. a link attached to it), it requests the action through its session with Physical Unit Services.

A similar situation applies to the Logical Unit Services: they are present in every Logical Unit, and the SSCP can control the LU through a session with the LU Services, or, alternatively, the end-user can request services from the SSCP through the Logical Unit Services.

For the control of resources in other domains, the SSCP must rely on the cooperation of other SSCPs (see later). The concept for the control of an SNA Network is one of cooperating SSCPs, which 'distribute' part of their function across Physical Units and Logical Units. This means, in the case of a one-domain network, that the control of network operation is fully centralized. In multi-domain networks, this control is shared among the SSCPs. In these networks, the resources can be assigned to the SSCPs as the network designer sees fit and they are then controlled by that SSCP only. However, if that SSCP fails, the resources can be dynamically taken over by another SSCP. There is no architectural concept of a 'master' SSCP that takes priority over the others. It is however possible during the definition of an SNA network to allocate all resources outside the type 5 PUs to only one node, but no others. Effectively one has then created a network with a 'master' SSCP.

System Services Control Point

A System Services Control Point provides Network Services to other Network Addressable Units (NAUs) in its control domain and it requests these services from them. For the communication with the other NAUs, a set of *Network Services Request Units* has been defined.

These requests flow on the sessions between the SSCP and the other NAUs. This means that, before any function can be performed in the domain, the SSCP must establish sessions with all NAUs involved. These sessions (a form of 'control channels') are usually established when the network is activated and they remain active for the 'life' of the network.

The Network Services that the SSCP can provide or request are currently defined as:

a *Configuration Services*. These have to do with the physical configuration of the network. The function is used to configure the network and to modify it if required.

b *Session Services*. These support the activation of sessions between Logical Units.

c *Management Services*. These assist in the management of the network. In early SNA publications [5] these were called Maintenance and Management Services. In current publications [21], however, the name Management Services is used exclusively.

SSCPs communicate with each other and with Physical and Logical Unit Services via sessions. The messages (RUs) on these sessions are usually structured (formatted) in a predefined way. The Request Header indicates that the RU is formatted through the Format Indicator, similar to the Function Management Headers. In Fig. 7.5 the basic layout of the Network Services RU is given. Further layout depends on the particular RU. This layout of Network Services RUs can be found in [12].

For the Management Services, a new RU has recently been defined, which uses a self-descriptive layout. This NMVT (Network Management Vector Transport) RU is very important in the SNA Network Management architecture. Its basic difference with the other RUs is that it does not have a predefined format. It is encoded according to a certain, more or less self-descriptive scheme which is more flexible. It is based upon the definition of *major vectors* and *subvectors*, a scheme similar to the General Data Stream variables which are discussed in Chapter 8. All network management functions that were not covered with the RUs originally defined, are now described using NMVT. As Fig. 7.5 shows, the RU contains a major vector, which starts with a two-byte length field, followed by a two-byte key. This key defines the particular management function to be provided. The actual specification of the function and the relevant data is carried in one or more subvectors. The subvectors in turn also start with a length field and a key identifying the subvector. Some of the subvectors are quite unique for the major vector in which they appear, others may appear in several major vectors. These are called *common subvectors*. They carry such general information as date, SNA addresses, etc. The role of the NVMT is further discussed on page 111.

We should also mention here that Physical Unit 2.1 is again a special case. Since it was conceived as a Physical Unit that could operate in a 'stand-alone' environment (i.e. two PUs 2.1 linked together), the concept of a *System* Services Control Point does not apply. PU 2.1 has its own Control Point (also called the Peripheral Node Control Point) that is responsible for the node and its resources. It contains Session Services, Configuration Services and the Address Space Manager (Section 4.5). These services have local significance only. Their real function becomes apparent in Advanced Program-to-Program Networking (APPN), which is discussed in Chapter 11. When a PU 2.1 node is attached to a major network (through a Boundary Node), it operates like a regular PU 2.0 with respect to the major network, i.e. control is shared between the SSCP and the PNCP.

In the following sections we will discuss the three types of Network Services for an SSCP controlled network in more detail.

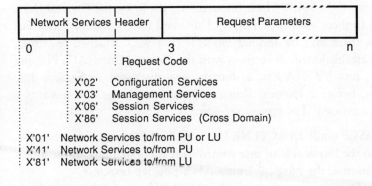

(a)

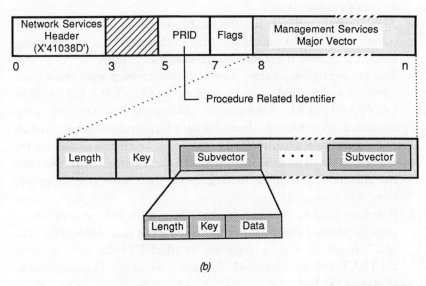

(b)

Fig. 7.5 Layout of the Network Services Request Unit: (*a*) general type and (*b*) Network Management Vector Transport (NMVT)

Configuration Services in the SSCP are responsible for the resources in the domain of the SSCP. These resources are the links, the Physical Units attached to them with their Logical Units and their outgoing links. For each link there may be another Physical Unit with attached resources, etc. The establishment of sessions with the Physical Units (ACTPU) and Logical Units (ACTLU) in a domain was discussed in Section 5.3. However, before a Physical Unit can be activated, the link towards it must be activated. The typical sequence is

1   The SSCP sends an ACTLNK (Activate Link) Configuration Services RU to the Physical Unit that controls the requested link. If the link is operational, the Physical Unit sends a positive response.

2   The SSCP next sends a CONTACT RU to the Physical Unit, specifying the network address of the node that must be contacted. The Physical Unit knows the link-station address of that node from its configuration data.

3   The Physical Unit instructs the local link station to poll the remote station and after a successful XID exchange and a mode-setting SDLC command, the stations have link-level contact.

4   The Physical Unit informs the SSCP that contact with the remote station has been established by sending the CONTACTED RU. The CONTACTED RU also indicates whether the Physical Unit in the contacted node must be loaded with its control program. Not all nodes have local program load capabilities, and if that is the case the remote node responds with the SDLC response RIM (Request Initialization). If remote loading is not necessary, the procedure continues with step 7.

5   If remote loading is necessary, the SSCP must have a copy of the required control program (part of the network generation task). The SSCP sends it with a sequence of IPLINITIAL, one or more IPLTEXT and an IPLFINAL Request Unit to the Physical Unit in charge of the link.

6   The Physical Unit sends the load module to the adjacent station using the SDLC command SIM (Set Initialization Mode) and several I-frames to transfer the program code. (Architecturally, UI frames must be used.) The sequence is terminated with SNRM and a UA response.

7   Now that contact with the remote node is established and the control program is present, the session between the SSCP and the Physical Unit can be activated. The SSCP sends ACTPU and the Physical Unit responds with a positive response.

8   If the new node also contains Logical Units, the SSCP will now send
    ACTLU to each of them.

The procedure can be repeated for all links and Physical Units attached
to the newly attached node and so on, for all the Physical Units in the
domain of the SSCP.
   Other Configuration Services include the control over switched connections, i.e. when nodes dynamically attach to a node, and the dynamic
address management needed for parallel sessions (Section 2.1) and for
Network Interconnection (Chapter 9).

Session Services

In this section we will first discuss the functions of the SSCP from a
one-domain viewpoint. Then, we expand the concept to multi-domain
services.

Single-Domain Session Services   In Fig. 7.6, the activation of a session
between two Logical Units is shown. Both Logical Units are already in
session with the SSCP. Assume that Logical Unit B represents a type-
writer terminal and Logical Unit A some kind of application program.
When the terminal end-user types in 'Logon A', this message is interpreted by the Logical Unit Services function in Logical Unit B. These
services represent the Services Manager in LU-B for the (SSCP,B) session.
A message is created for the SSCP, to request a session with Logical Unit
A. The philosophy is that LU-B must ask this from the SSCP since LU-B
does not yet know whether LU-A is active or what its address is. The
Network Services command that flows on the (SSCP,B) session is
INITSELF. The parameters in this message indicate the name of the
requested LU (i.e. 'A') and some information about the requesting LU
('B'). The message is interpreted by the SSCP (Network Services) and the
necessary checks are made: Is B an acceptable LU? Is A active? And so
on.
   If all checks are satisfactory, the SSCP sends a message on its (SSCP,A)
session to the Logical Unit Services component in A. This message,
CINIT (B), indicates that a session is requested by Logical Unit B and
that A should start the session. For that purpose, the CINIT request also
contains the network address of B, and other information about B that
was in the SSCP's tables. That information is used by A to build the
BIND request. The BIND request flows on the (not yet existing) session
(A,B) and it is sent to the Session Control (SC) component of the newly
assigned TCE(A,B). If all the session parameters that are suggested by A

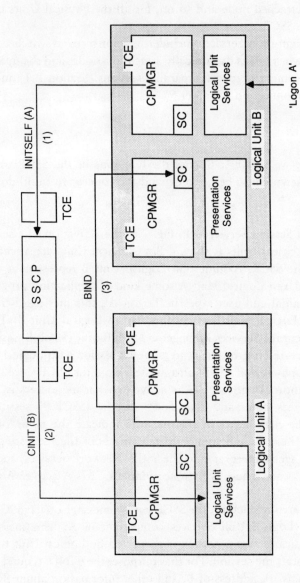

Fig. 7.6 LU-LU session activation

via the BIND are acceptable to B, B sends a positive response back to A. The session is now established, and A sends a *notification* RU to the SSCP (SESSION STARTED) to inform the SSCP of the success of the BIND.

In this example, the role of Common Session Control (see page 75) is left out, since the purpose here is to emphasize the Session Services requests INITSELF and CINIT.

If the secondary Logical Unit sends a negative response to the BIND, the primary informs the SSCP through the BIND FAILURE (BINDF) RU, which includes a reason code to explain why the BIND failed. To close the triangle, the SSCP informs the secondary through the NET-WORK SERVICES PROCEDURE ERROR (NSPE) RU of the failure. This is necessary, even where the secondary caused the BIND to fail, since the services manager in LU-B has received a positive response to the INITSELF and is thus expecting that the session will be set up. The NSPE tells it, therefore, that the session will not be established.

In some very simple networks, e.g. two Physical Units type 2 connected directly, there is no SSCP in the full sense, i.e. the Control Points in the PUs will perform an SSCP-like function. The session between the two Logical Units can then be initiated by either one via the BIND, without a CINIT from an SSCP. It is then not known, however, what profiles, etc., to use since that information is normally in the SSCP's database and supplied via CINIT. In this particular situation, the BIND is *negotiable*, i.e. the secondary may modify some of the parameters through its response to the BIND (Fig. 7.7). The negotiable BIND is also used on sessions between LUs that support program-to-program communication (LU type 6 and 6.2, see below). This makes a more dynamic choice of the parameters possible than would be the case if all parameters were held by the SSCP.

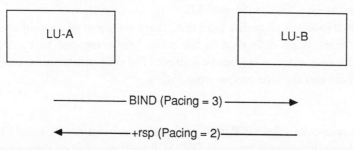

Fig. 7.7 Negotiated BIND. Some of the session parameters may be changed in the response to the BIND. Here, the pacing count that was suggested by the Primary is changed

Cross-Domain Session Services   The Logical Units in an SNA network should not be aware of whether they are part of a single-domain or a multi-domain network. They communicate for session services only with the SSCP that owns them. If they engage in a cross-domain session, they should see exactly the same conversation as described above for a single domain. The SSCPs involved will handle everything that has to do with the multi-domain aspects. It is therefore necessary that the SSCP's have sessions established between them, before any cross-domain activity can take place. This session establishment works in much the same way as the session establishment between the SSCPs and other Network Addressable Units. The Session Control component of Transmission Control is here again responsible for the actual session set-up. The Request Unit for this case is the *Activate Cross-Domain Resource Manager* (ACTCDRM).

Now let us look at the establishment of a session between two LUs which are in different domains. In Fig. 7.8, a Logical Unit *BETA* in the domain of SSCP *B* wants a session with LU *ALPHA* in the domain of SSCP (Cross-Domain Resource Manager) *A*. As in a single-domain network, an INITSELF request is sent to SSCP *B*. This request specifies, among other things, that LU *BETA* cannot play the primary role. *B* analyses the request and finds that *ALPHA* is not in its own domain, but is owned by *A*. Therefore, a request, the *Cross-Domain Initialize* (CDINIT), is sent to SSCP *A*. This request also indicates that LU *BETA* will be secondary in the session and another RU is sent, the *Cross-Domain Control Initialize* (CDCINIT), which contains the information about *BETA* that *A* must know. *A* then builds the CINIT (that is, if *ALPHA* is capable of being primary) and sends it to *ALPHA*. *ALPHA* sends in the normal way a BIND to *BETA*, whose address was contained in the CDCINIT and CINIT, and *BETA* responds with a positive response if the BIND is acceptable. *ALPHA* tells *A* about the positive result through the *Session Started* RU, and *A* in its turn tells *B* with the *Cross-Domain Session Started* RU.

It is important to realize here that, from the point of view of the two LUs, there is no difference in the procedure compared to the single-domain case which was discussed above. The only difference is conversation between the two cooperating SSCPs.

SSCP take-over   An SSCP may lose its sessions with the PUs and LUs in its domain for several reasons. The SSCP itself may fail or somewhere in the Path Control network a failure may occur that results in the deactivation of the Explicit Routes and Virtual Routes on which the

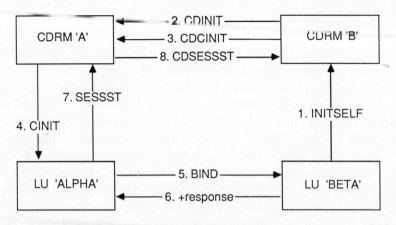

Fig. 7.8 Cross-domain session activation. (All responses, except that to the BIND, have been omitted to simplify the diagram)

sessions were carried. If such a failure occurs, it does not automatically mean that existing LU-LU sessions are failing as well. As long as the Virtual Routes supporting those sessions remain available, these sessions can go on. A typical example is the case where a host computer with an SSCP goes down. With it also, all the Logical Units in that host (application programs) go down. LUs in the domain of this SSCP, but outside the host, that have sessions with LUs in other domains, may continue their sessions. Actually, they are only aware of the loss of their sessions with the SSCP. Physical Units type-4 in the 'failing domain', i.e. the domain controlled by the failing SSCP, that are also controlled by other SSCPs, can signal to those other SSCPs that one SSCP was lost. Implementation and installation-dependent procedures can then be started to establish SSCP sessions with those resources that were exclusively owned by the failing SSCP. The Request Units used for that 'take-over' are the same as those for the initial establishment of the sessions with the SSCP, the *Activate Physical Unit* (ACTPU) and the *Activate Logical Unit* (ACTLU), except that the Error Recovery option is used in order not to reset existing sessions. Once the lost SSCP is accessible again, either because the route becomes available or because it has been restarted, similar procedures can be used to regain control over its resources.

Network Management Services are defined in SNA to assist users in the overall network management task. Network Management is a complex, mainly organizational process, that has to do with the planning, the organization and the operational control over a networked information system. The total task cannot be provided by a communications architecture, since its importance is wider than just the (technical) communications resources. However, for the proper network management to be implemented, tools must be provided also for the technical tasks. This is the area where the SNA Management Services lay the ground rules for the exchange of management-oriented data in the network.

Although a number of important services have been defined, the current SNA Management Services do not yet cover the total range of services considered to be part of network management. This does not imply that such services are not available in SNA networks. Indeed, many powerful tools are available on a product basis. However, these are product (implementation) defined and therefore not discussed in the context of this book.

Usually, network management is defined in four major categories:

- *Problem Management.* This involves
  a   *determining* that a problem exists in the network (i.e. communication is not or not adequately possible),
  b   a *diagnosis* of the problem (i.e. what is wrong),
  c   a *bypass* for the problem such that communication can carry on as well as possible until the problem is solved,
  d   a *solution* that corrects the actual error situation and
  e   a mechanism for *tracking* and *controlling* the problem from the determination all the way through to the correction.

In SNA only the first two steps are supported by architectural definitions, although one might say that the third step, problem bypass, is implicitly provided in the architecture per se: this may involve setting up different routes, changing the parameters of LUs, etc. The other steps are more of an administrative nature, and are usually provided in specific products

● *Performance and Accounting Management*
This aspect of management has to do with keeping track of a
quantitative measure of how well the network is doing and taking
corrective action if the performance is below required service levels.
Furthermore, the accounting services enable the network manager to
implement mechanisms for usage charging on the basis of the actual
usage of the various network components. The SNA management
services only provide for *response-time monitoring*

● *Configuration Management*
Where Configuration Services (page 102) were involved in establishing the current configuration through the activation of the various
resources, Configuration Management keeps track of information
about the actual status of the configuration. It involves keeping track
of addresses, unit ('box') identification, *where* components are actually (physically) located, how they can be reached (e.g. telephone
numbers), who is responsible, etc. The SNA Configuration Management Services allow the network operator to retrieve the *physical
identification* information of resources in the network, and also
session-dependent information.

● *Change Management*
These Management services are concerned with changes to the
components in the network. These changes may be necessary because
of needed extensions or because of corrective action as a consequence
of problem management. Change Management assists in the planning, control and application of changes to both the hardware and
the software in the network. Currently SNA does not define specific
Change Management services.

The architectural context in which the Management Services operate is a
hierarchy of *Control Point Management Services* (CPMS) and *Physical
Unit Management Services* (Fig. 7.9). Locally the CPMS communicate
with the Network Operator, the local Session Services and Configuration
Services, and the SSCP-PU session with Physical Unit Management
Services (PUMS) in the various Physical Units in the domain of the
Control Point. Note that no Cross-Domain Management Services have
been defined: the Control Point is only responsible for its own domain.
   The overall management of the total network is realized through the
network operators in each domain. These network operators can be
human operators, but they can also be network management application
programs. SNA defines the protocol boundary between the control point

and the operator as for an application. (For that reason, in Fig. 7.9 the network operator is shown *inside the SNA node*.) This implies that in an actual implementation the operator will always communicate with the control point via some intermediate application program. The communication between network operators is modelled as a cross-domain session between these programs (LUs) and *not* the control points.

PUMS are part of the Physical Unit and they control the resources in the node and those attached to it. This control is exercised through implementation-defined protocols with

a   Local Management Services for *Physical resources* (the attached devices, storage, microcode, etc.), *Logical Units, Data Link Control Manager* and the *Path Control Manager*.
b   The half-session of the SSCP-PU session. On this session the Network Services RUs flow between the SSCP and the PU Management Services.
c   The PU Session Manager which provides information about the currently active sessions.
d   The PU Configuration Services, which provide information to uniquely identify the hardware and software of the node and the active Logical Units.
e   The PU Address Space Manager, which assigns addresses for local resources as well as providing information about these addresses. This component plays a major role during session establishment in, for example, SNA Network Interconnection (Chapter 9) and in Physical Unit 2.1 (Section 4.5).

In Physical Unit 2.1, the Physical Unit Management Services themselves perform the role of the Control Point. In that case no distinction is made between the Control Point and the Physical Unit. Obviously, the SSCP-PU half session does not exist in the case of PU 2.1.

The session between the SSCP and the PU carries the flow of management RUs. This flow may either be unsolicited or a request/response flow. The unsolicited flow is used to report sudden conditions (e.g. alerts about overflowing counters or errors) without a specific request from the SSCP. Request/Response flows are used when the SSCP wants to invoke a specific service at the target PUMS. The service request may involve only one resource or it may involve several resources (e.g. all currently active LUs). When several resources are involved, PUMS may send the results in a sequence of reply RUs. Since more requests may be in process at the same time, the Procedure Related Identifier (PRID) is used to make sure that the replies are correlated with the appropriate requests (Fig. 7.5).

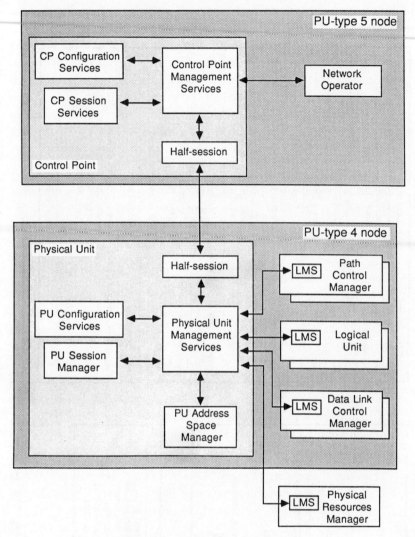

Fig. 7.9 Control Point structure

In Fig. 7.10 a summary is provided of the Network Management Services RUs defined so far and the Major vectors and Subvectors which have been defined for the Network Management Vector Transport (NMVT) RU. A full discussion of all these vectors and their sub-fields is far beyond the scope of this book. By looking at the names of the RUs and the vectors the reader should get some idea of the type of function provided. Further detail can be found in [21].

Network Management Request Units

ACTTRACE	Activate Trace
DACTTRACE	Deactivate Trace
DISPSTOR	Display Storage
ECHOTEST	Echo Test
ER-TESTED	Explicit Route Tested
EXECTEST	Execute Test
NMVT	Network Management Vector Transport
RECFMS	Record Formatted Maintenance Statistics
RECSTOR	Record Storage
RECTD	Record Test Data
RECTR	Record Test Results
RECTRD	Record Trace Data
REQECHO	Request Echo Test
REQMS	Request Maintenance Statistics
ROUTE-TEST	Route Test
SETCV	Set Control Vector
TESTMODE	Test Mode

NMVT Common Subvectors

Text Message	Product Set ID
Date/Time	Product Identifier
Hierarchy Name List	Relative Time
SNA Address List	Correlation
Hierarchy Resource List	Data Reset Flag
Name List	Sense Data

PD   Problem Determination
RTM Response Time Monitor

NMVT Major Vector	Subvectors
Alert	Basic Alert information / Detail Qualifier
Request Trace	Modify SIR Control / Query SIR Data
Trace	Reply SIR Control / SIR Common Data / SIR Control Block Data
Request PD Statistics	Request Link Connection Subsystem Data
PD statistics	X.25 Counters / Link Connection Subsystem Data / Data Link Traffic Counters
Request Response Time Monitor	RTM Request / RTM Control
Response Time Monitor	RTM Status Reply / RTM Data
Request Product Set ID	Request Product Set ID
Reply Product Set ID	Product Set ID
Request Link Resource Control	Set Link Station Attributes / Query Link Station Attributes / Set Link Attributes / Query Link Attributes
Reply Link Resource Control	Reply Link Station Attributes / Reply Link Attributes

Fig. 7.10 Network Management Request Units and NMVT vectors

8 Logical Unit types

8.1 Introduction

In Section 2.2, we defined the concept of architectured subsets of the SNA functions. At the level of the Logical Units, these subsets are defined in terms of LU *types*. All products implemented according to the SNA definitions are classified according to these LU types, which specify what functions the product can perform when it is in session with other SNA products. In Section 2.2, we also introduced the concept of the *profile*, the definition of a particular set of options in one layer of SNA. These profiles are defined for the three layers in the LU that participate in a session, Transmission Control (*TS-profile*), Data Flow Control (*FM-profile*) and Presentation Services (*PS-profile*). A summary of the TS- and FM-profiles was provided in Fig. 5.2. Each profile combines a set of functions related to the relevant layer. When a session is established, these functions are selected via a number associated with the appropriate profile. Both session partners must, of course, agree on the same profiles. It is, however, not always sufficient to request just the profile; sometimes more information is needed related to the profile. This is the case, for example, when in the TS-profile it is specified that pacing will be used; the pacing windows will still have to be set. This is done through the *profile usage fields* in the session establishment request (BIND). These usage fields can therefore be considered a further specification of the particular profile.

With each LU type, a specific set of profiles is defined. The LU type is classified through a number, which is the same as the PS-profile number (Fig. 8.1). LU types are described in detail in [20, 22, 23, 24]. A short summary description is given below of each of the LU types defined so far. Although these LU types play an important role in existing implementations, they will not be discussed in detail. An exception is made for LU 6.2 since it is the basis for the future.

LU-type	TS Profile	FM profile	FM Headers
0	2,3,4,7	2,3,4,7,18	N.A.
1	3,4	3,4	1,2,3
2	3	3	--
3	3	3	--
4	7	7	1,2,3
6	4	18	4,5,6,7, 8,10
6.2	7	19	5,7,12

Fig. 8.1 Summary of Logical Unit types

0 LU type 0 is used to classify sessions that do use SNA-defined protocols for both Transmission Control and Data Flow Control, but not for Function Management Data Services, i.e. for Session Presentation Services. At that level, the protocols are end-user or product defined.

1 LU type 1 is used between application programs and data processing terminals that can have either one or more devices attached to them. In this LU type, Function Management Headers can be used to select the appropriate device on which the data is to be presented. The data stream used is the SNA Character String (SCS).

2 LU type 2 is used specifically in sessions between an application program and a single display terminal using the SNA 3270 data stream. It is mainly used for compatibility with existing pre-SNA 3270 application programs.

3 LU type 3 is used similarly to LU type 2, but for a single-printer device that uses the SNA 3270 data stream.

4 LU type 4 can be used in two ways:

a For sessions between two terminals, which may be multiple devices. In this case, no network with a separate SSCP is required, i.e. the two terminals must handle SSCP-like functions themselves. These sessions can be used when two terminals are connected point-to-point, without any further network. The negotiable BIND is required in this case to allow for the selection of certain session parameters like pacing windows, etc.

b For sessions between application processes and terminals that may have multiple devices. In this case, the LU type is very similar to LU type 1, but more data streams are possible, e.g. for word processing.

5 LU type 5 has not been defined.

6 LU type 6 is defined for communication between application programs that cooperate in a distributed processing environment, for example transaction processing sub-systems. In this LU type, various data streams can be selected, such as the SNA Character String, but also specifically defined ones, such as a structured field data stream, a Logical Messages (LMS) data stream or even a user-defined data stream. An important aspect of this LU type is the synchronization of resources and update commitments in various parts of the transaction. The architectured vehicles for the exchange are the Function Management Headers FMH-4 through FMH-8 and FMH-10. The 'ultimate' version of LU type 6 is LU 6.2, which is the subject of the next section.

8.2 Logical Unit type 6.2

In the preceding sections a certain structure of the Logical Unit was presented and from that perspective several Logical Unit types were briefly described. It was also mentioned that the definition of LU types was seen as a logical consequence of defining subsets of SNA protocols (e.g. through the profiles) and trying to avoid a proliferation of differing, incompatible subsets. However, as time progressed, new communications requirements arose and it became apparent that the existing LU type definition was not adequate. Therefore, a new route was chosen and the 'ultimate' LU-type was defined. Since it is based on concepts defined for LU 6.1, it was called LU-type 6.2. It has however a much wider significance: it is not just another LU-type, but it is the *only* LU-type that will be used in the (foreseeable) future. Its strategic significance has been stressed by IBM several times. It is therefore appropriate to describe LU 6.2 in more detail than was done for the other LU-types (of which probably no new implementations will be made by IBM).

The design objectives for LU 6.2 have been described in the literature [25]. We summarize them briefly since these objectives clarify some of the aspects of LU 6.2. The more important objectives were

● Full program-to-program communication, independent of the node (-type) where the programs reside. This illustrates the recognition that communication is really between programs and not, as in the early days of SNA, between a person at a terminal and an application program in a host computer.

- A much higher level of *abstraction* from the internals of SNA for the programs using LU 6.2, i.e. less 'SNA knowledge' required from those writing these programs.
- The set of primitives made available to the using programs must be *semantically complete*. All functions that must be performed should be represented by appropriate primitives (*verbs*). This applies not only to sending/receiving data, but also to such things as selection of transport characteristics (delay, cost, etc.), commitment control, recovery from failures, accounting support, etc.
- *Efficient* implementations must be possible.
- It should be possible to make the defined primitives available in various *high-level languages*, to support a range of products.
- Operators must be able to *control* the operation of a set of LUs, particularly where multiple parallel sessions are involved.
- It must be possible to *subset* the LU 6.2 architecture since not all products need the full function. Obviously a printer (output only) does not require support for multiple sessions and two-way data transfer. However, the subsetting must allow for maximum connectivity between programs.

The basis for the definition of LU 6.2 is the concept of distributed transactions, that consist of Transaction Programs engaged in *conversations* to perform certain tasks. Thus in Fig. 8.2, Transaction Program (TP)-A has a conversation with TP-B to perform a task. If during the conversation TP-B finds out it needs the help (e.g. some additional information) from TP-C to complete its part, it sets up a conversation with TP-C for that purpose. In this way complicated distributed transaction structures may be defined, according to the need of the application. However complex the structure may be, the basic element is always the conversation between two Transaction Programs. The LU 6.2 architecture provides the tools to manage and control this (potentially) complex environment. As a consequence, some authors view the Logical Unit in the LU 6.2 context no longer as the end user's port to the communication

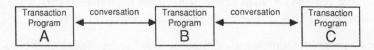

Fig. 8.2 Three transaction programs engaged in conversations

system, but as part of a distributed operating system. This distributed operating system manages various types of local and remote resources. The communication resource (i.e. the SNA session) which is used for the conversations is just one of these resources.

Another concept in LU 6.2 new to SNA is the concept of the *protocol boundary*. This term is somewhat unfortunate, since it is the equivalent of the OSI *service* boundary! Nevertheless, LU 6.2 is the first time IBM has provided a service description in SNA. This description takes the form of a *generic verb* interface. These verbs are the equivalents of the OSI service primitives. How the verbs (and their associated parameters) are implemented in a particular product, has to be defined by that product. However, a distributed transaction can be designed without reference to a particular product, using the generic interface [23].

As was said before the basic concept of LU 6.2 is the conversation. These conversations are allocated to SNA sessions with the appropriate characteristics. These sessions can be taken from a pool of free sessions or be initiated as required. On the SNA session, the conversation is the equivalent of the *bracket* (refer to Section 6.2).

To illustrate the operation of LU 6.2, it is best to follow some simple flows, both from the TP point of view and from the LU point of view. The examples discussed below are constructed from the standard flows in the LU 6.2 Format and Protocol Reference Manual [24]. Similar examples are described by Gray et al [25]. After the explanation of these examples we will discuss some of the properties of LU 6.2 in more detail.

Example 1

This example consists of a simple transaction in which there is a data

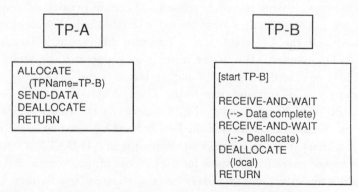

Fig. 8.3 Verbs used in a simple one-way transaction

flow in only one direction (Fig. 8.3). TP-A has some data that must be sent to TP-B for further processing. No feedback from TP-B is required.

The first thing TP-A does is to issue the verb ALLOCATE naming TP-B as the target transaction program (and also the name of the LU at which TP-B is located). Next TP-A issues the SEND-DATA verb, passing the data to be sent as a parameter. Since all TP-A wanted to do was to invoke TP-B and send some data to it, it is now ready to quit. TP-A thus ends the conversation by issuing the DEALLOCATE verb.

At some time, LU-B will start Transaction Program TP-B. How this is actually achieved is transparent to the transaction program. By design (remember, TP-A and TP-B are designed together as one distributed transaction) the first thing TP-B does, after some initial housekeeping, is to issue the RECEIVE-AND-WAIT verb. This verb places the TP in the wait state if no data is yet received. When data is received, control is returned with the indication DATA-COMPLETE. TP-B processes the data and when it has finished doing so, it issues another RECEIVE-AND-WAIT. This time control is returned with the indication DEALLOCATE, so TP-B knows that TP-A has deallocated the conversation resources and it can delete whatever local information was kept about the conversation. It continues its processing until the end of its designed task and then it terminates its existence by returning control to the local control program.

So far, we described the behaviour of the two TPs mainly from the point of view of the transaction programmer (whether the actual flow consisted of one BIU or more is completely transparent to the programmer). Now we look somewhat closer and understand the SNA mechanisms used by the Logical Unit. It was already mentioned, that the conversation is mapped onto the SNA bracket. Therefore, when the ALLOCATE verb is issued, the LU will verify that a free session with the target LU exists. It also verifies whether the session has the appropriate characteristics. If there is no free session and certain pre-defined session limits are not exceeded, a new session is established. The session is allocated and the LU constructs a Function Management Header-5 (ATTACH), naming TP-B as the transaction program to be attached. The FMH is placed in the LU's buffer, but it is not necessarily sent immediately. This is transparent to the TP. The LU also sets the Begin Chain (BC) and Begin Bracket (BB) indicators in the Request Header (both the Begin Bracket BB and the End Bracket EB must be in the first BIU of a chain, refer to Chapter 6). When the SEND-DATA is issued, data is passed to the LU. Assume for the purpose of the example that the data is not too short, so it exceeds the maximum size of one Request Unit (RU). The first part of the data is placed in the buffer to complete the RU

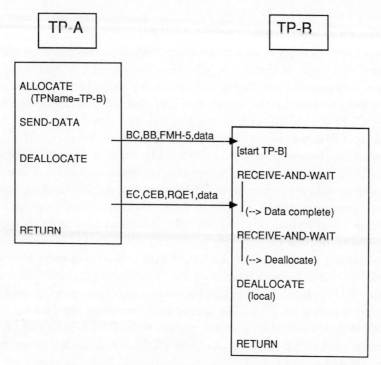

Fig. 8.4 SNA data flow for the simple transaction of Fig. 8.3

and subsequently a first-in-chain BIU[*] is sent to TP-B (Fig. 8.4). The remainder of the data is placed in the LU buffer—for the sake of simplicity we assume that now it will fit in one RU. Next, TP-A issues DEALLOCATE. This means to the LU that the buffer contents must be sent to complete the transmission from TP-A. The BIU to be sent will be the last BIU in the chain. So, the End-of-Chain (EC) indicator is set in the RH. However, DEALLOCATE also means that the bracket (= the conversation) must be terminated. Here, the architects encountered a problem that they had caused themselves: the End Bracket indicator must be set, but it can only be set in the first BIU of the chain, which was already sent to TP-B.

The options to solve this dilemma are:

1 to redefine the EB indicator, or
2 to send a separate RU (e.g. LUSTAT) with EB to terminate the bracket, or
3 to define a new mechanism.

---

[*] The Basic Information Unit (BIU) is the combination of the Request/Response Unit (RU) and the Request/Response Header (RH); refer to Chapter 2.

Option 1 was not acceptable since too many products implement tests to make sure that the architecture is followed. Changing EBI would have meant many changes in existing products. Option 2 was not acceptable either, since one of the design objectives for LU 6.2 was efficiency. Therefore, option 3 was chosen and a bit in the RH, which was reserved until then, was used as the *Conditional End-of-Bracket Indicator* (CEBI). This CEBI is only allowed on the *last* RU of a chain. The 'old' End Bracket (EB) is not used at all by LU 6.2. Thus the reason for CEBI is the autonomous buffering and sending by the LU. When the first BIU is sent, the LU does not yet know whether the conversation (i.e. the bracket) must be terminated or not. Since TP-A did not request any confirmation, the response-type requested is set to RQE (Exception Response only).

From LU-B's point of view, the SNA indicators have the following effect. The BB bracket indicator in the first BIU tells LU-B that a new conversation is started. The ATTACH Function Management Header (FMH-5) results in the activation of the Transaction Program. The data in this BIU is placed in the buffer, but since it is not complete, control is not yet returned to TP-B. The second BIU completes the data, so the RECEIVE-AND-WAIT now completes with DATA-COMPLETE†. Because of the CEB Indicator, the next RECEIVE-AND-WAIT returns with DEALLOCATE.

It will be clear from the example that the verbs used by the transaction programs are simple and straightforward. They are aimed at the task to be performed and not at the various SNA mechanisms involved. This first example was a fairly simple case, where one TP invokes another TP and sends data to it, but no further feedback was necessary. In the next example we look at a somewhat more complicated situation.

Example 2

The transaction again consists of two Transaction Programs, TP-A and TP-B (Fig. 8.5), but now TP-B also sends data to TP-A, in reply to the data it received (and, of course, because of the common design of TP-A and TP-B, TP-A expects this data).

The beginning of the example is the same. TP-A issues the ALLO-CATE verb, then sends some data with SEND-DATA. Now, since TP-A expects a reply from TP-B it uses the verb PREPARE-TO-RECEIVE to tell the LU that data is expected. Next it issues RECEIVE-AND-WAIT,

---

† LU 6.2 allows various mappings between the data from the TP's point of view and the buffers in the LU and the TP. Although some additional explanation will be provided later, a full description is outside the scope of this book

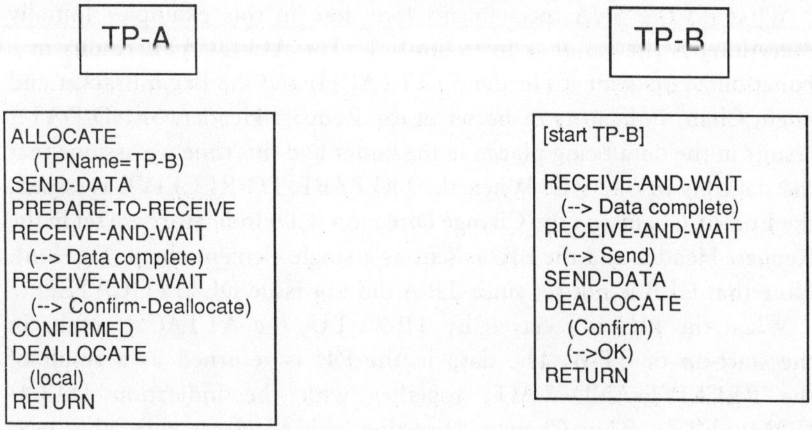

```
┌─────────┐                          ┌─────────┐
│  TP-A   │                          │  TP-B   │
└─────────┘                          └─────────┘

┌──────────────────────────┐        ┌──────────────────────────┐
│ ALLOCATE                  │        │ [start TP-B]             │
│   (TPName=TP-B)           │        │ RECEIVE-AND-WAIT         │
│ SEND-DATA                 │        │   (--> Data complete)    │
│ PREPARE-TO-RECEIVE        │        │ RECEIVE-AND-WAIT         │
│ RECEIVE-AND-WAIT          │        │   (--> Send)             │
│   (--> Data complete)     │        │ SEND-DATA                │
│ RECEIVE-AND-WAIT          │        │ DEALLOCATE               │
│   (--> Confirm-Deallocate)│        │   (Confirm)              │
│ CONFIRMED                 │        │   (-->OK)                │
│ DEALLOCATE                │        │ RETURN                   │
│   (local)                 │        └──────────────────────────┘
│ RETURN                    │
└──────────────────────────┘
```

Fig. 8.5 Verbs used in a simple two-way transaction

after which it will not regain control unless data is received. Before that, we look at TP-B's side. When TP-B is started, it issues RECEIVE-AND-WAIT and gets the indication DATA-COMPLETE. After the next RECEIVE-AND-WAIT the return code is SEND, meaning that TP-B is now in the SEND state. It issues a SEND-DATA for the reply to TP-A and then terminates the transaction by DEALLOCATE-ing the conversation. However, TP-B wants to make sure, before the conversation is actually deallocated, that the whole transaction was successful. Therefore, the parameter TYPE = CONFIRM is passed with the DEALLOCATE. TP-B does not get control again unless a confirmation is received from TP-A. This confirmation is then indicated in the return code OK. This ends the conversation and eventually TP-B terminates and returns control to the local control program.

What happens on TP-A's side in the meantime? When data is received from TP-B, TP-A gets control again, with the indication DATA-COMPLETE. It processes the data and issues another RECEIVE-AND-WAIT. Control returns with the indication CONFIRM-DEALLOCATE, meaning that TP-B wants a confirmation and will deallocate the conversation when the confirmation is received. If everything is OK, TP-A issues the verb CONFIRMED and then also deallocates from its side (i.e. deletes the information about the conversation).

What do the SNA mechanisms look like in this example? Initially everything is the same as in example 1. The ALLOCATE results in a Function Management Header 5 (ATTACH) and the Begin Bracket and Begin Chain Indicators to be set in the Request Header. SEND-DATA results in the data being placed in the buffer and this time we assume that the data fits in one RU. When the PREPARE-TO-RECEIVE is issued, the End-of-Chain *and* the Change Direction (CD) Indicators are set in the Request Header and the BIU is sent as a single element chain (Fig. 8.6). Note that CEB is not set since TP-A did not issue DEALLOCATE.

When the BIU is received by TP-B's LU, the ATTACH results in the start-up of TP-B. The data in the RU is returned as a result of the RECEIVE-AND-WAIT, together with the indication DATA-COMPLETE. The Change Direction takes effect with the next RECEIVE-AND-WAIT which completes with the indication SEND.

TP-B's SEND-DATA results in the data being placed in the buffer (it fits in one RU). Also, the Begin Chain (BC) indicator is set in the RH. Next the DEALLOCATE verb results in the setting of the End-of-Chain (EC) and Conditional End-of-Bracket (CEB) indicators. Since TP-B wants a confirmation of its reply, a definite response is requested via RQD2 and the BIU is sent. On TP-A's side, the RECEIVE-AND-WAIT is completed with DATA-COMPLETE and on the next RECEIVE-AND-WAIT the CEB plus the RQD2 result in the indication CONFIRM-DEALLOCATE. When TP-A issues the CONFIRMED verb, this is 'translated' into a positive response (+ DR2) to TP-B's chain. According to the rules of bracket termination, the LUs only return to the Between Brackets state when the positive response is sent or received.

In the preceding examples we have given a brief illustration of the use of LU 6.2 verbs in transaction programs. Before we look at these verbs in more detail, we look at the data passed between the two transaction programs. First, we have to know that LU 6.2 supports two types of conversation, the *mapped* conversation and the *base* conversation. These conversations are linked to the structure of the Logical Unit.

As illustrated in Fig. 8.7 application transaction programs normally use the mapped conversation protocol boundary, which gives the highest level of abstraction. Inside the LU there are also transaction programs. These are called *Service Transaction Programs*, since they provide services to the user (i.e. the application transaction program) or the logical unit. These services are available to the user through the mapped conversation protocol boundary. The Service Transaction Programs themselves have access to the basic functions of the logical unit through the basic conversation protocol boundary. This protocol boundary

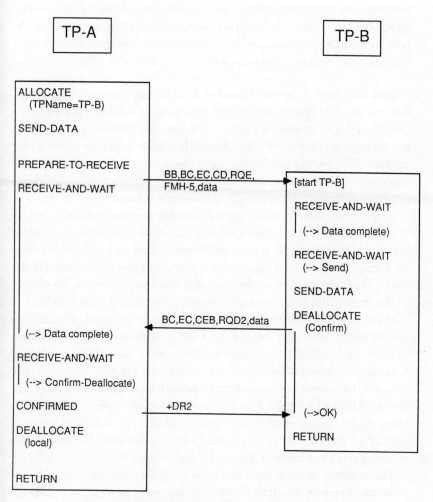

TP-A   TP-B

ALLOCATE
  (TPName=TP-B)

SEND-DATA

PREPARE-TO-RECEIVE
                          BB,BC,EC,CD,RQE,
RECEIVE-AND-WAIT   FMH-5,data   [start TP-B]

                                              RECEIVE-AND-WAIT

                                                | (--> Data complete)

                                              RECEIVE-AND-WAIT
                                                (--> Send)

                                              SEND-DATA

                          BC,EC,CEB,RQD2,data DEALLOCATE
                                                (Confirm)
(--> Data complete)

RECEIVE-AND-WAIT

  | (--> Confirm-Deallocate)

CONFIRMED   +DR2
                                              (-->OK)
DEALLOCATE
  (local)   RETURN

RETURN

Fig. 8.6 SNA data flow for the transaction of Fig. 8.5

provides less abstraction than the mapped conversation boundary. Of course, if more control of detail is needed for a particular transaction program, the basic conversation protocol boundary can also be used by an application transaction program. However, an application cannot use both the basic conversation and the mapped conversation protocol boundary in the same conversation.

Now let's look at some of the detail of the two protocol boundaries. First of all, the verbnames used are (marginally) different: the verbs for the mapped conversation are equal to the ones for the basic conversation, but they are prefixed with MC-. Then, they differ in the parameters they support. The parameters for the basic conversation allow more detailed control over the conversation. Also the format of the messages which are exchanged between the transaction programs differs.

In the base conversation, the transaction programs have to use a standard record format. They exchange *Logical Records* which consist of the data, preceded by a two-byte length field (LL, Fig. 8.8). The maximum length of a Logical Record is 32 kbytes (including the LL field). The high-order bit of the LL field is reserved. It is the responsibility of the transaction program itself to include the proper length field.

In the mapped conversation the transaction programs do not have to worry about the form of the data or maximum length. The data transferred is called a *data record*. The type of data and the internal structure are purely a matter of agreement between the two TP's. The actual (total) length of the data is passed as a parameter with the MC-SEND-DATA verb. The LU may optionally transform this data using a user-defined *map* that describes the data record. If mapping is used, the name of the map is passed with the MC-SEND-DATA. The resulting record is called a *Mapped Conversation Record*.

The mapped conversation component of the Logical Unit uses the basic conversation interface to send the mapped conversation record. It 'packs' the record in a *General Data Stream* (GDS) Variable to tell its counterpart what type of data is being sent. The General Data Stream Variable starts with a GDS-Header, followed by the data. The Header contains a two-byte LL-field, followed by a two-byte ID-field, which describes the type of variable. The ID-field of the GDS variable that is used to send the mapped conversation record has a value ID = X' 12FF' (application data).

Because of the LL field, a GDS variable is a logical record from the base conversation point of view (Fig. 8.8). If a GDS variable exceeds the 32 kbyte maximum length of a logical record, it may be segmented into several logical records. The high-order bit of the LL-field is used for

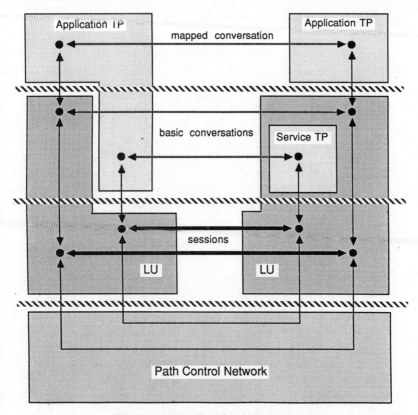

Fig. 8.7 Mapped and Basic conversations

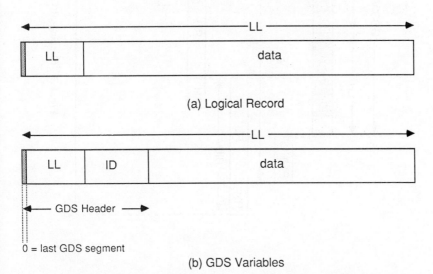

Fig. 8.8 Logical Records and General Data Stream variables

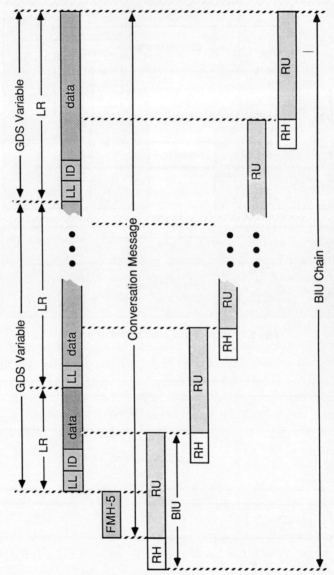

Fig. 8.9 Mapping of Conversation Messages onto Basic Information Units

segmentation control. It is set off in the last segment of the GDS variable. Obviously, only the first segment contains the ID-Field.

The purpose of the GDS Variable is more general than just describing the mapped conversation record. Any transaction program using the basic conversation interface can use GDS variables to describe the data exchanged. Specific ID fields have been assigned for specific purposes. For example, the value X'12xx' is used by the internal LU 6.2 Service Transaction Programs like CNOS and RESYNC (to be described later). SNA Distribution Services (SNADS, Section 10.4) uses mainly variables with ID = X'C3xx', whereas Document Interchange Architecture (DIA, Section 10.3) uses X'C0xx' through X'CFxx'. Depending on the specific use by the Transaction Program, the remainder of the GDS variable may also be structured. An example is the DIA Interchange Unit. Complete definitions of GDS variables can be found in the relevant IBM literature, e.g. [12] and [26].

The sequence of mapped conversation records in one direction (i.e. consecutive MC-SEND-DATA verbs) is called a *Mapped Conversation Message*. The total length of a mapped conversation message depends solely on the transaction programs involved. The mapped conversation records may each be segmented into several logical records, each with a maximum length of 32 kbytes. However, for each session a maximum RU-size is agreed which is usually smaller. Logical Units have their own buffers, limited in size and number, whereas the basic transaction programs may have buffer sizes smaller than the logical record. So, there can be various mappings between data records, mapped conversation records, logical records and finally the SNA Request Units exchanged between the LUs. This is illustrated in Fig. 8.9. The LU uses chaining to send a conversation message that exceeds the maximum RU length. The details of the various mappings and the relationship with the parameters and return codes on the (MC-)SEND-DATA and the (MC-)RECEIVE verbs are beyond the scope of this book. The reader is referred to [24] for additional detail.

Verbs for LU 6.2

In the preceding examples we introduced some of the verbs that LU 6.2 provides. In Fig. 8.10 a full list of the verbs for both the mapped and the basic conversation is provided, as well as the verbs that are type-independent and the Operator Control verbs. Although a detailed treatment of all verbs, their parameters and options is far beyond the scope of this book, some additional discussion is provided here, as far as it pertains to the concepts of LU 6.2. Most verbs are described for the mapped conversation. The description is very similar for the basic conversation, except for the detail of the parameters, which is not provided here anyway.

MC-ALLOCATE

The allocation verb is used by the transaction program to get into a conversation with another transaction program. Although this transaction program may reside at the same logical unit, we will assume it to be remote. The actions involved are

a a session is allocated to carry the conversation messages;
b the remote transaction program is started;
c the characteristics of the conversation are defined.

The transaction program specifies with the MC-ALLOCATE verb the name of the logical unit where the other transaction program resides and the name of that transaction program. In addition the required characteristics of the session (security, class of service, etc.) are specified as in a typical SNA log-on request from a terminal. The logical unit will first try to allocate a session that already exists. For this purpose the LU maintains a pool of free sessions. For each remote LU this pool contains sessions with various characteristics like 'who wins bracket contention', 'class of service', etc. How many free sessions are contained in the pool depends on the number of sessions in use and on various session limits defined for the logical unit. These limits may be changed by the LU Control Operator (relevant verbs will be discussed later).

The logical unit will try to allocate a session which fulfills the session requirements and for which it is the contention winner. If it is the winner, it can start the bracket (= conversation) immediately. If such a session is not available, the LU tries to find a session for which it is the contention loser. If such a session is found it requests permission to start a bracket. LU 6.2 never uses the explicit BID (FM profile 19). Instead it always uses implicit BID (refer to 6.2). If neither type of session is available, the LU will try to start a new session, provided the various session limits are not exceeded. If they are, control is returned to the application program with a return code indicating 'session not available'. For a successful allocation the return code indicates OK.

The MC-ALLOCATE verb can be used to attach more than one transaction program to the same initiating TP. It can also be used by an attached TP to attach a 'next level' transaction program and so on. In this way complex structures can be created which will perform truly distrib-

Mapped Conversations	L	R	Basic Conversations	L	R
MC-ALLOCATE	B	B	ALLOCATE	B	B
MC-CONFIRM	B	B	CONFIRM	B	B
MC-CONFIRMED	B	B	CONFIRMED	B	B
MC-DEALLOCATE	B	B	DEALLOCATE	B	B
MC-FLUSH	O	B	FLUSH	O	B
MC-GET-ATTRIBUTES	O	--	GET-ATTRIBUTES	O	--
MC-POST-ON-RECEIPT	O	--	POST-ON-RECEIPT	O	--
MC-PREPARE-TO-RECEIVE	O	B	PREPARE-TO-RECEIVE	O	B
MC-RECEIVE-AND-WAIT	B	--	RECEIVE-AND-WAIT	B	--
MC-RECEIVE-IMMEDIATE	O	--	RECEIVE-IMMEDIATE	O	--
MC-REQUEST-TO-SEND	B	B	REQUEST-TO-SEND	B	B
MC-SEND-DATA	B	B	SEND-DATA	B	B
MC-SEND-ERROR	B	B	SEND-ERROR	B	B
MC-TEST	O	--	TEST	O	--
Type-independent verbs					
BACKOUT	O	O	SYNCPT	O	O
GET-TYPE	O	--	WAIT	O	--
Control Operator Verbs					
Change number of Sessions			LU Definition		
CHANGE-SESSION-LIMIT	O	B	DEFINE-LOCAL-LU	O	--
INITIALIZE-SESSION-LIMIT	B	B	DEFINE-REMOTE-LU	O	--
RESET-SESSION-LIMIT	B	B	DEFINE-MODE	O	--
PROCESS-SESSION-LIMIT	B	B	DEFINE-TP	O	--
Session Control			DISPLAY-LOCAL-LU	O	--
			DISPLAY-REMOTE-LU	O	--
ACTIVATE-SESSION	O	B	DISPLAY-MODE	O	--
DEACTIVATE-SESSION	O	B	DISPLAY-TP	O	--
			DELETE	O	--

L = Local Support   B = Base set
R = Remote Support   O = Option set
                       -- = Not applicable (does not invoke remote processing)

Fig. 8.10 The verbs for LU 6.2

Simple

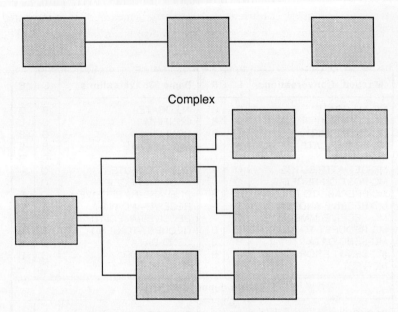

Complex

Fig. 8.11 Possible structures of distributed transactions

uted processing. The actual structure depends on the nature and design of the application. In Fig. 8.11 two possible structures are illustrated.

In addition to the names of the remote logical unit and the transaction program to be attached, the initiating transaction program can specify initialization, security and synchronization information for the conversation. The initialization information consists of parameters to be passed to the remote TP when it is invoked. The security parameters define whether the user-ID and passwords can/must be used to control or restrict access to certain transaction programs (refer to page 141).

The synchronization information defines the extent to which the LU should take responsibility for the integrity (consistency) of the data associated with the conversation. This does not apply only to data actually transmitted, but also to databases updated in the course of the transaction. This is particularly useful in distributed applications, where a failure in one session or LU (e.g. due to network or hardware failures) may cause uncertainty about the status of the various databases.

LU 6.2 provides three levels of synchronization: NONE, CONFIRM and SYNCPT. In case NONE is specified, no synchronization support will be provided by the LU and relevant verbs are not accepted. If CONFIRM is specified, the transaction program may, during the conversation, request confirmation of a certain message. It is indicated to the remote transaction program that confirmation is requested. The requesting TP will not regain control until the confirmation is received. (This was illustrated in Example 2.) The confirmation indicates that the message was properly received at the remote TP. The TPs themselves have to keep track of the state of the data in case recovery is necessary.

If a synchronization level of SYNCPT is specified, the LU will take responsibility for the integrity of the data, the 'protected' data. When failures occur, the LU will, after restart of the session, use a special Service Transaction Program RESYNC, to resynchronize the protected data to a defined state. This (re)synchronization mechanism will be described later with the appropriate verbs.

MC-DEALLOCATE

This verb is used when a conversation is to be terminated and the associated resources can be freed. In addition, synchronization actions are performed as required by the synchronization level. Which transaction program issues the MC-DEALLOCATE depends on the design of the transaction: for certain transactions it will be the TP that also allocated the conversation; in other situations it will be the 'attached' TP. In either case, one TP issues MC-DEALLOCATE, which brings the conversation in *deallocation state*. To complete the deallocation, the other TP must also issue MC-DEALLOCATE, but with the mandatory parameter LOCAL. This frees the resources held locally for the conversation.

MC-SEND-DATA and MC-FLUSH

When a transaction program wants to send data to its counterpart, it uses the MC-SEND-DATA verb. The length of the data to be sent is specified as a parameter. There is no restriction on the type of data, but optionally the data can be mapped before it is transmitted. The mapping process is user-defined and it must be defined in advance. The definition is called a *map* and the name of this map is specified with the MC-SEND-DATA when mapping is required.

Each time the MC-SEND-DATA verb is issued, the mapped conversation handler creates an appropriate GDS (Generalized Data Stream) variable to contain the data. If a map name is specified, it is carried in a separate GDS variable. The GDS variables are not necessarily transmitted immediately. They may be buffered by the LU and transmitted at the LU's convenience. If the transaction program wants to force transmission, it can issue the MC-FLUSH verb. The LU will then transmit whatever is left in its buffers.

MC-PREPARE-TO-RECEIVE and MC-RECEIVE-AND-WAIT

When a transaction program wants to receive data, it issues the MC-RECEIVE-AND-WAIT verb. This verb specifies the maximum length of data that can be received (depending on the TP's own available buffer space). If the data received by the LU (i.e. the GDS variable) is longer, the first part, up to the requested length, is returned and a return code DATA INCOMPLETE is also sent. The transaction program should then issue one or more additional MC-RECEIVE-AND-WAITs to complete the data.

The data exchange protocol used by LU 6.2 is always half-duplex, i.e. one TP is sending while the other is receiving. If a sending TP wants to receive, it can go to receive state by issuing the MC-PREPARE-TO-RECEIVE verb. This will flush the buffers in the LU and an indication is sent to the other TP that it should now start sending. The next time this TP issues MC-RECEIVE-AND-WAIT it gets this indication through a return code SEND.

Using the MC-PREPARE-TO-RECEIVE is one way of going from send state to receive state. Optionally the transaction program may use the MC-RECEIVE-AND-WAIT immediately. This will also result in flushing the buffers and going into receive state. However, the MC-PREPARE-TO-RECEIVE allows more control over the synchronization associated with the state transition.

MC-REQUEST-TO-SEND

Above we discussed the transition from send state to receive state. This can be done at will by the sending TP and the other one is just told about it (of course, there is also the overall design which ensures a 'mutual understanding' between the two TPs). The reverse situation is more complex, i.e. when the receiving TP wants to start sending. It cannot do this at will, since the other may still be sending. So, it must indicate its desire to send to the sending TP and await permission to start sending. The MC-REQUEST-TO-SEND verb is the mechanism used to indicate to the LU that the receiving transaction program wants to send. As a result, the other TP will get return code REQUEST-TO-SEND RECEIVED in response to an MC-SEND-DATA. (The SNA mechanism used on the session is the Data Flow Control SIGNAL RU.) There is no architectural obligation for the sending TP to relinquish control. Therefore, the requesting TP must continue to issue MC-RECEIVE-AND-

WAIT until it receives the return code SEND. Obviously, the overall design of the transaction has to ensure proper behaviour on both sides.

Control Operator verbs

In Fig. 8.10 the Control Operator verbs are also listed. These verbs are used to control the environment in which the transaction programs operate. Conceptually the verbs are issued by a Control Operator Transaction Program, operating at the mapped conversation protocol boundary. This Control Operator Transaction Program (COTP) may communicate with a human operator or it may execute certain procedures at, for example, fixed times or it may communicate with other COTPs. In this way the control of a distributed environment can either be centralized with one human operator or be spread across several, depending on the needs of a specific implementation or installation.

The Control Operator verbs can be used to change the various session limits mentioned before. The verbs to do this use the CNOS (Change Number Of Sessions) Service Transaction Program. Other verbs are used to start or to deactivate sessions or to change the parameters of the logical units. When LU parameters are changed, this can apply to either the local LU or the remote LU. However, in the latter case no changes are made to the actual remote LU parameters, but only to the parameters kept locally. That is, the local LU's *view* of the remote LU is changed. Parameters that can be changed are for instance the LU-name, whether parallel sessions are supported, whether password verification at the LU level is required, etc.

Synchronization

In the description of the LU verbs the synchronization capabilities of LU 6.2 were introduced. Simple synchronization support relies on the CONFIRM verb, which must be responded to with the CONFIRMED verb. Eventually, the requestor of CONFIRM gets a return code OK. The SNA mechanism used to realize the CONFIRM is the RQD2 on a request and +DR2 on the response as a result of the CONFIRMED verb. This was illustrated in example 2.

A more powerful synchronization mechanism is available through the SYNCPT verb. The mechanism is enforced through SyncPoint Services (SPS) in the various LUs. These SyncPoint Services, together with the Resource Managers, keep track of all changes to protected resources (e.g. databases and other conversations). The Resource Managers also provide locking mechanisms to prevent concurrent updates from

133

different transactions. The changes to the resources are kept in a *logfile* on permanent storage. If a SYNCPT procedure fails, the logfile is used to undo any changes made to the protected resources and thus restore the situation of the previous syncpoint. After a successful syncpoint the entries in the logfile are deleted and the changes are thus permanent. The sequence of syncpoints structures the conversation into Logical Units of Work, which have more or less 'atomic' characteristics. Once they are complete, they need not be worried about any more.

The syncpoint mechanism used by LU 6.2 is a so-called two-phase commit protocol. In the first phase, messages flow through the distributed transaction to verify whether all transaction programs are ready to commit, i.e. make the changes to their protected resources permanent. In the second phase a similar 'wave' of messages makes the actual changes happen.

In Fig. 8.12 this process is illustrated for an over-simplified situation with only two transaction programs, TP-a and TP-b. Their respective logical units are called LU-a and LU-b. TP-a takes the initiative for the syncpoint by issuing the SYNCPT verb. It is called the *initiator* of the syncpoint. TP-b is called an *agent*. These roles are in no way related to who allocated the conversation! At which point in the conversation should which TP start the synchronization process is a design consideration.

When the initiator issues SYNCPT to start the synchronization, the local resource manager verifies the state of the internal resources. Next LU-a sends a message (PREPARE) to LU-b. When TP-b issues the next RECEIVE-AND-WAIT verb, it receives a return code telling it to take a syncpoint. When it is ready to do so, it also issues the SYNCPT verb. LU-b will check its local resources and then send the message REQUEST COMMIT to LU-a. LU-a now knows that its local resources are ready to commit as well as TP-b (which is a protected resource for TP-a). It sends COMMITTED to LU-b to request the actual changes to be made for TP-b.

After these changes have been made, LU-b erases the log entries for this Logical Unit of Work, sends FORGET to LU-a to report the successful syncpoint, and finally returns control to TP-b with a return code OK. When the FORGET is received by LU-a, it also erases the log entries in its logfile and returns control to TP-a with return code OK.

It should be clear from this description that the only involvement from the transaction programs is the SYNCPT-verb. Eventually this verb will be completed with returncode OK. TP-a issues SYNCPT spontaneously, as an initiator, whereas TP-b does it in response to a return code TAKE SYNCPT. The remainder of the mechanism is handled completely by the

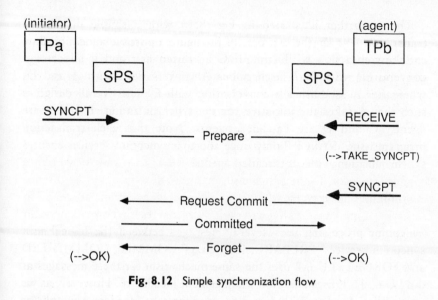

Fig. 8.12 Simple synchronization flow

resource managers and SyncPoint Services and it is thus transparent to the transaction programs.

Let's elaborate a little more on what happens to TP-b. It gets the indication TAKE SYNCPT and when it is ready to do so, it issues the SYNCPT verb. SyncPoint Services, together with the local resource managers, makes sure that *all* associated resources are ready for the syncpoint. This means not only the database(s), but also all other conversations that TP-b may be engaged in. So, before LU-b can respond to the PREPARE it must synchronize the other conversations. To these conversations TP-b appears to be acting as the initiator, with the other TPs being *cascaded agents*. Only after REQUEST COMMIT has been received from all of them, SyncPoint Services in LU-b can assume that all resources are ready and send REQUEST COMMIT to LU-a.

This is further illustrated in Fig. 8.13 with a simple distributed transaction flow. In the first part of the figure a possible allocation flow for the transaction is illustrated. C is started first and it allocates a conversation with B. B itself allocates conversations with A and D, whereafter A establishes a conversation with E. The overall design is such that A takes the initiative for the synchronization. B and E are agents; C and D are cascaded agents. Note that each transaction program issues SYNCPT only once and that syncpoint services ensures synchronization with all cascaded agents.

Presentation Services Headers

Syncpoint processing uses several messages between the logical unit syncpoint services: PREPARE, REQUEST COMMIT, COMMITTED and FORGET. LU 6.2 uses the same mechanism for these messages as did LU 6(.1). It uses Function Management Header 10. However, as we saw earlier (Section 7.2), Function Management Headers can only be present in the first RU of a chain and their presence must be indicated by the Format Identifier bit in the Request Header (RH). Since LU 6.2 may buffer several logical records before actually sending them, it is possible, especially for the PREPARE, that it ends up at the end of a chain! Obviously, a solution could have been to force a flush of the buffers and then send a separate RU containing only FMH-10. That would have been inefficient and therefore a 'trick' is used. The FMH is preceded by two LL-bytes, with a value of X' 0001' , i.e. an *illegal* value for an LL-field (LL-fields always include their own length, i.e. the minimum value is two). The combination is called a *Presentation Services Header*. It is recognized as a Presentation Services Header since it is a code violation, therefore not a regular logical record. In addition the header layout is adapted to the more powerful LU 6.2 synchronization mechanism.

Synchronization errors

The synchronization mechanism was introduced in SNA to ensure consistency of the protected resources across Logical Units of Work. This implies that the mechanism shows its real strength when something goes wrong, not while everything is alright! Actually, things may go wrong in two different ways. Firstly, one of the participating transaction programs may find out during the process that it cannot commit the requested changes. Secondly, the actual communication may fail due to logical unit or session (network) failures.

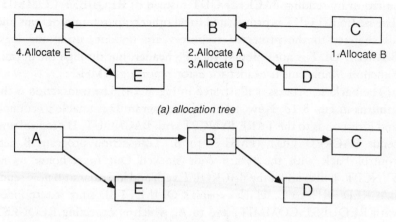

(a) allocation tree

(b) synchronization tree

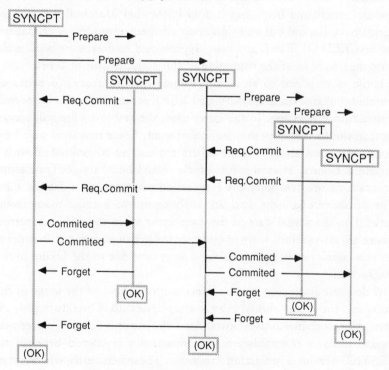

Fig. 8.13 Distributed synchronization flow

In the first situation, there is not really an error from the commu nications point of view and the SyncPoint Services can handle the situation by sending BACKED OUT instead of REQUEST COMMIT. The BACKED OUT is propagated to all other transaction programs and all changes to the protected resources are undone, using the logs. BACKED OUT is not reported via a PS header, but through the normal Function Management header for error reporting, FMH-7.

The backout process is illustrated in Fig. 8.14. The transaction is the same as in Fig. 8.13. Now, transaction program D is unable to commit and it responds to the TAKE SYNCPT with BACKOUT. D's logical unit sends BACKED OUT (FMH-7) to B. Transaction program B gets control back with the return code Backed Out in response to its SYNCPT. B also issues the BACKOUT verb and logical unit B now sends BACKED OUT to C, which expects COMMITTED since it responded with REQUEST COMMIT, and to A, which is expecting REQUEST COMMIT in response to the PREPARE. It is invisible to A where the backout originated from, but it does know that B and all its cascaded agents have backed out and thus restored their resources. A propagates the BACKED OUT to E and now all protected resources are back in the state they were in at the beginning of this Logical Unit of Work.

If the error is due to an actual communication error, it depends on whether the error occurred during SYNCPT processing or during normal transaction processing. In the latter case, the resources are still consistent; in the former they may be inconsistent. Some resources may have been committed already, while others are not yet committed. If such a situation occurs, it is the job of the RESYNC Service Transaction Program to resynchronize the transaction programs to a defined state. The actual mechanisms used are fairly complex, because many things depend on the actual state of the transaction when the failure occurred. There are also various ways to optimize the performance, e.g. in order to prevent databases being locked for a long time due to the failure of one transaction.

A detailed discussion of the subject matter is beyond the scope of this book and the reader should refer to the relevant IBM literature [24]. In brief, the procedure is as follows. After the communication between the logical units is re-established, a conversation is started between the RESYNC Service Transaction Programs. These first verify whether they are both using the appropriate log datasets. (The names of these data sets are exchanged when the conversation with SYNCLEVEL = SYNCPT is allocated.) If the log datasets are correct, the situation that existed before the failure is recreated from the log. After the state of the transaction is compared between both sides and found to be OK, the transaction can be

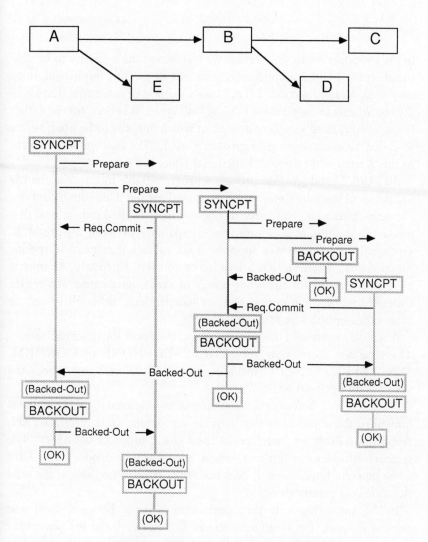

Fig. 8.14 Example of backout processing

completed. Otherwise the equivalent of the backout is performed and the logs are erased.

Subsetting

In the introduction to this section we mentioned the necessity to be able to subset the LU 6.2 architecture, since not all product implementations may need the full function. LU 6.2 uses a method of subsetting that again distinguishes it from previous Logical Unit types. Whereas, for the earlier types, several fixed sets were defined of which one was to be used, here a so-called 'base-and-options' approach is used. (The concept is equivalent to the 'Kernel and optional' Functional Units in OSI.)

All LU 6.2 products that provide a programmable interface at the LU 6.2 protocol boundary *must* implement the base set. This subset contains the verbs, parameters and return codes (with associated indications) that guarantee minimum communications capability between all products. Optionally, products may support other subsets that provide specific functionality. These subsets are called option sets. Currently, 41 subsets have been defined for the whole range of verbs, parameters and return codes. Most of these option sets are independent, although in certain cases other option sets are a prerequisite.

A typical example of this subsetting is the support for synchronization. The base set allows only for SYNCLEVEL = NONE or CONFIRM. SYNCLEVEL = SYNCPT (including the SYNCPT verb and associated verbs) is an optional set.

As mentioned before, the requirement to implement the base set is limited to those products that provide a programmable interface (API, Application Program Interface) at the LU 6.2 protocol boundary. The requirement does not apply to certain 'fixed function' products that have some inherent limitations. It does not make sense to implement the send function in a printer device.

In the subsetting a further distinction is made between local and remote support. *Local support* means that the verb (or the parameter or ...) is available for use by the local transaction program. *Remote support* means that the LU must be able to handle the result of the use of the verb by the remote transaction program. Often, something that is optional for local support is in the base set for remote support.

A good example is the PREPARE-TO-RECEIVE verb. It was mentioned earlier that a transaction program need not use PREPARE-TO-RECEIVE, but might issue RECEIVE-AND-WAIT instead at the expense of less synchronization control. PREPARE-TO-RECEIVE is indeed in the option set for local support. However, if the remote transaction program does issue PREPARE-TO-RECEIVE, the LU must understand the signal it receives (CD, Change Direction) and pass it on to its transaction program. Therefore, PREPARE-TO-RECEIVE is in the base set for remote support. For certain verbs or parameters that have no immediate remote effect, the remote support requirement is not applicable. This is always the case for return codes and associated indications. It is also true for most Operator Control Verbs. In Fig. 8.10 it is indicated for each verb whether local (L) or remote (R) support is in the base set (B), in an option set (O) or not applicable (--). For more detail, also with respect to the parameters and return codes, the user should consult the appropriate IBM documentation [23].

LU 6.2 Security

In Section 5.4 we have described how session-level cryptography can be used to protect data flowing on the session from exposure or interference. LU 6.2 provides for additional (optional) mechanisms to verify the identity of two LUs before the session is actually started and, in addition, to verify the validity of a transaction program to access a secure resource.

When the Logical Unit is defined (through the Control Operator verbs), User-IDs and passwords can be specified for those users allowed to access the resources. If this level of security is specified, these IDs and passwords must be used when the ALLOCATE verb is issued. They are sent in the ATTACH FM Header (FMH-5) to be verified by the target LU. This provides for *conversation-level security*.

It is also possible to mutually verify the identity of two logical units when they try to establish a session. For this purpose an LU-LU password must be defined *in advance* for each LU-LU pair. When the session activation is started, the Primary LU (PLU) sends a 64-bit random number as part of the user data structured subfield [12] in the BIND. The Secondary LU (SLU) enciphers this random number, using the DES algorithm with the password as a key. The result is returned in the response to the BIND, together with a second 64-bit random number which is generated by the SLU. The enciphered PLU random number is deciphered by the PLU and, if it is found wrong, the PLU discontinues session establishment by sending UNBIND. If the result is OK, the SLU is apparently the right one. Now the PLU must prove itself to the SLU. It enciphers the SLU random number (again using the password) and sends the results in a Function Management Header FMH-12, which is specifically defined for this purpose. If the SLU, after deciphering, finds the results equal to its random number, it accepts the session and partner

LU verification is complete. Otherwise it rejects the session by sending UNBIND.

Note that these mechanisms only verify the identity of the partners when the session or conversation is established. It does not prevent an intruder from taking over in a network that is not secure. It also relies completely on external procedures for the management of the passwords. If a network is not secure, session-level cryptography should also be used since it gives continuous protection and is less sensitive to external procedures because of the session key generated for each session. When both levels of security are used, the CRV (Cryptography Verification) RU flows first after the response to BIND, since it is a Session Control RU. After the response to CRV, an FM data RU is sent, which only contains the FM Header-12. It must be the first FMD Request on the session.

9 SNA Network Interconnection

In Chapter 7 we discussed the cooperation of SSCPs in setting up a session between LUs in different domains. The *domain* concept was introduced in SNA as a network management tool; each SSCP is responsible for its own domain. Network Addressable Units in the domains are identified by their network names. These network names have to be unique in the domain only. If an NAU must be accessed from another domain, it must have a name that is also unique in that domain, or it must have a unique alias. All domains together form the complete SNA network. This is the 'management' view, applicable in the Function Management layer.

At the Path Control level, the network is composed of subareas, with a subarea node in the center of each subarea and the peripheral nodes around it. The subarea node is identified by the subarea part of the network address and each Network Addressable Unit inside the subarea is identified by a unique element address in that subarea. The network address is thus unique across the network.

SNA Network Interconnection (SNI) extends the communications capabilities of Network Addressable Units outside the limits of their own network [27]. It allows NAUs in one network to communicate with NAUs in another network, while the two networks remain fully autonomous. Why is this autonomy so important? Supposedly, if two NAUs in different networks have to communicate, they could be made part of the same network by integrating the two networks. However, based on what was said above, this would mean that the address spaces of both networks should be mutually exclusive in order to keep addresses unique. Care must also be taken to avoid unnecessary restrictions on the names used.

There is another reason why integration is not wanted. Suppose the networks belong to different companies or two divisions within the same company. Normally, most communications will be local to each network but only occasionally there will be a need for communication between NAUs in both networks, for example for placing a purchase order. Nobody would argue that the two networks should be integrated just for this occasional communication. It would imply that the addresses (and possibly the names) used by company A could not be used by company B. It would be much better if both networks could remain completely autonomous, with as little knowledge about the other network as possible. (Later we will show that it is possible with SNI to have no *exact* knowledge at all about the other network.)

SNI not only guarantees the autonomy of the two networks at the level of names and addresses, it also guarantees the integrity of the networks at the operational level. Neither network can seize control over the other network, nor can malfunction of one network (e.g. inappropriate flow control) cause problems in the other.

The level at which the interconnection takes place is the Virtual Route Level. The higher protocols (i.e. the session protocols) are end-to-end across the networks, but they appear to be local to their own network only. It is completely transparent to an LU (and its end-user) that the partner LU is in another network. This is achieved by translating the *network specific* names and addresses in a *gateway* when traffic flows from one network to another.

As we know from earlier sections, names are used mainly in the Network Services requests which flow to or from SSCPs. Addresses are used mainly in the Transmission Header, for the routing of the messages in the subarea nodes. Therefore, SNI defines a gateway which consists of a *gateway SSCP* and a *gateway node*. The gateway SSCP (SSCP-GW) is responsible for name translations. The gateway node is a subarea node where the addresses are translated as messages pass through. Viewed from one network, all resources that can be accessed in the other network appear to be just other-domain resources, belonging to the gateway SSCP. All traffic with the other network flows to and from the gateway subarea. In other words, the accessible resources (NAUs) in the other network are mapped into the own network.

The mapping implies that cross-network resources must have names and addresses in their own network but also in the other network from which they may be accessed, which seems in contradiction with our earlier statement of full autonomy of each network. SNI solves this problem with a minimum impact on the address spaces. There is also minimum user awareness about the names in both networks. An example (Fig. 9.1) will illustrate this.

Company A has a network (NETA), in which there is an application PAYROLL. The application is owned by SSCP1. The PAYROLL application must communicate with an application in the network of company A's bank (NETB) in order to transfer money into the employees' accounts. This application is known in NETB as IMS and it is owned

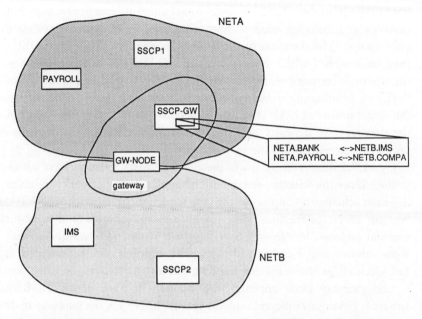

Fig. 9.1 Name translation between interconnected SNA networks

by SSCP2. Since the name IMS could already be in use in NETA, an *alias name* is assigned in NETA. Let's use for this banking application the alias name BANK. In other words, the application IMS in NETB is known in NETA as application BANK. As far as NETA is concerned, SSCP-GW is the owner of BANK. In SSCP-GW the translation is made between BANK and NETB.IMS. Note that the gateway prefixes the name with the network ID. Similarly, application PAYROLL must have an alias assigned in network B's name space. Here we will use the name COMPA. This alias is also stored in the tables of SSCPP-GW*.

When PAYROLL and IMS are in session, the session traffic flows through the gateway node. Note that it does *not* pass through the gateway SSCP, but only through the subarea node that physically connects the two networks. This is similar to multi-domain SNA, where the SSCPs are also only involved during session establishment. In the gateway node, the (NETA) address of PAYROLL is translated into some alias address in NETB, and the (NETB) address of IMS is translated into

---

* For the time being, SSCP-GW is shown to be in NETA. Later we will look at other configurations.

an alias address for use in NETA. The mechanism is very similar to that used in the Boundary Function (refer to Section 4.4) except that now full network addresses are used on both sides. Since the alias addresses are only used for the duration of the session between PAYROLL and IMS, they are assigned when the session is established and freed again when the session is terminated. In this way the number of addresses required in the gateway subarea can be kept reasonably small. It is not dependent on the total number of NAUs that can be accessed in the other network. On the contrary, it depends only on the total number of simultaneous sessions between LUs in the two networks.

Figure 9.2 illustrates the use of the alias addresses. First we have a look at the addressing scheme used in both networks. Both networks are given different schemes to emphasize the independence. In network A (NETA) we use 16-bit addressing with a 4-bit subarea address and a 12-bit element address. In network B we also use 16-bit addressing, but with 8-bit subarea and element addresses. The addresses are represented in hexadecimal (without the surrounding quotes: X' ').

The gateway node appears as a subarea in both networks. Both subareas belong to different address spaces! In NETA the gateway node is subarea 3; in NETB it is 04. The full network address of LU 'PAYROLL', which has element address 013 in NETA, is 6013. PAYROLL thinks it is in session with LU 3211. When it sends a message to 3211, this message is routed to the gateway node (since that is subarea 3). In this gateway node the address 3211 is recognized as an alias and the destination address is changed into 0725 (element 25 in subarea 07), which is the actual (NETB) address of LU 'IMS'. After the message 'crossed the border' between NETA and NETB, the address of PAYROLL is changed into 0415, which is its alias address in NETB, so IMS thinks it is in session with 0415. Neither LU is aware of the fact that the session is actually cross-network.

Since the SNA Network Interconnection operates at the Path Control level, with translation of the network addresses, the Explicit and Virtual Routes remain local to the interconnected networks. The benefit is that Virtual and Explicit (!) route numbers need not be coordinated between the networks. Again, this preserves the autonomy of both networks. However, the implication is that Virtual Route Flow Control cannot be used end-to-end. It must be performed in two stages: from the PLU-subarea to the gateway node and from the gateway node to the SLU-subarea (and the reverse of course). This makes the gateway node vulnerable for congestion. To protect the gateway node, SNI defines a simple local mechanism.

A counter is associated with each Virtual Route that ends in the

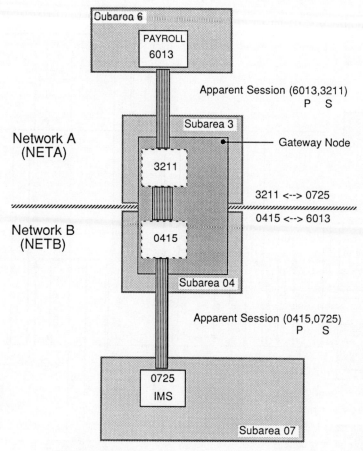

Fig. 9.2 Address translation in the Gateway Node

gateway node. This counter is increased by one for each message that enters the gateway node via the associated Virtual Route. When one of these messages leaves the gateway node again, the counter is decreased. Thus the counter keeps track of the number of messages that arrived on a certain VR and are still around in the gateway node. Recall from Section 4.3 that a VR endnode sends a VR Pacing Response (VRPRI) to the other end of the Virtual Route, when another 'window' of messages may be sent. A gateway node will not send this VRPRI if the counter for that Virtual Route exceeds a certain (implementation-defined) threshold value. The side-effect of this could be that the window is increased, when the VRPRI is finally sent (if the window is not yet at its maximum value).

Fig. 9.3 Sample cross-network session activation flow

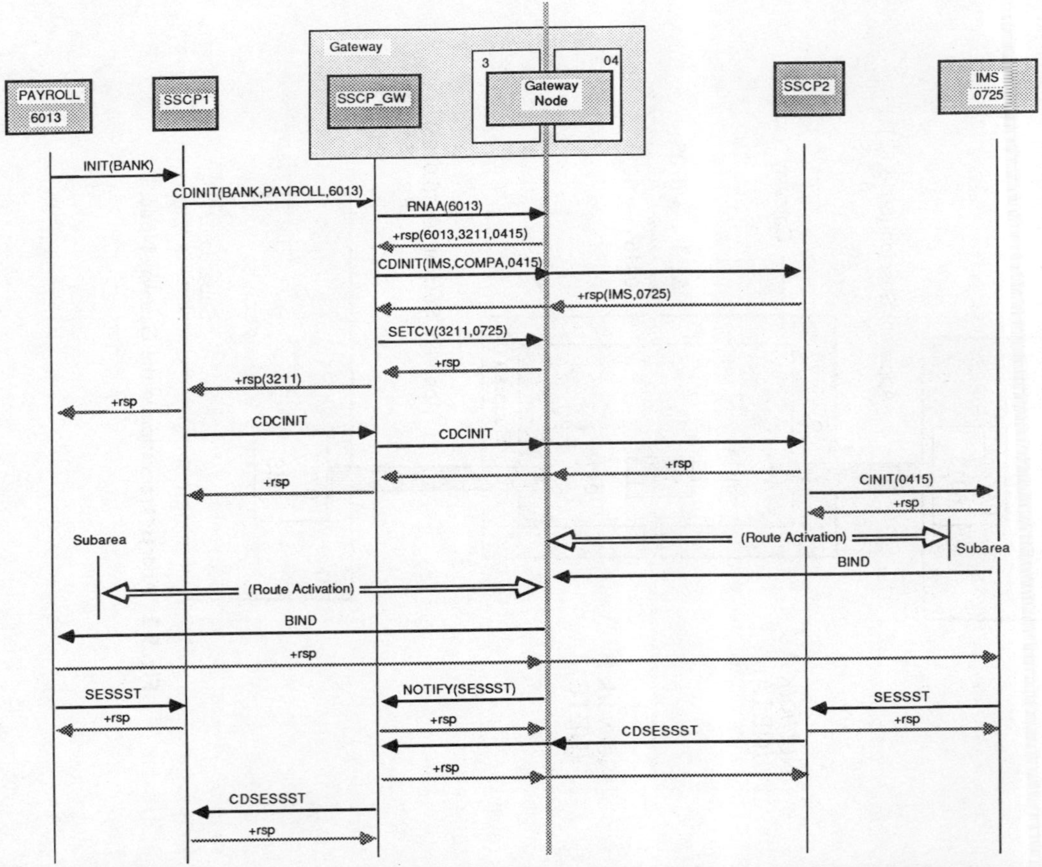

The Gateway Node may, depending on a second threshold value, also send the Change Window Reply Indicator (CWRI) to prevent this increase and instead decrease the window. Effectively this indicates that the gateway node suffers minor congestion.

In Chapter 7 we discussed session establishment, both for the single domain and the multiple domain situation. We will now look at session activation for the cross-network case and notice again that there is no difference from the point of view of the LUs. The awareness of the other networks exists only in the Gateway (SSCP and gateway node).

The session establishment is illustrated (in simplified form) in Fig. 9.3 We use the same configuration as in Fig. 9.2, with application PAYROLL in NETA and IMS in NETB. The qualified alias in NETA is NETA.BANK for IMS. In NETB it is NETB.COMPA for PAYROLL. We let PAYROLL take the initiative for the session, so it sends an INITSELF request to its SSCP (SSCP1) indicating it wants a session with application BANK. SSCP1 recognizes that BANK is a cross-domain resource, owned by SSCP-GW. SSCP1 sends a CD-INIT to SSCP-GW indicating that PAYROLL (with address 6013) wants a session with BANK. It also indicates that PAYROLL will act as a Secondary LU. SSCP-GW receives the CD-INIT and recognizes BANK as being a cross-network resource. It replaces the LU-name BANK with the real (NETB)name IMS and also replaces PAYROLL with its alias COMPA. Before it can forward the CD-INIT to SSCP2 however, it must also have an alias address to represent PAYROLL in the address space of NETB. A request is sent to the Physical Unit in the Gateway Node (RNAA, Request Network Address Assignment) to request the assignment of alias addresses. The RNAA carries the address of PAYROLL (6013); the response of RNAA carries the alias to be used for PAYROLL (0415) and also the alias address (3211) that will be used in NETA for BANK (i.e. IMS). Note, however, that the real address of IMS is not yet known!

Now that the alias addresses have been set up, SSCP-GW forwards the CD-INIT to SSCP2, which handles it as it would any other cross-domain request. It locates its resource IMS and verifies that it can act as a Primary Logical Unit. It then sends a response to the CD-INIT. This response also carries the (real) address of IMS (0725). When SSCP-GW receives the response, it first sends a Set Control Vector (SETCV) to the Gateway Node, to complete the address translation table. When this is done, it replaces the IMS address (0725) in the CD-INIT response by its NETA alias (3211) and forwards the response to SSCP1, which can then send a positive response to the INITSELF from PAYROLL. This positive response means that the resource is available and that session activation will be started.

The remainder of the activation procedure is quite similar to the normal cross-domain situation. SSCP1 sends a CD-CINIT (as the owner of the secondary LU) with information pertinent to PAYROLL (BIND image, etc.). Although the general responsibility of SSCP-GW is to translate names, it must sometimes also translate addresses. This happens when addresses are contained in the Network Services requests themselves as is the case for the CD-CINIT. Since the CD-CINIT also carries LU-names, SSCP-GW performs the necessary alias transforms and forwards the CD-CINIT to SSCP2. SSCP2 can now build CINIT and send it to LU IMS.

IMS must send BIND to LU 'COMPA' with address 0415. Before it can do this, Explicit and Virtual Routes between its subarea and the gateway node may have to be activated (refer to Section 4.3). In this particular example we take the activation for granted and send the BIND to the gateway node (actually to 'ghost' LU 0415). The BIND is intercepted and the addresses are translated. Since the BIND also contains LU-names, the gateway node must replace these as well in this particular case. This is similar to the occasional address translation in SSCP-GW (see above). The information for the transform is supplied in the SETCV. After the appropriate route activation in NETA, the BIND is sent to PAYROLL, which sends a positive response to BANK (IMS).

Both LUs do send a Session Started (SESSST) Network Services request to their SSCP, with SSCP2 forwarding it as a CD-SESSST to SSCP-GW and SSCP1. In order to make sure that the gateway tables remain synchronized with respect to active sessions, the Gateway Node, when it forwards the positive response to the BIND to IMS, also sends a NOTIFY to SSCP-GW to tell it that the session has been established.

Interconnection Configurations

We have so far looked at the basic structure of a Gateway, which consists of a Gateway SSCP and a Gateway Node, and at the basic functions performed by the gateway in order to maintain autonomy and independence of both networks. One of the design goals of SNI was the preservation of this autonomy and, on the other hand, maximum flexibility in configuring interconnected networks. We will now discuss some of the configuration options and illustrate how this can also be used to ensure even more autonomy than with the configuration in the preceding examples. The various configurations are shown in Fig. 9.4.

Figure 9.4(a) is the configuration which we used in the example above. It implies that the Gateway-SSCP, which is part of one of the networks, has some knowledge about the other network. Isolation between both

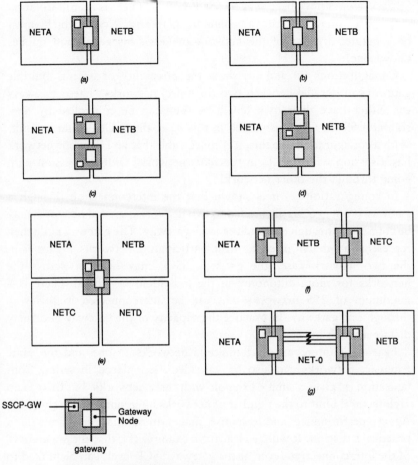

Fig. 9.4 SNA gateway configurations
  (a) simple case
  (b) split SSCP-GW responsibility (shared control)
  (c) parallel gateways
  (d) parallel gateways with shared SSCP-GW
  (e) multiple networks, one gateway
  (f) cascaded networks
  (g) cascaded networks with 'null' network

networks can be enhanced through configuration (b), where the gateway responsibility is split across two SSCPs. Each SSCP only knows *aliases* for the other network, but no real resource names and addresses. In the previous example, the SSCP-GW could have been split in SSCP-GW-A and SSCP-GW-B. In that case, SSCP-GW-A would have translated PAYROLL into COMPA and then forwarded the CD-INIT to SSCP-GW-B, which would have translated BANK into IMS. Similarly, the

SETCV would have been sent by SSCP GW D. There is no full isolation yet, since there is still a common Gateway Node which must be generated by one of the network owners (this generation implies knowledge).

Configurations (c) and (d) show the possibility of having multiple gateways in parallel between two (or more) networks. These gateways can either have their own SSCP, or they can be controlled by one, common SSCP. Obviously, also in this case, the SSCPs could be split. With a configuration like this, it is conceivable that an LU in one network has a session with an LU in the *same* network, with the session path going through the other network!

In configuration (e) it is shown that the interconnection through a gateway is not necessarily limited to two networks: several networks may be connected through one and the same gateway. The gateway node then represents a subarea in each of the participating networks. Again as in the two-network case, the gateway SSCP may be split across the networks for more autonomy in the individual networks. There is a maximum of 255 networks that can be interconnected in this way through one gateway. In practice the capacity of the gateway node may dictate a much lower limit.

Instead of interconnecting multiple networks to one and the same gateway, networks can also be 'cascaded', i.e. placed in series. Configuration (f) gives a simple example with three networks, but there is no architectural limit to the number of networks interconnected in this way. Again, performance and response time criteria may set limits in a practical situation. It will be clear from example (f), that the 'awareness' of the interconnection, even at the gateway SSCP level, can be limited to awareness about the immediate neighbour network. If an LU in NETA requests a session with an LU which, its SSCP thinks, belongs to NETB, the session request may actually be routed to the next gateway SSCP, which then decides that the requested LU is in NETC.

An extreme situation, where awareness of the interconnected networks about each other is completely reduced, is given in configuration (g). Here, the middle 'network' in a cascade consists of physical links only, interconnecting two gateway nodes. So, the middle network only has two subareas, with the addresses in the two mapped directly onto each other. This mapping is known to both gateway SSCPs, but *not* the mapping onto the real resources in each other's network: both are fully autonomous and the impact on their own network is the reservation of a few element addresses in one of their own subareas, which then becomes the gateway node. Of course, the gateway SSCPs must have a mutual agreement about the alias names they will use for each other's resources, but the real names and addresses need not to be known. A configuration of this type is dubbed a *null-network* (NET-0) because of the rudimentary nature of the middle network. Obviously, more than two networks can be connected to the same null-network, thus creating a 'star-topology' of networks that can communicate together but have no other awareness about each other than a set of alias names. For certain organizations this could be an attractive alternative to configuration (e) for the creation of a corporate-wide overall network, consisting of individually autonomous networks.

10 Related architectures

10.1 Introduction

There are a number of architectures which are very closely related to SNA, and are considered part of the SNA. They build on top of SNA's communications capabilities, but could be used in other environments as well. They are either related to communications themselves, or they use the communications environment to provide a certain functionality. Distributed Data Management is an example of the latter. Since its main emphasis is not communications, it will not be discussed in the context of this book. The other ones are Document Interchange Architecture and SNA Distribution Services. Their main purpose is communications and for that reason they are described in this chapter. A third architecture is Document Content Architecture, which provides a 'formal' description of documents in order to make interchange of documents easier. As such it is closely related to DIA and therefore we start with a brief description of it. After that, Document Interchange Architecture is described and finally SNA Distribution Services.

10.2 Document Content Architecture

The purpose of Document Content Architecture (DCA) is to describe text documents as they are exchanged between (office) systems. DCA documents come in two flavours: final-form-text and revisable-form-text. The first form is a stream of text characters with embedded control characters that allow the text to be presented on a visual medium like a printer or a display. It does not allow any additional formatting or editing of the text. Revisable-form-text on the other hand allows for the revision of both the text and the format control in the document.

Since this is not a book on word processing, we will not discuss DCA in great functional detail, i.e. we will not describe the meaning or the result of, for example, a SYLLABE HYPHEN. Mainly because of the relationship with Document Interchange Architecture (DIA) we will however give a brief overview of the concepts of both final-form-text and revisable-form-text and describe the general structure of the datastreams for both. The interested reader may find the additional detail in the IBM publications [28, 29].

Final-form-text

Final-form-text datastreams contain the bare minimum required to present the data stream on a visual medium. This means that it contains the text itself and control codes that control this presentation and the operation of the presentation device (e.g. the printer). These control codes are either one-byte EBCDIC controls, like X' 0D' for Carriage Return, or multi-byte controls as defined for SNA Character String (SCS, Section 7.2). These multi-byte controls all start with the 'multi-byte ESCAPE', X' 2B'.

The one-byte controls have in general an immediate effect, such as the beginning of a new line or a new page. The multi-byte controls may have a long-term effect. They control, for instance, the line spacing, the character set, the font, underscoring, etc. A typical data stream will start with some initiation (multi-byte) controls. Thereafter the lines of text follow, each terminated by a line-end (and sometimes a page-end). However, additional one- or multi-byte controls may occur within or in between lines of text. In Fig. 10.1 a simple illustration of such a data stream is given.

Revisable-form-text

In revisable-form-text the document format is not *controlled* immediately as in final-form-text, but rather it is *described*. This description is based on a series of structured fields, some of which contain the document text, with or without embedded one- and multi-byte controls. Obviously most of the controls used in final-form-text can also be embedded in the revisable-form-text stream, if direct control over the result is required (e.g. a required hyphen or a required carriage return).

A basic concept in the revisable-form-text is the page image. The layout of this page image is described in terms of size (page width and depth), margins, indentations, etc. The layout and the various relevant parameters are illustrated in Fig. 10.2.

The structured fields used to construct the data stream are General Data Stream variables as defined for LU 6.2 (Section 8.2). Each structure starts with a five-byte introducer, optionally followed by the *content* field. The content itself may contain structured fields, but DCA uses

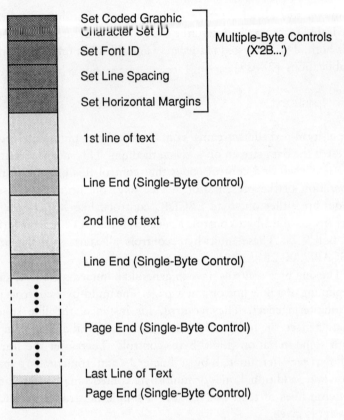

Set Coded Graphic
Character Set ID

Set Font ID

Set Line Spacing

Set Horizontal Margins

Multiple-Byte Controls
(X'2B...')

1st line of text

Line End (Single-Byte Control)

2nd line of text

Line End (Single-Byte Control)

Page End (Single-Byte Control)

Last Line of Text
Page End (Single-Byte Control)

Fig. 10.1 Example of Final-Form-Text data stream

one-level nesting only. As is usual in GDS, the first two bytes of the
introducer specify the *total* length of the structured field (including the
length bytes). The next two bytes (the GDS ID field) specify the class and
type of the structured field. IDs used by DCA are summarized in
Fig. 10.3. This summary also provides an illustration of the type of
control available through DCA structured fields. The final introducer
byte is the format byte, which is always X' 00' for DCA.

A DCA revisable-form-text document is composed of several components, each of which is a sequence of structured fields. The components
are the Format Units 1 and 2 (and optionally 3), the Text Unit(s) and the
End Unit. The structure is illustrated in Fig. 10.4.

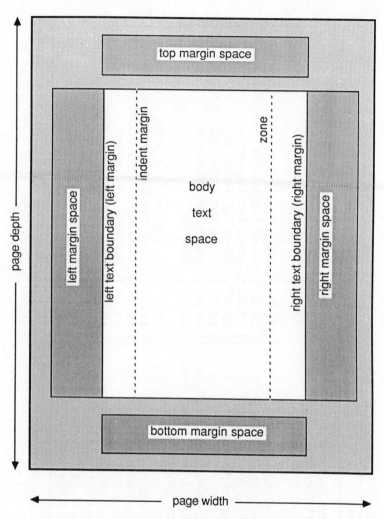

Fig. 10.2 Layout of page image

GDS ID	Name	GDS ID	Name
E1 03	Format Unit Prefix	E6 01	Line parameters
E1 04	Text Unit Prefix	E6 02	Tab Parameters
E1 06	End Unit Prefix	E6 03	Line Numbering
E2 01	Primary Master Format	E8 01	Margin Text, top, all
E2 02	Alternate Master Format	E8 02	Margin Text, top, odd
E2 04	Text Unit Format Change	E8 03	Margin Text, top, even
E2 05	Document Parameters	E8 04	Margin Text, bottom, all
		E8 05	Margin Text, bottom, odd
E3 01	Establish Primary Master Format	E8 06	Margin Text, bottom, even
E3 02	Establish Alternate Master Format	E8 07	Body Text
E3 03	Return to Master Format		
		E9 01	Punctuation Format, arithmetic parameters
E4 02	Print Medium	E9 02	Punctuation Format, character parameters
E4 03	Operator Message	E9 03	Note Format Parameters
		E9 04	Auto-outline Parameters
E5 01	Margin Text Parameters, top	E9 05	Page Formatting Parameters
E5 04	Margin Text Parameters, bottom		
E5 07	Page Image Parameters		
E5 08	Page Image Numbering		

Fig. 10.3 Summary of GDS IDs used for Revisable-Text-Form

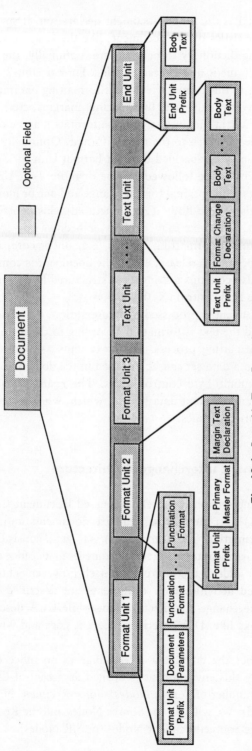

Fig. 10.4 Revisable-Text-Form document structure

159

Format Unit-1 is the initial document declaration. It specifies several overall characteristics of the document, like the Graphic Character Set and the spelling dictionary to be used and, optionally, the punctuation formats for arithmetic and character fields. Format Unit-2 describes the *master format*. In this format the default formatting parameters, including the page layout (page size, line spacing, margins, etc.), are defined. Even though later in the data stream the formats may be changed, it is always possible to return to the master format. Optionally an alternate master format may be specified through Format Unit-3.

The format units are followed by one or more Text Units. Each of these may contain an optional format change and one or more Body Text structured fields. These Body Text structured fields contain the actual document text. The text may contain embedded one- or multi-byte controls for further formatting control (e.g. underscore, font change, begin/end keep, margin release, etc.). The document is completed by an End Unit. It also contains a Body Text structured field, which can only contain a Page End control (X' 0C').

When a document is processed for presentation, the various units are interpreted and the text is formatted according to the formats specified. During the formatting process other text units as well as data from specific fields in a data set can be included in the document. This is also controlled via multi-byte control codes. The result of the formatting process is a final-form-text data stream, which, when printed, results in one or more printed pages.

10.3 Document Interchange Architecture

In the preceding section we briefly discussed Document Content Architecture (DCA) as a method to structure documents and specify their layout and formatting. The aim of DCA is to get a consistent document definition to ease the interchange of documents in an office environment. DCA does not address the interchange itself however. This interchange and the related activities with documents are described by DIA, the Document Interchange Architecture. So, while DCA describes what a document looks like, DIA describes where it goes and what should be done with it.

DIA describes the document interchange in an office environment. Architecturally this environment is defined as a central *Office Systems Node* with a number of *Source Nodes* and/or *Recipient Nodes* attached to it (Fig. 10.5). We will call the Source Nodes and the Recipient Nodes collectively the Source/Recipient Nodes (or S/R Nodes).

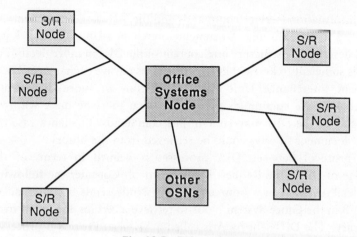

Fig. 10.5 DIA configuration

The Office System Node (OSN) provides DIA services to receive, store, route and deliver documents to/from S/R nodes, usually at their request. Actually, the S/R nodes do send and receive documents on behalf of their end-users, the *sources* or *recipients*. In practical (i.e. implementation) terms the OSN can be seen as a departmental system, with the S/R nodes being the various workstations around it (personal computers, word processors, etc.). The Office System Node thus has more responsibilities, based on its central position in the organization (and presumably its more powerful configuration).

Conceptually, the OSN can also exchange documents with other OSNs (Fig. 10.5) given the appropriate transport network. SNA Distribution Services (SNADS) uses the DIA protocol structure to define general distribution services across systems. These services are described in Section 10.4. In the current section we will concentrate on the 'local' situation, i.e. one Office System Node with various Source/Recipient Nodes around it. In this context it should also be mentioned that the term 'document' is used in a very broad sense in DIA. It may be a document as described by DCA, or it can be any collection of data that users want to exchange.

In relation to the basic SNA architecture, it should be pointed out at this point that the 'attachment' of S/R Nodes to the OSN is defined at a logical level. Although physical attachment is a prerequisite for communication, this is not visible in DIA. DIA relies on the SNA LU 6.2 architecture to make the communication possible.

The information (service commands and the associated documents) is exchanged in DIA through Document Interchange Units (DIUs). Later we will describe the structure and content of the DIU in more detail. For now it is sufficient to know that DIA processes always exchange DIUs. A Document Interchange Unit may contain one or more documents, together with the commands that define what must be done with the document; or the DIU may contain just commands. In such a case the subject document (if any) could be retrieved from the library.

The protocol between DIA processes is defined in terms of the exchange of DIUs, the Request/Reply protocol. Consider the following example. Process A in a Source/Recipient Node sends a command to process B in the Office System Node to retrieve a certain document from the library. The DIU sent by A is called a *Request*. Process B processes the request, retrieves the document and sends it together with the DELIVER command in a DIU to A. This DIU is now called the *Reply*.

The sender of a request may specify that a reply must be sent immediately (Synchronous Reply Requested, SRR), at some later time (Asynchronous Reply Requested, ARR) or, in certain cases, that a reply is not necessary (No Reply Requested, NRR). An example of a synchronous reply is the delivery of a document from the library as used above. An example of an asynchronous reply is the sending of a memo to another user. In that case a reply can only be sent after the addressee has actually read the message, which may happen much later since the addressee may not be present at the workstation (typical Electronic Mail situation). If we take this example a little bit further, we realize that, when the other user sends a reply, a reaction is again wanted. So, we must indicate also on the reply that a reply (asynchronous) is requested. Such a sequence of DIUs would stop when No Reply Requested is indicated. Another example of NRR is the acknowledgement of a received document. In that case there is no need to reply to the acknowledgement, so it indicates NRR.

It follows from this discussion that the reply-class is not only indicated on a request, but also on a reply and a whole chain of events may result. Another possibility is that more than one reply results from a single request. For example, when a request is sent to the OSN to deliver all messages received since the last session, there may be several. Each of the messages is sent in a separate reply. Depending on the situation each reply may also specify a certain reply class.

Particularly in the asynchronous class and in the situation with multiple replies, it is important to know to which request a particular reply is related. Each DIU (request or reply) is therefore assigned a unique identifier (DIU-ID), which can be referred to in later DIUs as

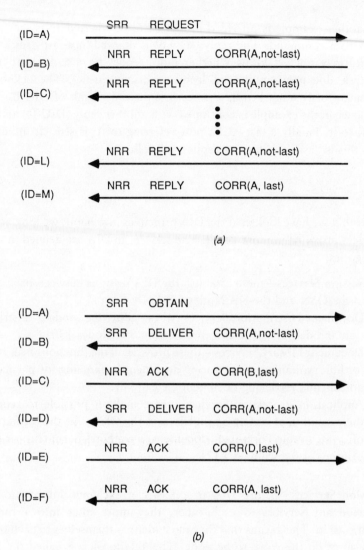

(a)

(b)

Fig. 10.6 DIA Request/Reply flows

the *correlation ID*. In Fig. 10.6(a) such a sequence is illustrated. A request carries DIU-ID = A and it results in several replies (identified as B, C, ..., M). Each of these replies refers back to the original request (CORR = A) and specifies No Reply (NRR). Furthermore, in the CORR field of each reply, except the last one, it is indicated that these replies are not the last. Reply M however is marked last and thus concludes the sequence of replies.

Another example is provided in Fig. 10.6(b), where data is sent as a reply to a command. The reply (ID = B) is marked 'not-last', since the sender may not yet know whether more replies have to be sent (e.g. multiple documents requested from a message queue). The acknowledgement of B is marked 'last' since it is the only result of DIU-B. The sequence in the example is continued with another reply (DIU-D) and an ACK to it. Finally a last ACK, now referring to A, is sent. It indicates that this is 'last', so no more replies will follow.

DIA Services

Now that we have looked at the DIA principles in general, we look at the services provided in more detail. The services in DIA are defined in four categories:

- Session Services—these establish the DIA sessions between processes in the OSN and the S/R Nodes [26].
- Document Distribution Services—these allow the sending, distribution and delivery of documents to/from S/R Nodes [30].
- Document Library Services—these provide all the functions necessary for library management: storing documents, searching for particular documents, retrieving documents, etc. [31].
- Application Processing Services—these make it possible to request the execution of certain applications in the OSN, like the formatting of a Revisable-Form-text document into Final-Form-text or the printing of a document [32].

Session Services Before DIA processes can exchange information or provide any services to each other, they must enter into a certain relationship. This means that they must identify themselves to each other and agree on the work to be done. This relationship is called the *DIA Session*. This DIA session is not immediately related to the SNA session. Actually, the two are defined at different levels of abstraction. The DIA processes are (Service) Transaction Programs from an LU 6.2 point of view and in order to get the DIA session, they start an LU 6.2 conversation (Fig. 10.7). Eventually, the conversation will be allocated to a (SNA) session between the two LUs.

DIA Session Services help the two processes to establish the DIA session. The basic command is the SIGN-ON, in which the requestor provides identification and the necessary information about authorization, accounting, etc. The type of work to be done is specified in the SIGN-ON through the *Function Sets* (see below). The SIGN-ON reply is

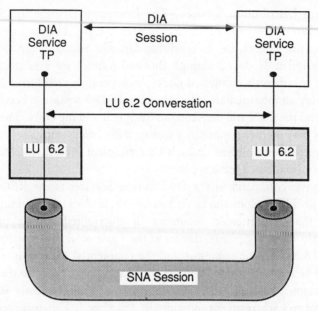

Fig. 10.7 Relation between DIA sessions and SNA sessions

used to agree on the requested Function Sets or propose different functions. However, the newly proposed functions must be a subset of the functions originally requested.

The SIGN-OFF command is used to terminate the DIA session. This command may be sent by either partner and it does not require a reply.

Another Session Services command is the ACKNOWLEDGE, which was already introduced in the example flows in Fig. 10.6. It is a general-purpose command, in that it can be used to report either successful or unsuccessful completion of a previous DIA command. In the event of unsuccessful completion, the data field contains an exception code, which provides a description of the type problem encountered. If appropriate, the data field may also contain a recommended action for recovery. The Correlation parameter must always be present in an ACKNOWLEDGE, because it always refers to an earlier command.

Finally, the SET-CONTROL-VALUE command can be used to change passwords for both users and documents. Obviously, if it is used to change the password for a user other than the signed-on user (e.g. an operator or supervisor), an authorization password is also needed.

Document Distribution Services The Document Distribution Services are the heart of Document Interchange Architecture. They can be used to distribute documents, i.e. to send them from a Source Node to one or more Recipient Nodes. Although this can happen on a bilateral basis between two directly connected nodes, in general an Office System Node would play an intermediate role, whereby the DIA session is between the Source and the OSN and between the Recipient and the OSN. The role of the OSN may involve temporarily storing a document until a session with the recipient is established and until the recipient is ready to receive the document (mailbox function).

The basic command in the Distribution Services is the REQUEST-DISTRIBUTION command. A Source Node uses this command to request that a particular document be distributed to one or more recipients. These recipients may be at the same or at different Recipient Nodes. (Actually, the requestor and the recipient(s) may be at the same node.) The requestor need issue the command only once with the names of all recipients. The Office System Node will subsequently send the document to each recipient individually ('fan out'). The document itself may be present in the DIU that carries the command (see below under Document Interchange Unit), but it is also allowed that the command just carries a reference to a document in the library. A short message may be appended to the document; this message will be delivered to all recipients.

Associated with the REQUEST-DISTRIBUTION is the DELIVER command. With this command documents can be sent from an OSN to a recipient. Normally, the document will be present in the DIU and a short message may be appended (the same message used in the REQUEST-DISTRIBUTION command).

The DELIVER command can also be used to send documents from the source to the recipient directly, when two Send/Receive DIA processes have a DIA session directly, i.e. without the OSN.

When documents are submitted to an OSN for delivery to a recipient, these documents are queued in the OSN if the recipient does not have an active DIA session or if unsolicited distribution is not allowed. A recipient can request information about documents queued for him by sending the LIST command. If any documents (or messages with delivery status about other documents) are queued, a list is returned by the OSN with the DELIVER command. The recipient may request subsequent delivery with the OBTAIN command or may request that the documents are removed by sending the CANCEL-DISTRIBUTION command. An OSN may indicate to a Source/Recipient Node that something is available by sending the STATUS-LIST command. This command is always sent unsolicited. The S/R Node may retrieve the documents (with OBTAIN) or first get the status via LIST.

A final command for the Distribution Services is PROCESS-BIT-STRING. It is used for bit-image (facsimile) devices. These devices are normally only equipped to send bit-coded images of original documents. In order to indicate the kind of function requested, coded cover sheets may be used, on which the user marks the requested function, etc. Depending on the sophistication of the device, it may or it may not be capable of interpreting the bit-representation of this cover sheet. If it is capable of doing so, it will send the appropriate DIA commands with the image of the document, e.g. in a REQUEST-DISTRIBUTION command. If the device is not capable of doing the interpretation, it sends the bit image of the cover sheet to the OSN, using the PROCESS-BIT-STRING command. The OSN should then be capable of interpreting it. (Of course, this is pre-arranged via the function set that was agreed for the session.)

Document Library Services   An essential aspect of DIA is the description of the services for the use of document libraries. These library services are complementary to the distribution services in that they allow the storage of documents. Copies of documents can then be distributed from the library or a number of users may have access to the documents and retrieve a copy or even modify them (given proper authorization). In summary, the library services allow users to:

file a document in the library;

retrieve a copy of a document;

delete a document from the library;

search for documents in the library which satisfy certain criteria.

For a proper management of the library, it is necessary to protect documents from inadvertent access by unintended users. DIA defines for this purpose the concepts of *owner*, *delegates*, *access codes* and *user affinity*. Before we discuss these concepts, we must first describe how documents are stored in the library. Of course, this is a conceptual description since a particular implementation defines how the library is actually organized. From an architectural point of view, each document is stored in the library under a Library Assigned Document Name (LADN), which includes a timestamp to make it unique. The name assigned by the user is not used by the library as such, but stored as one of the descriptors of the document in the profile (see below). The user-assigned name need not be unique, since the LADNs are unique. This makes it possible to have several versions of one document and still be able to uniquely identify them. For instance a user may retrieve a copy of document 'SNA book', make some editorial changes to it and file it again. The new version would get its own LADN, so both versions are uniquely identifiable. The user may subsequently decide to delete the old version or to keep it for some time.

All information that describes a document is stored with the document in the *Document Profile*. This profile is initially defined by the user, although some information is filled in by the library services (e.g. the LADN). Normally the Document Profile is transferred with the document in the Document Interchange Unit (DIU, see below). Users may define their own profiles and so may the implementors of certain products, to contain information about a document that is relevant to them. IBM has defined one standard profile for use within DIA. This profile is called *Interchange Document Profile*.

The IDP consists of one or more sub-profiles. The first one, the BASE sub-profile, is defined within IDP and it is mandatory. Other sub-profiles are usually product specific, e.g. the IBM 5520 uses its own sub-profile. DIA uses a separate sub-profile, the DIA Application sub-profile, to contain information necessary for Document Library Services and Document Application Services. In Fig. 10.8 a summary of the information in both the BASE sub-profile and the DIA Application sub-profile is provided. A detailed definition can be found in [33].

When a document is stored in a library, the requestor is normally listed in the profile as the *owner* of the document. This *primary owner* may specify other users as *owner-delegates* by including their names in the appropriate field in the profile when the document is filed. These owner-delegates can perform the same operations on the document as the owner, except for the change of the access authorization. For non-owners of the document, access is controlled via *access codes*. This access can only be read-only, since only the owner(-delegates) have write access.

Access codes are defined when a document is filed. They are four-digit decimal numbers, ranging from decimal '0000' (no access restrictions) to decimal '2047'. If no access code is defined for a document, access is limited to the owner and owner-delegates. The access codes can be used to group the users, according to their needs to have access to certain documents. A particular user may be a member of several 'user groups' (several access codes). On the other hand, a document may have several access codes assigned to it, which means that several user groups may access it. The definition of access codes and the association with users and documents is completely installation defined. It depends on the actual organization of the office in which DIA products are being used.

IDPA Base Sub-profile	
Required	*Conditional*
Document Name Document Type Profile GCID	Revisable-form-text Parameters Library Assigned Document Name System Code
Optional	
Author Copy List Creation Date/Time Document Class Document Date Document GCID	Document Size File Cabinet Reference Last Changed Date/Time Owner Subject

DIA Application Sub-profile	
Optional	
Expiration Date File Date/Time Keywords	Owner Delegate Ownership

Fig. 10.8　IDPA Base and Application Subprofiles:
Required—parameter always present
Optional—parameter presence depends on using product architecture
Conditional—parameter presence depends on certain conditions

Another concept that allows organised access to DIA resources is the *User Affinity*. In an affinity relation, a user (the *surrogate*) may act on behalf of another user (the *principal*). For instance a secretary could modify a report in the library which is actually owned by the manager. Two lists are associated with the mechanism, the *authorization list* and the *affinity list*. The authorization list is associated with a principal and lists all users that may act on the principal's behalf, i.e. authorized users. The affinity list is associated with a surrogate and it contains the names of all principals for whom the surrogate may act, i.e. with whom affinity is ratified. Both lists are complementary in that a user who has affinity to somebody else must also be in that person's authorization list.

When a user wants to store a document in the library, the user sends a DIU with the FILE command, the document profile and the document itself. The profile may specify the owner and owner-delegates, the access codes and further characteristics of the document. When the command is successfully executed, an ACKNOWLEDGE DIU is returned. This ACKNOWLEDGE contains the Library Assigned Document Name (LADN) which can be used for future unique identification.

When a document must be removed from the library, the owner (or owner-delegate) uses the DELETE command. This command does not actually delete the document from the library, but it removes the requestor's ownership for that document. Only after all owners (primary and all delegates) have removed their ownership is the document physically deleted from the library.

In order to obtain a copy of a document (or a document profile or both) from the library, the RETRIEVE command is used. The requestor must have the proper access authority for the document and in certain cases of affinity additional password protection can be requested. One RETRIEVE command can request access to one document only. However, the request DIU may contain multiple commands (see below) if more than one document is required. For each document requested, a DELIVER command is returned, which contains the document. Again, one DIU may contain several DELIVERs, or multiple DIUs may be sent. Only the last DIU in a reply will be marked 'last', as was discussed earlier.

In the above commands DELETE and RETRIEVE, reference to a document can be made using the unique LADN. However, it is also possible to precede the request with a SEARCH command in which certain criteria for the search are specified. The result of the search action is usually a list with one or more documents (LADNs), together with some document-related parameters, as specified in the SEARCH. This list is also stored as a document under a user-provided name. The list can be used in DELETE and RETRIEVE requests to identify a certain document (list name and position in the list) as an alternative for direct LADN specification.

Application Processing Services   In addition to the Document Distribution Services and the Document Library Services, which are the very heart of DIA, there are some more general services that may be requested from an Office System Node. These services are grouped together in the Application Processing Services. They allow the user to request:

- Execution of processes in the OSN. These processes can be any user-defined programs or procedures. They can also be specific programs for the formatting of documents. A special command is defined for the latter case.

- Modification of certain document-related parameters in library documents.

The general command to invoke a program or procedure in the OSN is the EXECUTE command. Although is command is an SRR class command, the requested program is executed asynchronously. The EXECUTE itself is replied to with an ACKNOWLEDGE command to indicate that the EXECUTE is accepted, i.e. the program is scheduled for execution. Optionally, one or more documents may be specified on the command, if these are needed by the program. The documents may be included in the DIU or the DIU may contain references to library documents. Other parameters, that are passed to the program, can also be specified on the command. The result of the execution may be one (or more) new documents. Since the program is executed asynchronously, these resulting document(s) cannot be returned in reply to the EXECUTE. The server process must use Document Distribution Services (DELIVER) for this purpose, or it should use Document Library Services to store these documents in the library.

A request for a more specific type of process is the FORMAT (SRR) command. This command is used to request the execution of a *formatting* process, i.e. a process that will convert a document into another form. An example is a program that takes a DCA revisable-form-text document and prepares it for printing on a specific printer. The resulting formatted document is then a final-form-document. Since the FORMAT command always results in an output document, the disposition of the output document is specified with the command (unlike EXECUTE). If a name is specified for the formatted document, it is stored in the library under this name. The server sends an ACKNOWLEDGE (NRR) reply to the requestor to signal successful completion of the formatting. If no name is specified, it is assumed that the formatted document must be returned to the requestor. The server uses the DELIVER (NRR) command to return the document when the formatting is complete.

Finally, the Application Processing Services can also be used to modify certain parameters of documents in the library. Where Library Services are only concerned with the *handling* of documents, the MODIFY command is used to change document control information. This information can be the access code (i.e. which group of users may access the document) and the search parameters as they appear in the document profile. These can be such parameters as the subject, author, dates, keywords, etc. Of course the requestor of this service must have appropriate authorization (affinity) to change the parameters of a particular document.

In the preceding paragraphs we have discussed the various services that can be requested in a DIA environment. Normally, these would not all be required at the same time or in the same implementation (product). Thus, DIA also allows subsetting of functions. This means that products may choose to implement only certain subsets, which are relevant for that product. The subsets are called *Function Sets*. Each Function Set is defined in terms of the DIA commands that must be supported and the role each of the parties will play.

This role can be either as the *requestor* of the service or as the *server*, i.e. providing the requested service. So, Function Set 3 for example (Fig. 10.9) provides for unsolicited delivery of documents to a recipient by the OSN. That means the documents are delivered without a specific request from the recipient node. The DIA process in the OSN is the server in this case, so it must be able to *send* the DELIVER command, whereas the requestor process must be able to *receive* the command. In this Function Set the ACKNOWLEDGE command can be sent either

Command	Command	roles	
	Class	Server	Requestor
DELIVER	SRR	send	send
ACKNOWLEDGE	NRR	send/receive	send/receive
SIGN-ON Request	SRR	receive	receive
SIGN-ON Reply	NRR	send	send

Fig. 10.9 Function Set 3, Unsolicited Delivery from OSN to Recipient Node

nr.	description
2.	Solicited delivery from OSN to Recipient Node
3.	Unsolicited delivery from OSN to Recipient Node
4.	Input to OSN from an Image Source Node
5.	Document Distribution Request from Source Node to OSN
6.	Image S/R node to Image S/R node (without OSN)
7.	S/R Node to S/R Node (without OSN)
8.	Document Library Services
9.	Application Processing Services
10.	Session Services (Create, change or delete DIA control variables)

Fig. 10.10 Summary of DIA Function Sets

way, so both server and requestor must be able to send/receive the command. The requestor process does take the initiative for the session, so it sends the SIGN-ON command. In Fig. 10.10 a summary description of all Function Sets defined so far is provided. The actual definition of these Function Sets is provided in [26].

Document Interchange Units

The Document Interchange Unit was introduced earlier as the basic unit of exchange between DIA processes. It is now time to look at the structure of the DIU in more detail. Since DIA is a Service Transaction Program in LU 6.2 it is clear that it follows the rules for the General Data Stream. Actually, the DIU is composed of a number of structured fields, in a fixed sequence. Each of the fields is a GDS variable and may be sub-structured (Fig. 10.11).

As usual, the GDS variables start with the GDS Header, LLID. Each DIU component has a unique first byte in the ID, with the second byte being used for further specification of the substructures in the field. The five basic components of the DIU are:

a the DIU Prefix (ID = ' C0xx')
b the Command Sequence (ID = ' C1xx' or ' CDxx')
c the Data Units (ID = ' C6xx')
d the Document Units (ID = ' C9xx') and
e the DIU Suffix (ID = ' CFxx')

Each structured field in the DIU begins with the DIU Introducer. It contains the GDS Header (LLID), a one-byte Format field (F), a one-byte Segmentation Control field (I) and a two-byte Segment Sequence Number (SS). The ISS part of the Introducer is optional; it is called the DIU Introducer Extension. Its presence is indicated via a bit in the F-field. Note that this segmenting control is different from the segmenting performed by the mapped conversation handler in LU 6.2, which uses the high-order bit of the LL-field. The DIA mechanism is conceptually more powerful, since it specifies a sequence number field. However, in the current definitions this field is not used.

We now briefly describe the five components of the Data Interchange Unit (Fig. 10.11). Where required, the reader may find additional detail in [26].

The DIU Prefix consists of the Introducer and the (Optional) DIU-ID field. The Introducer defines this structured field as the Prefix. The DIU-ID is generated by the user and must be a 1–16 byte value. This ID

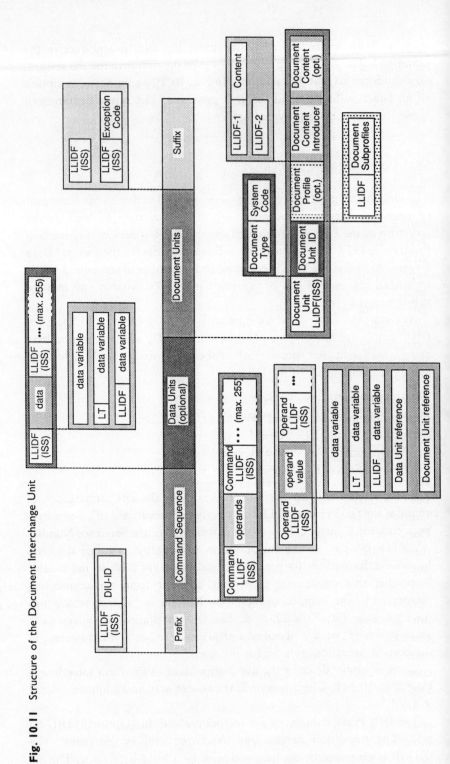

Fig. 10.11 Structure of the Document Interchange Unit

174

is used to correlate replies to this request. If no reply is requested (i.e. all commands in the DIU are of the NRR class), the DIU-ID may be omitted. Its presence can be deduced from the LL value.

The Command Sequence consists of one or more (maximum 255) commands that specify actions to be performed. The commands must be processed by the receiver in the order in which they are present in the DIU. Each command is a structured field, with LLID specifying the length and the particular command (code point). Operands may be included with the command, containing either immediate data or reference to data units or to document units. The presence and the format of the operands depends on the particular command and on the F-field in the introducer of the operand field. The operand is another structured field with its own introducer, which specifies the particular type of operand, e.g. a CORRELATION operand or a SIGN-ON-ID and so forth. If the value of the operand is immediate data, this data can be just the data itself, or another structured field with an LLIDF introducer or it can be a 'length-type' variable (LT). Length-type variables are preceded by a one-byte length (L) and a one-byte type indication (T) as illustrated in Fig. 10.11.

The Data Unit is optional (it is for instance not used by SNA Distribution Services), but there may be as many as 255 Data Units. For reference purposes they are implicitly sequentially numbered. If a Data Unit is present, it contains operand data for the commands in the Command Sequence. This operand data could also have been provided in the operand field of the command. Therefore, the rules for the structure of the operand data are the same as for the operand data had it been contained in the Command Sequence. Operand data in the Data Unit is referenced by a Data Unit Reference structured field in the Command Sequence operand field. This Data Unit Reference specifies the GDS-ID of the operand to look for. It also specifies the sequence number of the Data Unit where the operand data can be found.

The next component of the DIU, the Document Unit, is again optional, i.e. it depends on the type of command whether it is present or not. The maximum number of Document Units that may be present in one DIU is 255. Each Document Unit completely describes one document that is referred to by a command in the command sequence. Its contents depend on the Document Unit type, which is defined by its Document Unit Introducer (LLIDF). Several Document Units have been defined, but a range of codes (ID = X′ C980′ −X′ C9FF′) has been reserved for user assignment. An important Document Unit is the Interchange Document Unit type-3 (IDF = X′ C90301′), which is used for all exchanges between IBM-defined DIA processes. This Document

Unit has three fields, the Document Unit Identifier, the Document Profile and the Document Content (with its introducer).

The Document Unit Identifier defines the datastream used in the document and the system on which the document was produced. The datastream can be DCA final-form-text (code X′0002′) or revisable-form-text, but also other datastreams like the IBM-3730 Text DS (code X′0007′) or a customer-defined datastream can be used. A complete list of assigned datastreams can be found in [26]. The system code part of the Document Unit Identifier is a unique identification of the system, IBM or other, on which the document was created.

In the Interchange Document Unit type-3 (see above) the document profile structured field is an important field that describes the attributes of the document. In the Interchange Document Profile [33] the various fields and subprofiles define such things as author, creation date, date of last change, location where hardcopy of the document is stored ('file cabinet reference'), content keywords, etc. The purpose of this profile is to make document handling like classification, storing and searching in a library easy, without scanning the entire contents of the documents.

The Document Profile field is followed by the Document Content Introducer and (optionally) the actual contents of the document. Whether or not the contents follow is indicated in the introducer.

The DIU is completed with the DIU Suffix which indicates whether the DIU was completed normally (type-1 suffix) or abnormally (type-2 suffix). In the abnormal termination case the suffix LLIDF is followed by a data variable which contains an exception code to describe the reason of the abnormal termination. These exceptions are called 'sender detected' and they prevent completion of the DIU. An example of such an exception is an I/O error while the DIA process is reading a document for transmission. Exception reporting via the DIU suffix is part of a general exception reporting scheme. Other exceptions are reported via the ACKNOWLEDGE DIU (see below).

This brief description of the Document Interchange Unit (DIU) should give the reader sufficient 'feel' for the generality of the DIU definition. Various fields have been predefined to accommodate IBM products and procedures, but for most fields blocks of codes have been reserved as 'customer defined', to leave room for further expansion by either the customer or other suppliers. Some coordination will be required, however, even for customer definitions, if the objective of interchange is to be achieved.

10.4 SNA Distribution Services

In the preceding section we alluded albeit briefly to SNA Distribution Services in its relationship to Document Interchange Architecture (DIA). DIA describes basically a protocol structure for various document services around an Office System Node. SNADS builds on top of this and uses the DIA concepts to define a more general service for the distribution of 'documents' across a small or a large network or, for that matter, across several networks if these are interconnected with SNA Interconnection.

In DIA we emphasized also that the relationship between Source/Recipient Nodes and Office System Nodes was not a physical one, but in the first place a logical one: DIA sessions are created as *conversations* on top of LU 6.2 sessions. These in turn make use of the physical connectivity of the underlying SNA network. For SNADS we should stress this even more. An SNA network consists of interconnected physical systems in which Logical Units may reside. The Logical Units can engage in sessions to exchange data. These sessions require that two LUs that are in session must be 'present' (or 'active') at the same time, i.e. the sessions have a 'synchronous nature'. A SNADS distribution network (Fig. 10.12) consists of *Distribution Service Units* (DSUs), interconnected by LU 6.2 conversations. This network has an 'asynchronous nature'. When a DSU sends a document to another DSU, a conversation with the destination DSU is not necessary. The document will be sent to

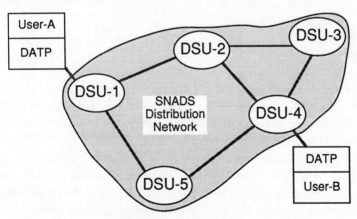

Fig. 10.12 The SNADS distribution network
DSU = Distribution Service Unit
DATP = Distribution Application Transaction Program

177

the next DSU on the 'route' to the destination. The distribution network is a true *store-and-forward* network, based on an underlying synchronous packet switching network. The structure of the SNADS distribution network is therefore highly influenced by organizational aspects and much less by the physical characteristics.

In Section 8.2 the concept of Service Transaction Programs in LU 6.2 was introduced and SNADS was mentioned as an example of such a Service Transaction Program. Now we can be more specific. As is indicated in Fig. 10.12, the DSUs are the actual Service Transaction Programs. They serve their users, the Originators and Recipients of documents, through Application Transaction Programs. The distribution network is 'formed' by LU 6.2 conversations between DSUs. These conversations are allocated as required.

When (Fig. 10.12) a document (*distribution object*) must be transferred from user A to user B, it is first handed over to DSU-1, in A's system. This DSU now has the *Origin DSU* role and, like in any store-and-forward network, it is now responsible for correct delivery of the document. User A may even log off from the system and trust that the document will be delivered (or might later get a message that a serious error prohibited delivery of the document). Now, DSU-1 establishes the next step in the route through the network, based on service requirements (see below). In the example the document is handed over to DSU-2, which for this distribution plays an *Intermediate role*. DSU-2 is now responsible for the document, so DSU-1 may forget about it. This procedure continues, until the document reaches DSU-4, which serves under B, so it is the *Destination DSU*. DSU-4 may have to store the document for some time, until user B logs on to the system and requests delivery of queued documents.

Distribution Units

It was mentioned in Section 10.3 that SNADS uses the Document Interchange Architecture for its exchange of user information. That is, all communication between DSUs is structured in Document Interchange Units (DIUs) as they are defined for DIA. The DIU used by SNADS is called the *Distribute Interchange Unit*. It consists of (refer to Fig. 10.11) the Prefix, the Command Sequence (which contains the SNADS distribution command, ID = X'C105', and several operands), the Document Unit (which contains the distribution objects) and the suffix. The DIA Data Unit is not used by SNADS. A detailed specification of the Distribute IU is given in [12, 34].

Whenever something goes wrong after the distribution network has taken over responsibility for the distribution object (e.g. a catastrophic failure of the responsible DSU), the originator must be told about this failure. This is done through the ACKNOWLEDGE DIU, which is used in DIA for both positive and negative reporting. SNADS does not use it for positive acknowledgement, but uses the LU 6.2 CONFIRM mechanism instead. This mechanism leads to a +DR2 response exchange in the SNA protocol between the LUs but not to an exchange at the SNADS level. This is considered more efficient than sending a separate DIU.

Naming and Addressing

In any distribution network it is necessary to have global conventions for naming and addressing in order to uniquely identify a user and also the location where this user is. In SNADS a choice is made for a structured naming scheme that is completely independent of the addressing scheme. The objectives for these schemes [35] were to insulate users as much as possible from changes in the structure of the distribution network or the location of other users, to avoid large tables with addressing information, and to allow for either centralized or distributed management of such tables.

The user name in SNADS is formally called the *Distribution User Name* (DUN) and the user address, i.e. the DSU where the user resides, is called the *Distribution Service Unit Name* (DSUN). The Distribution User Name consists of two parts, the *Distribution Group Name* (DGN) and a *Distribution Element Name* (DEN), each with a maximum length of eight bytes. Although the architecture does not attach a special meaning to the DGN or the DEN, in a typical situation the DGN could be a department name within an organization (e.g. SALES) and the DEN a person's last name (e.g. Hart). Mr. Hart in the Sales department would thus be identified as SALES.HART. Distribution Element Names must be unique *within* one Distribution Group. Distribution Group Names are *not* associated with a certain location but with an organizational entity and are thus by default unique across the distribution network. When the DGN appears at more than one DSU in the distribution network, it is just considered one distributed group by SNADS.

The address, the Distribution Service Unit Name (DSUN), is also structured in two components, each of which also can be eight bytes in length. The components are called the *Routing Group Name* (RGN) and the *Routing Element Name* (REN). Routing Element Names must be unique within their Routing Group, while Routing Groups must be unique in the network. Contrary to the Distribution Group and Distribution Element Names, the Routing Group and Routing Element Name do have an association with physical location, since they identify a specific DSU. The Routing Group Name (RGN) can be used in a way similar to the subarea in Path Control, i.e. to group a number of 'destinations' in order to make routing tables smaller. In Fig. 10.13(a) the naming concepts are illustrated.

As the figure shows, there are several end-users, belonging to four departments: laboratory (LAB), manufacturing (MAN), sales (SALES), and administration (ADMIN). One of the departments (SALES) is distributed across three DSUs. The distribution name for Mr. Hart in the sales department is SALES.HART, for Mr. Rogers it is SALES.ROGERS. In Fig. 10.13(b) the addresses are illustrated. DSU-A is located in Uithoorn (UH), DSU-B in Utrecht (UTR), DSUs C and D both in Amsterdam (AMS), and DSU-E in Zoetermeer (ZTMR). Although this is not shown in the example, the DSU names need only be unique within the Routing Group, i.e. all, except C or D, could have been called DSU-A.

For the remainder of our examples we will not use the routing groups explicitly, but only the DSU names A through E and assume that the Routing Group Name is implied.

Directories

Since there is no immediate correspondence between the user name (e.g. SALES.HART) and the routing name (e.g. C), a mechanism, a directory, is needed to associate the two. In SNADS the directory can be structured and distributed in various ways. The objective is, as was stated before, to allow easy updating with either centralized or distributed management and no mandatory large tables.

In Fig. 10.14(a) the full directory reflecting Fig. 10.13 is shown. It is possible to have such a complete directory in every DSU, but maintaining consistency would become very difficult when the number of users increases. Therefore a DSU may contain only a subset of the directory, with the information relevant to that DSU and 'pointers' to where additional information can be found, if necessary. If we look at distributions originating in DSU-A (Fig. 10.13), it is clear that, for all departments except LAB, distributions have to go through DSU-B. So, there is no need to maintain information about the other departments at A. The directory in A is shown in Fig. 10.14(b). It has a *default* entry (similar to a 'wild card') for the other departments. So, we find entries for Smith and Parry (who are in department LAB and reside at A) and also a default entry that indicates that all other names in department LAB are an error. All other users names are referred to DSU-B. This means that

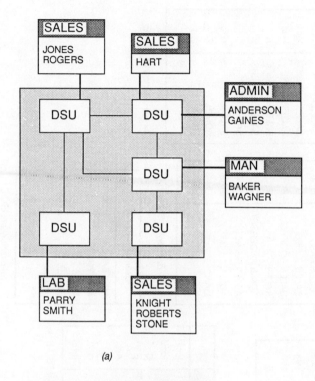

(a)

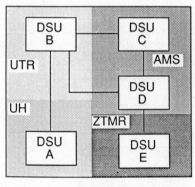

(b)

Fig. 10.13 Naming and addressing

(a) Full directory

User Name	DSUN
SALES.JONES	B
SALES.ROGERS	B
SALES.HART	C
SALES.KNIGHT	E
SALES.ROBERTS	E
SALES.STONE	E
LAB.SMITH	A
LAB.PARRY	A
ADMIN.ANDERSON	C
ADMIN.GAINES	C
MAN.BAKER	D
MAN.WAGNER	D
.	error

(b) directory at DSU-A

User Name	DSUN
LAB.SMITH	local
LAB.PARRY	local
LAB.*	error
.	B

(c) directory at DSU-B

User Name	DSUN
SALES.JONES	local
SALES.ROGERS	local
SALES.HART	C
SALES.*	E
LAB.*	A
ADMIN.*	C
MAN.*	D
.	error

(d) directory at DSU-C

User Name	DSUN
SALES.HART	local
SALES.JONES	B
SALES.ROGERS	B
SALES.*	E
ADMIN.ANDERSON	C
ADMIN.GAINES	D
ADMIN.*	error
MAN.*	D
.	B

(e) directory at DSU-D

User Name	DSUN
MAN.BAKER	local
MAN.WAGNER	local
MAN.*	error
SALES.*	E
ADMIN.*	C
.	B

(f) directory at DSU-E

User Name	DSUN
SALES.KNIGHT	local
SALES.ROBERTS	local
SALES.STONE	local
SALES.JONES	B
SALES.ROGERS	B
SALES.HART	C
SALES.*	error
ADMIN.*	C
MAN.*	D
.	B

Fig. 10.14 Directories

any distribution originating from A for departments other than LAB is directed to B. In Fig. 10.14(c) the directory in B is shown. Here we find a reference to three people in SALES (Jones, Rogers and Hart) who are located at B and C. For all other salespeople there is another default entry, which points to E. User names from manufacturing are referred to D, from administration to C, and from laboratory to A. Other user names (i.e. other departments) are invalid and thus an error.

Now let's look at the sales department again. In B we find entries for all people in B and C, all other names being directed to E. Supposedly, in E there should be a directory with the names of Knight, Roberts and Stone. Now, how should the other salespeople at B and C be listed in E? If we were to use a default entry SALES.* again, to redirect other names to B, distributions with invalid names (e.g. SALES.PETER) would forever bounce back and forth between B and E! To avoid this situation, we must take care that for a given Destination Group Name at least one DSU contains the full directory for that DGN. One possibility is for instance to have the full directory for a destination group in the DSU where the major responsibility for that group (e.g. department) is located. This could be different for each department. Alternatively we may choose to have one DSU responsible for a complete directory for all destination groups and only minimum directories at all other DSUs. Similarly, there should also be at least one DSU which has all valid Distribution Group Names and a default error entry to catch invalid DGNs. It is the task of the system administrator of the distribution network to make sure that the directories are complete and consistent. In Fig. 10.14 a possible set of directories with distributed responsibilities is given for the configuration of Fig. 10.13.

Routing

Based on the information in the directories, the DSUs are able to find out how to move a Document Interchange Unit (a DIU or a 'distribution') through the SNADS network. The first step to take is the *directing* step at the originating DSU. Based on the user name (DUN), the destination Distribution Service Unit Name (DSU Name or DSUN for short) is found from the directory. The destination user is either located at that DSU, or the directory in that DSU will contain re-direction information (see below). The DSU Name is placed in the operand field in the command sequence of the Distribute IU, together with the user name. Given this DSU Name, the DSU selects the next DSU in the route towards the destination (*routing* step). The actual selection mechanism depends on the DSU implementation, the overall network definition and the *Dis-*

tribution Service Level (DSL, see below). The DIU is now sent to the next DSU, where the next hop is determined. Note that in these intermediate DSUs only the destination DSUN is used, not the user name.

In the destination DSU, the DSU name is recognized as the local name and *now* the directory is again consulted. If in this directory the user name is marked 'local', the DIU is placed in a queue for local delivery. If the user is at some other DSU, that DSU's name is placed in the DIU as the destination DSUN (re-directing) and the DSU is moved on. Using again Fig. 10.13 and the directories in Fig. 10.14, we find that a distribution from Baker in Manufacturing to Hart in Sales first goes to DSU-E and then is re-directed to C (through D again!).

Distribution Service Levels

For certain aspects of a distribution, users may request a specific *level of service*. SNADS users may specify their requirements for *priority*, *protection* and *capacity*.

With respect to priority, SNADS distinguishes between *data* distributions and *status* distributions. For data distributions the user may request any of sixteen priority levels. However, there is an implementation option that maps the eight higher levels to HIGH and the eight lower levels to LOW, which effectively means only two priority levels in certain implementations. Distributions of a certain priority will be handled by SNADS before any distributions of lower priority. The user also has the option FAST, which is the highest priority, but can only be used for short messages (see below under *capacity*). Finally, there is a separate priority for status messages, either generated by SNADS or by the user. With these messages the status of a distribution can be reported back to the originator. Status messages therefore have higher priority than data distributions, but they are still lower than FAST. Status reporting about FAST messages, if required, also happens at priority FAST.

The priority service level dictates how SNADS should service the various queues. It also relates to the SNA Class of Service (i.e. which Path Control routes are used). Conversations between successive DSUs will be allocated to sessions that have the proper 'mode' (Class of Service) for the type of priority required.

Another distribution service level aspect is *protection* against failures of a DSU that has responsibility for a distribution. This type of protection is required in store-and-forward systems like SNADS, since responsibility for the distribution is handed over between successive DSUs, as the message progresses through the network. If 'no protection' is selected, a distribution (DIU) may be lost after a DSU failure. If protection is selected, the DSU will be able to recover the DIU (e.g. from permanent storage). The protection provided is only associated with communications and systems failures. It does not provide for medium failures like a head-crash on a disk device after the DSU stored the DIU.

A final service level aspect is *capacity*. It has to do with the storage capabilities of the DSUs in the distribution network to handle large objects. SNADS defines two levels of capability. Either LIMITED or INDEFINITE. LIMITED means that distributions should be smaller than 4 kbytes. All DSU implementations are required to support this minimum capacity. Therefore, any route through the distribution network will satisfy this capacity requirement. INDEFINITE means that there is no restriction on the size of a distribution A DSU may not instantaneously be able to handle a large distribution, but eventually it will have sufficient capacity available. It is part of the routing strategy to find a route where all DSUs have indefinite capacity if that is requested for a distribution.

The allowed combinations of (priority, capacity and protection) are (FAST or STATUS, LIMITED, NO PROTECTION) and (DATA 1-16, INDEFINITE, PROTECTED). Routes through the distribution network are selected based on the capabilities of the DSUs. Obviously, all DSUs along a route must be able to provide the same Distribution Service Level.

Temporary re-direction

The distributed architecture of the directory, as described above, allows for temporary local changes without the need for synchronized overall changes. The overall change is either not desired because of the temporary nature of the change, or it is postponed until another major update. Suppose Jones (Fig. 10.13) is temporarily assigned to the sales office at DSU-C. The directory entry for Jones in B is changed to point to C, while Jones is added as 'local' in C. No other changes are necessary, not even in E, which has overall responsibility for the SALES directory. Note also that the changes in B and C may not happen at exactly the same time. They are made by local administrators and there may even be a time-zone difference between the two DSU locations.

If Baker (manufacturing in D) now sends a document to Jones, this document is first routed to E, according to D's directory. In the destination E it is found that the actual destination should be B and the DSU is re-directed to B. When it arrives in B, the user name is checked against the directory and this time it is found that the destination is C.

Once more the DIU is re-directed. Obviously, this may not result in the most efficient routing, but this *temporary re-direction* is very useful for changes of a temporary nature or until a major update of all directories is made.

Hop count

With a directory structure and routing mechanism as described above, it is possible that directory entries are temporarily inconsistent. Jones may already have been removed from B, but not yet entered at C. And, of course, inconsistencies may also occur due to errors in the definition of the directories. Such inconsistencies may give rise to DIUs bouncing back and forth between the DSU with the full directory and the DSU which is the supposed location. Definition errors may even result in loops in the network. In order to prevent eternal life for distribution documents, every DIU which is initially created by an origin DSU gets a *hop count* assigned to it. This hop count is the maximum number of times the DIU may be handed over from DSU to DSU. With each hand-over the hop counter is decremented and, if it reaches zero before it reaches the destination, an error is signalled.

Fan-out

When a document is distributed to several users, SNADS tries to minimize the number of copies actually transmitted. So, if for all destinations the next DSU on the route is the same, only one copy is sent to that intermediate DSU. When at a certain DSU the next DSU is different for certain destinations, the DSU creates as many copies as is necessary, i.e. one copy for each 'next DSU'. Each copy then moves along independently to its destinations and it may fan-out further if that is necessary.

In the example of Fig. 10.15 user Parry (LAB in A) sends a report to Hart in Sales and to Baker and Wagner in Manufacturing. Since Parry is not aware of the actual locations, he issues one distribution command with a name list for the three people. The routing process in DSU-A finds that for all three the next DSU is B, so only one copy of the report is sent to B. In B the routes split. For Hart a copy is sent to C, while for Wagner and Baker one copy is sent to D. Local services in D will deliver a copy of the report to both Wagner and Baker.

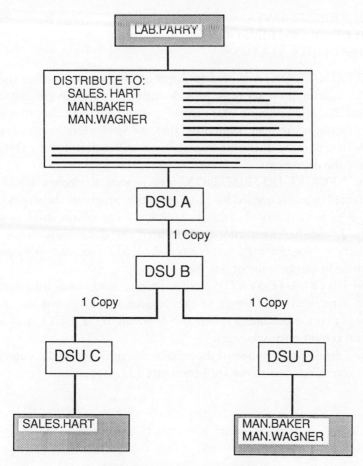

Fig. 10.15 Distribution fan-out

SNADS verbs

It was mentioned before that a SNADS implementation is a Service
Transaction Program in LU 6.2. It uses Basic Conversation verbs like
ALLOCATE, SEND-DATA, etc. SNADS users get access to the services
through local Application Transaction Programs, which in turn use the
SNADS verb interface. Conceptually this protocol boundary is at the
same level as the Mapped Conversation boundary. SNADS supports only
three verbs:

- DISTRIBUTE-DATA
- RECEIVE-DISTRIBUTION
- DISTRIBUTE-STATUS

DISTRIBUTE-DATA is used to distribute documents to other users. The transaction program must provide such parameters as the distribution list (list of destination user names), a correlation identifier to which status messages can refer (similar to DIA), the service level required, and the document to be distributed or sufficient information for the DSU to retrieve the document.

The RECEIVE-DISTRIBUTION verb is used to receive whatever distributed object is queued for this application program. On return, the type of object (status or data) is indicated. The object itself is also returned, together with information about the destination. Since the transaction program may serve more than one user, the destination information can be a list of names.

The DISTRIBUTE-STATUS verb is used to send status information about a received data object to the originator. This status can be a message that the document is actually delivered to the user; it may also contain certain error messages.

For a detailed description of these verbs and the associated parameters the reader is referred to the IBM literature [34, Appendix H].

11 Networks of small SNA systems

As we have seen before, SNA was historically defined for terminal access networks: the communication was thought to be between a host computer and a (person at a) terminal. This also led to the concept of a Primary Logical Unit and a Secondary Logical Unit. With the advent of program-to-program communication this differentiation in capabilities is much less significant, and it was recognized that most peripheral equipment with the current state of the art is also communicating as a 'program'. A lot more intelligence is built into the controlling code of even simple peripheral devices. These 'programs' need to communicate with each other. To accommodate this new requirement, Logical Unit 6.2 was defined, together with Physical Unit 2.1. This allows peripheral nodes to communicate with each other in so-called *peer-to-peer* connections.

Since there was also an enormous growth expected in the numbers of devices that could be addressed, a solution for the addressing problem and more importantly for the network definition problem was required. For such networks it is no longer possible to pre-define the topology, since the changes will be too many. Also, the definition of all possible routes—as in the SNA backbone network—becomes a nearly impossible task.

These developments led to the concept of networks composed of a (potentially large) number of small systems. This concept was first published by IBM authors as a research project called SNA/Low Entry Networking [36]. Later, the name SNA/Low Entry Networking was announced for a peer-to-peer architecture (based on PU 2.1), whereas the functions defined in the mentioned papers were announced as *Advanced Peer-to-Peer Networking* (APPN) for the IBM System/36. Although at the time of writing no further IBM commitments were made, it is clear from other publications [37] that APPN will evolve into a 'new' networking architecture for large networks of relatively small systems. The assumption behind the architecture is that in these large networks traffic volumes will be relatively low. Therefore, efficiency is not the key issue but connectivity. For high-volume networks the SNA backbone architecture will still be the solution. However, traditional peripheral networks may be replaced by APPN networks since the architecture is compatible with the Boundary architecture (Section 4.4).

In the following we will describe SNA/Low Entry Networking and APPN, together with some of the concepts of PU 2.1. We will use the generic name APPN, but it should be understood that the node-to-node protocols are based on SNA/LEN, while the overall protocols are part of APPN.

In Fig. 11.1 an example of an APPN network is given. The most significant features of the topology are the presence of various media (including Local Area Networks and X.25 networks) and the meshed structure (the traditional Peripheral Network was a strict star-topology).

In the APPN network, there are two types of node, both based on Physical Unit 2.1. The first one is the *Network Node*, the second one the *End Node*[*]. The two differ in the services they provide. The services provided by the Network Nodes are

- Connectivity Services (CS)—these handle changes in the physical connectivity of the network, i.e. when nodes and/or links are added to or removed from the network.
- Directory Services (DS)—the resources in the node (and in End Nodes attached to it) are identified, and resources elsewhere in the network are located on request.
- Route Selection Services (RSS)—the preferred route to a destination node (where a requested resource is) is selected, based on existing knowledge of the topology of the network.
- Session Activation Services (SAS)—a session with the remote resource is established and the preferred route is activated.
- Data Transport Services (DTS)—the actual communication between the two resources (LUs).

End Nodes can perform a subset of these services:

- Connectivity Services—only for the activation of links to neighbouring Network Nodes.
- Directory Services (for the local resources only).
- Session Activation (for the local resources only).
- Data Transport Services (only for local resources, i.e. no intermediate Data Transport).

[*] In the original publication the term 'Peripheral Node' was used. Later this was replaced with 'End Node'.

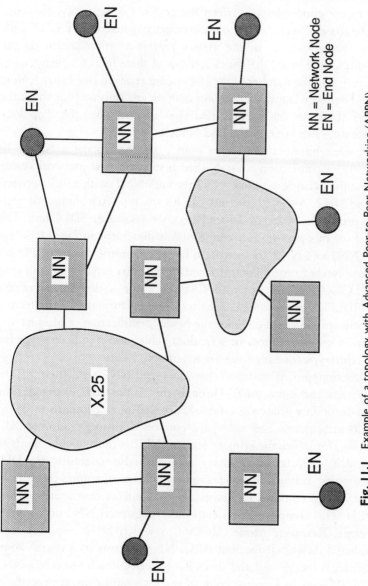

Fig. 11.1 Example of a topology with Advanced Peer-to-Peer Networking (APPN)

NN = Network Node
EN = End Node

We look first at the operation of Connectivity Services. In Fig. 11.2(a) a simple network is illustrated. Each of the Network Nodes in this network maintains a description of the current network topology in the Topology Database. The information in the Topology Database consists mainly of the connectivity between the nodes. Conceptually, the Topology Database is very similar to the connectivity matrix in Fig. 11.2(b). Each of the entries (x) in the matrix represents information on the availability of the links, the characteristics of these links (capacity, cost, delay, etc.), and the number of the last update received (see below). Note that the Topology Database does *not* contain any information about the resources (LUs) in the various nodes! Also note that the Topology Database does not contain the End Nodes.

Now, what happens when a new node attaches to the network? In Fig. 11.2(a) a connection is established between a new (network) node NN1 and the existing network (NN2 through NN7) with a link between NN1 and NN2. Although the link can be any type (telephone line with various protocols, X.25, or Token Ring), we assume an SDLC link. The protocol for this peer-to-peer connection is illustrated in Fig. 11.3.

Both NN1 and NN2 are instructed by their Control Point (the PU 2.1 Peripheral Node Control Point) to contact the other box. They both send the SDLC XID frame (refer to Chapter 2 for a description of the SDLC/HDLC commands). PU 2.1 uses a special format of XID, format 3. The information field contains the Node Identification (a product and installation specific number or a random value) and it indicates that the SDLC Primary/Secondary roles are negotiable [13].

In the example it is assumed that NN1 and NN2 send their XID at more or less the same time. Through this initial XID exchange, the primary-secondary roles are established based on a comparison of the Node Identification. The roles are confirmed through another XID handshake, for which the Primary Station (NN1 in the example) sends an XID which indicates its Primary role and also contains its SDLC characteristics (frame size and maximum number of frames that can be received). NN2 confirms its Secondary role and its characteristics in a final XID. This completes the identification sequence. NN1 now sends a Set Normal Response Mode (SNRM) to which NN2 responds with Unnumbered Acknowledgement (UA). NN1 informs its Control Point that contact is established and sends RR (Receive Ready) to NN2. NN2 now also informs its Control Point of the successful contact procedure.

Now that the link-level connection has been made, a session between the two adjacent Control Points (NN1 and NN2) can be established. This will be a regular LU 6.2 session, i.e. BIND is used instead of ACTCDRM. The BIND is sent by the Control Point which was identified

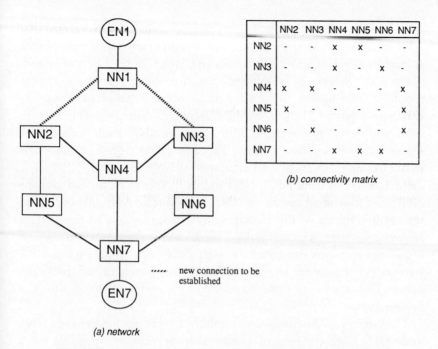

(b) connectivity matrix

(a) network

Fig. 11.2 Connectivity Services: sample network and connectivity

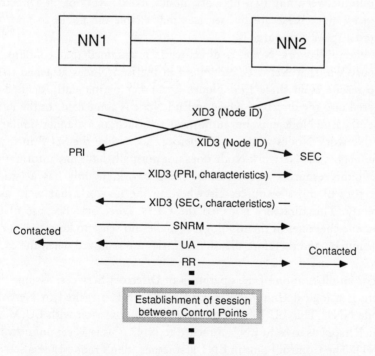

Fig. 11.3 Initial contact procedure between two Network Nodes

as such in the XID exchange. During this exchange it is also verified that NN1 is allowed to attach to NN2. This requires some registration, but it is local to a certain node: only nodes attaching to it need be authorized.

Once the session is established, the two Control Points exchange topology information by sending each other a series of Topology Database Updates (TDUs). So NN2 sends its Topology Database to NN1 and next NN1 sends its information to NN2. Each node is now required to send any changes in its Topology Database to its neighbours. In our example NN2 will send an update to NN4 and NN5, NN4 sends an update to NN3 and NN7, NN5 to NN7, NN3 to NN6, and perhaps NN7 tries to send an update to NN5, NN4 and/or NN6, depending on the relative timing of the messages. Each node assigns to the TDU a sequence number, which is unique for it, and it keeps track of the last sequence number received from its neighbours. In the initial exchange the two nodes compare the sequence numbers they have received from each other. This allows an optimization when a node still has up-to-date information.

The same procedure is used to establish the connection between NN1 and NN3. With the help of Connectivity Services it is possible for a Network Node to fully know the topology of the network and thus select a route between any two network nodes. Next, we look at Directory Services, since these are the services that enable the nodes to find out where a specific resource is.

In every Network Node, a directory is maintained that contains *all* resources in that Network Node and in the End Nodes attached to it. The resources in these End Nodes are either permanently defined or entered into the directory when an End Node is connected. In the latter case, the End Node must be 'authorized' to attach, in a manner similar to the Network Nodes as discussed before. So, unlike the SSCP in traditional SNA, the Network Node does not normally have any information about the resources in the rest of the network. It only has a (small) directory of those resources elsewhere in the network that were used recently. This directory is called the *Cache Directory*. Because of the dynamic character of the topology, it makes no sense to keep the entries indefinitely, and therefore the oldest entries are removed when the cache fills.

For an illustration of the operation of Directory Services, assume that there is a logical Unit *John* in End Node EN1, attached to Network Node NN1. This LU John wants to establish a session with LU *Mary*, which happens to be in EN7, attached to NN7 (this is as yet unknown to NN1). The Control Point in EN1 first issues John's request for a session with LU Mary to NN1, which searches its directory. Since Mary is not a local resource, it is not found in the local directory. In our example it is also unlikely that Mary is in the Cache Directory, since NN1 was just connected to the network. (More on the Cache Directory later.) NN1 starts a search through the network to find out where Mary is located. This search is a 'breadth-first' search, where the search message is propagated from a Control Point to all adjacent Control Points. In this way the search-time is roughly proportional to the number of hops to the node farthest away (the diameter of the network) and not to the total number of nodes as it would be when the message was forwarded to one Control Point at a time.

The search procedure is illustrated in Fig. 11.4(a). Each node forwards the search request to the nodes attached to it and it only sends back a reply if it has received a reply from these neighbours. In the diagram for instance, NN2 sends the request to NN4 and NN5. After a reply is received from NN4 and NN5, a reply is sent to NN1. NN1 knows that the search is complete when it has received the replies from both NN2 and NN3.

It is interesting to look at what happens in NN4. Assume that the request from NN2 arrives in NN4 first. This request is then forwarded to NN3 and NN7, which are NN4's neighbors. In the meantime NN3 has forwarded the request it received from NN1 to NN4 (and NN6). In NN4 this request can be interpreted as if it is a negative reply to NN4's request. Even if NN3 does have the resource, it will eventually be indicated on the

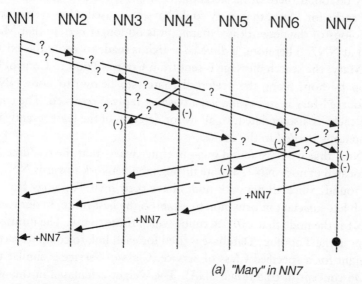

(a) "Mary" in NN7

Fig. 11.4 Directory Services: undirected search for a resource: (a) specific

'upstream' to NN1, so NN4 need not worry. Similarly, when NN3 receives the request from NN4, this is interpreted as a negative reply to NN3's request. Again, even if NN4 has the resource, the fact that it sends a request to NN3 means that it got a request itself along some other path and will report the resource along that path.

Something similar may happen in NN7. Assume that the first request it receives arrives via NN4. This request is now forwarded to NN6 and NN5, even though NN7 has the requested resource. In this way it is made certain that *all* instances of the requested resource are found. Doing so allows for the use of 'generic' resource names, such as 'quality printer' or 'tape backup'. In our example NN6 and NN5 also forwarded a request to NN7. These are interpreted as negative replies by NN7, whereas NN5 and NN6 interpreted the request from NN7 as a negative reply, so they return a negative reply to NN2 and NN3 respectively. NN7, after having received the (implicit) negative replies from NN5 and NN6, sends a positive reply to NN4, which can then send a positive reply to NN2. NN2 in turn sends a positive reply to NN1.

In Fig. 11.4(b) the flow is illustrated with the same timing, but now for a generic search for PRINTER. Resources with this name are located at NN4, NN6 and NN7. It is seen from the diagram, that all positive replies are concatenated, so NN1 receives the full information about where to find a resource PRINTER.

Resources located with the undirected search are entered into NN1's Cache Directory, so if at some later time the resource is needed again, it may be found there. If in the above example there had been an entry in the cache for Mary, that entry could have been used. However, since the topology of the network is dynamic, it is no longer certain that Mary is still at NN7. Therefore, a *directed* search is made to verify the existence of Mary: the search message is sent from Control Point to Control Point (hop by hop) along the preferred route (see below) to node NN7. If resource Mary is still available, a positive reply is returned. The entry in the cache is also updated, to allow for deletion of the least recently used, if space is needed in the cache.

Now that we have found out—in either way—that the resource Mary is located in node NN7, a route through the network towards NN7 must be found. Since all network nodes have their own Topology Database, each has sufficient information to establish the best route. In our example NN1 is the node that will determine which route to use. The information kept in the Topology Database is used for each link to compute a certain weight for a specified Class of Service (Class of Service is similar to the COS concept in traditional SNA). The weight calculated in this way is inversely proportional to the suitability of the link to be included in a

196

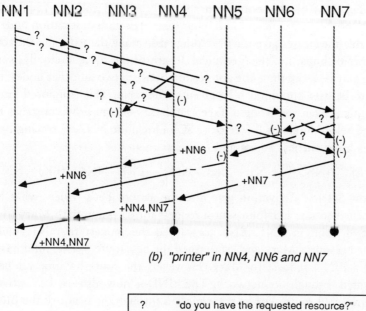

NN1   NN2   NN3   NN4   NN5   NN6   NN7

(b) "printer" in NN4, NN6 and NN7

?	"do you have the requested resource?"
–	"No"
(-)	received question interpreted as reply "No"
+NNx	resource present in Node NNx

Fig. 11.4 Directory Services: undirected search for a resource: (b) generic

route for the particular Class of Service (except for a weight of zero, which means that the link is not operational).

In Fig. 11.5(a) our example network is drawn again with weights assigned to the links for a certain Class of Service, say FAST.

Using a shortest path algorithm*, the Control Point in NN1 can construct a so-called Rooted Tree Database in which the shortest paths from NN1 to all other nodes (for the given Class of Service) are given. It is up to the node to decide when the Rooted Tree Database is constructed. This can be done either when a Topology Database Update is received, or when a route selection request is received.

*The algorithm suggested in the papers is a variation of Dijkstra's original algorithm [38, 39] optimized for a 'heap' data structure [36]. The execution time is proportional to $L*\log(N)$, where L is the number of links and N the number of nodes. However, the algorithm itself can be implementation defined.

In Fig. 11.5(b), the rooted tree is shown for NN1 and Class of Service FAST, both as a graph and in tabular form. For each destination node in the table the entries give the preceding node along the path and the total number of hops, i.e. the 'graphical' length of the route. Actually, since there may be more than one connection between two adjacent nodes, the link to be used should also be given in the table. This is ignored in the example. Given the Rooted Tree Database, we can now construct the Route Selection Control Vector (RSCV) for node NN7 by tracing back through the entries. So we find for

$$RSCV(NN7) = NN1 - (LK) - NN2 - (LK) - NN4 - (LK) - NN7$$

Now Session Activation gets into the action. Let's review what has happened so far. LU John sent a request for a session with Mary to its Control Point in EN1. EN1 forwarded the request to NN1, which located resource Mary and established the best route. Next, John has to send a BIND request to Mary. However, the route has not yet been activated through the network. The BIND is now also used to activate the preferred route. For its transmission through the network the BIND must be preceded by a Transmission Header (TH). PU 2.1 uses FID-2 headers (as in the Peripheral network in traditional SNA), with 2-byte addresses (OAF' and DAF') forming a four-byte Local-Form Session ID (Section 4.5). The Address Space Manager in NN1 selects a free LFSID, which is local to NN1's side of the link between NN1 and NN2, and places it in the TH. NN2 selects a new LFSID for the link to NN4 and so on.

The technique of exchanging the Session ID in each node is called *Session ID Swapping*. The significance of using FID-2 headers with OAF' and DAF' is that an APPN-node (PU 2.1) can also attach to a traditional Boundary node where it is impossible to tell the difference from another (traditional) PU 2.

In Fig. 11.6 the flow of the BIND between John and Mary is illustrated. Since the BIND contains the Route Selection Control Vector, each node can establish the next hop in the route, select an appropriate session ID and set up the swap.

Note that full compatibility with Boundary function requires not only session ID swap, but also reversal of the LFSID on the reverse route, e.g. X'2373' becomes X'7323', so the OAF'/DAF' roles are maintained. This might cause a conflict in the assignment when two adjacent nodes assign a session ID at the same time. To avoid this conflict, the ODAI (OAF'-DAF' Assignor Indicator) bit in the FID2 is used (Section 4.5). In the example, the role of ODAI is ignored.

The entries in the swap tables (i.e. the *Session Connectors*) are

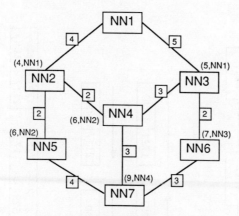

(w,NNx) = Total "cost" w, coming through node NNx

(a) "weighted" network

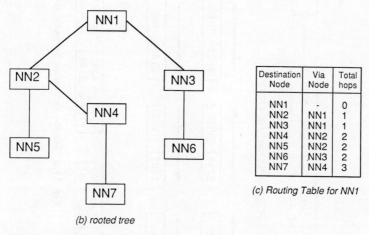

Destination Node	Via Node	Total hops
NN1	-	0
NN2	NN1	1
NN3	NN1	1
NN4	NN2	2
NN5	NN2	2
NN6	NN3	2
NN7	NN4	3

(c) Routing Table for NN1

(b) rooted tree

Fig. 11.5 Route Selection Services: weighted network and rooted tree

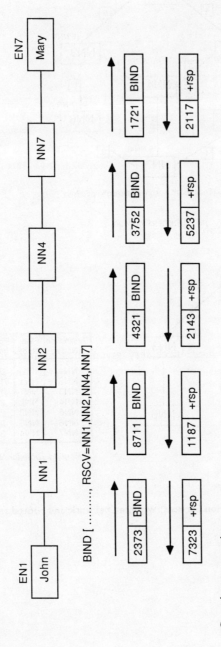

Fig. 11.6 Session Activation Services: setting up the session connectors

maintained as long as the session exists. Data messages flowing on the session will have their session ID's swapped each time they go through a network node.

Once the route (and the session) are established, the two LUs John and Mary can communicate using standard LU 6.2 protocols. However, because of the dynamic nature of the routing and multiplexing of session traffic on routes of arbitrary length, it is necessary to have additional flow control and priority mechanisms that did not exist in the traditional SNA peripheral network (because of its star-configuration).

Priority is handled the same as in the SNA backbone network, where it is associated with the Virtual Routes (Priority + Virtual Route Number defines the Class of Service). In APPN there is also a Network Priority for certain control messages (e.g. BIND, flow control, etc). Below this Network Priority, there are three Session Priorities, high, medium and low. These priorities are selected based on the required Class of Service and established via the BIND. Since the FID-2 header does not contain a Transmission Priority Field (as FID-4 does), a different mechanism is used. Each network node maps the priority on subsets of the session identifiers. This is purely a local matter which is used to decide which message must be transmitted next. It also depends upon the actual implementation how 'ageing' of messages (low-priority messages waiting forever to be transmitted) can be prevented. The only architectural requirement is that a prevention algorithm is implemented.

Flow Control across the APPN network is necessary to prevent congestion. This is the more necessary given the dynamic nature of session requirements and route-selection. The mechanism chosen is based upon the existing SNA session-level pacing, but executed on a hop-by-hop basis. Traditional SNA session-level pacing can be performed in two stages: Primary LU-to-Boundary and Boundary-to-SLU. Each of these stages can have its own window size, although that size is fixed once the session is active. In APPN the pacing mechanism has as many stages as there are hops along the route. Furthermore, the window size can be different for each hop. It is known from other networks (e.g. ARPA) that such mechanisms may cause deadlock if not enough buffers are available in a node to accommodate all incoming traffic. In order to prevent deadlock, APPN requires a node to pre-allocate buffers for a window it commits to a sender. Although this does not always make the most efficient use of available buffer space, it avoids the deadlock problems.

In this section we have described the most recent additions to the SNA framework, SNA/LEN and APPN. From our description it should be clear that these additions have some new features that make them particularly useful for large networks of (relatively) small computers. Since there is full compatibility with existing SNA, these networks may attach through a boundary node, to take advantage of services in the backbone SNA network. Since an APPN network can also operate 'stand alone' (i.e. without a backbone SNA network) there is even a future scenario possible in which the SNA backbone network would gradually disappear. However, this is unlikely to happen, since the SNA backbone network has characteristics that are different from those of an APPN network and it will thus continue to exist. It is likely, however, that dynamic features similar to the Topology Database Update, the directory search and dynamic route selection will also be made available for the backbone network [37, 40]. Lengthy, complicated network definitions are then no longer required.

Fig. 12.1 Comparison of the OSI and SNA layers

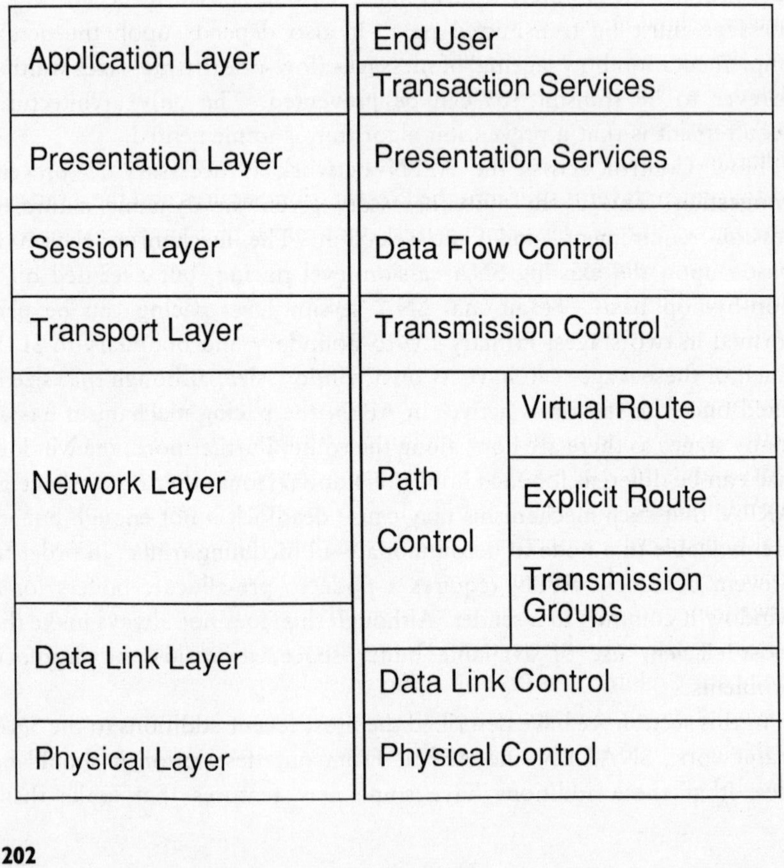

OSI	SNA	
Application Layer	End User	
	Transaction Services	
Presentation Layer	Presentation Services	
Session Layer	Data Flow Control	
Transport Layer	Transmission Control	
Network Layer	Path Control	Virtual Route
		Explicit Route
		Transmission Groups
Data Link Layer	Data Link Control	
Physical Layer	Physical Control	

12 Comparison with the OSI Reference Model

12.1 Introduction

From the description of the SNA layers in the preceding sections it will be clear that the SNA's layers are generally similar to the layers of the Reference Model for Open Systems Interconnection, as defined by the ISO [41].

In Fig. 12.1, the layers of both SNA and the Reference Model are shown side by side. The reader should realize that this way of drawing the comparison is subjective and time dependent. Earlier publications, for example [42], show a mapping that is somewhat different from the one presented here. The differences are mainly in the position of the ISO Transport and Network Layers relative to the SNA Layers. Since the definition of both layers changed while the Reference Model matured, it is not surprising that with today's definition the result of a mapping is different. On the other hand, with LU 6.2, the earlier SNA Function Management layer is split into the Presentation Services and the Transaction Services layer. This emphasizes, once more, that any such mapping is only relevant as an overall indication and can only properly be positioned in time since both the Reference Model and any proprietary architecture, including SNA, continuously evolve.

Several studies have been made, also by IBM [referred to in 37], of the mapping between OSI and SNA. The main reason for doing so is to get a better understanding for the building of gateways between SNA networks and the OSI world. If such gateways could be designed, they should operate similar to the SNA Interconnection gateway. This would make it transparent to the users whether they communicate with somebody in the same network, in another SNA network, in an OSI environment or even in a network of another architecture (via OSI). This would be the real objective of OSI, to interconnect systems of different make and architecture. Like SNA Network Interconnection (Chapter 9), it would leave the interconnected systems fully autonomous.

In the remainder of this chapter we will look at a number of ways in which OSI (and related standards) can be and have been supported in

SNA. Necessarily this discussion is much closer to actual implementation than the preceding part of this book. However, we will maintain as much as possible an architectural view of the various interconnection options.

12.2 SNA and X.25

The use of X.25 as a transport mechanism in an SNA network has been described in detail in [43]. There are two fundamentally different ways in which X.25 can be used in an SNA environment. The first one has been used by IBM in its earliest support of X.25 since 1980. It uses the X.25 Virtual Circuits in much the same way as SDLC links are used. This is illustrated in Fig. 12.2.

The X.25 Virtual Circuit is given the appearance of a single data link with end-to-end control. From an architectural point of view, one could say that the X.25 circuit is 'downgraded' to the level of a physical circuit. To achieve this a *protocol wrapping* technique is used, giving the necessary end-to-end functionality, equivalent to SDLC. It should be realized, that, although HDLC is used at X.25 level 2, it only covers the connection from the SNA equipment to the X.25 network (X.25 is a network access specification). The wrapping layer used is called Logical Link Control. It is similar to LLC used on the Token Ring, in that it only supports the functions necessary for end-to-end control across the X.25 network and not those for transparency and media access (e.g. polling). Data is transmitted in X.25 data packets, while SDLC-like control packets are transmitted using X.25 Qualified Data packets. The major product that provides X.25 support and also implements this technique is an extension of the Network Control Program (NCP) for the IBM 3725 Controller. It is called the NCP Packet Switching Interface (NPSI) [44]. Support is also provided through a stand-alone Network Interface Adapter (NIA, as in Fig. 12.2) or through integrated support in the Cluster Controllers.

Since this support of X.25 is at the link level, it is totally transparent to the using sessions. It is not really interconnection, because on both sides of the X.25 network the environment is SNA. A different approach is necessary when one wants to interconnect application programs in the SNA environment with application programs (or terminals) in the X.25 environment. The first step in this direction is the so-called Protocol Converter for Non-SNA equipment (PCNE, Fig. 12.3), which is part of NPSI. From an architectural point of view, this support concatenates the SNA session with the X.25 Virtual Circuit (i.e. now the SNA session is

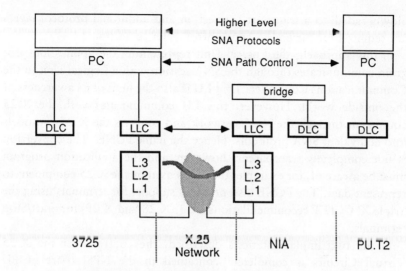

Fig. 12.2 Use of X.25 in an SNA environment

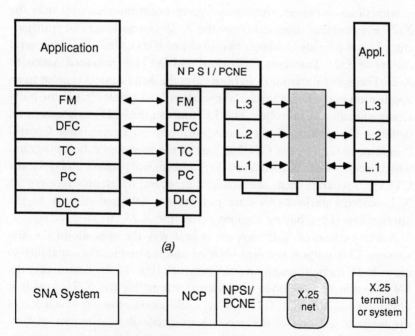

(a)

Fig. 12.3 Attachment of Non-SNA equipment through an X.25 network
(*a*) architectural view
(*b*) connection topology

'downgraded' to a transport connection and additional protocol layers are required for the end-to-end control, refer to Section 12.3).

In this approach, the Logical Unit representing the application program communicates through the SNA session with a Logical Unit in the Communications Controller. That LU is also the limit of its awareness of the outside world. However, this LU communicates with the X.25 equipment through the X.25 network and converts the X.25 protocols into equivalent SNA protocols. Hence the name PCNE. The conversion is not completely transparent, however, and the application program must be aware of, for example, the codes used by the X.25 equipment to represent data. The PCNE also provides support for terminals using the 'triple X' CCITT recommendations (X.3, X.28 and X.29) for Start/Stop terminals.

In the two implementations described, the control over the X.25 Virtual Circuits is completely contained in the NPSI (part of PU Configuration Services). When an SNA session is established for which an X.25 Virtual Circuit is required, the SSCP and the Physical Unit establish this circuit through a Link Activation procedure similar to the one used for SDLC links. Any X.25 control packets (e.g. RESET) are handled by the NPSI.

Sometimes, however, the user program needs more control over the X.25 environment (note that now the X.25 can no longer be transparent). This is provided through two IBM products called GATE (General Access to X.25 Transport Extension) and DATE (Dedicated Access to X.25 Transport Extension). In both cases the X.25 control is given to an application in the host through a session with a Logical Unit in the NPSI Communications Controller. This LU controls the X.25 environment on behalf of the application, the Communication and Transmission Control Program. In GATE, the CTCP is part of the user application program, which receives both X.25 data packets and control packets. In DATE the CTCP is a separate (dedicated) control program, which only receives the X.25 control packets. All data packets are delivered directly to the applications (LUs) having sessions across the X.25 virtual circuits.

A final version of X.25 support is in a way the opposite of the first version. This support is called SNA/XI and it provides the capability to carry X.25 traffic through an SNA network (Fig. 12.4). Essentially, the SNA session now behaves as a virtual circuit for the X.25 world. It illustrates the fact that X.25 is a network access protocol which leaves the internal working of the network unspecified! As a matter of fact, several public X.25 networks use proprietary protocols internally. SNA/XI uses SNA as such a proprietary protocol. One of the advantages is that X.25 traffic can be mixed with normal SNA traffic. A major factor

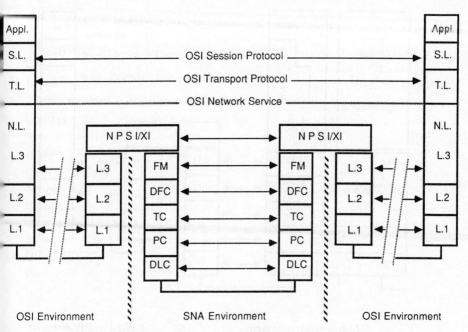

Fig. 12.4 SNA as an X.25 transport network

is also that this X.25 network can be managed using the SNA network management.

12.3 SNA and OSI

Based on the GATE support described before, IBM now also provides support for the layers of OSI above the X.25 Packet level (Fig. 12.5).

This support includes two levels. First there is a (CTCP) program, Open Systems Network Support (OSNS) [45] which adds the necessary functionality to the X.25 support in order to provide the OSI Network Service. On top of that, the Open Systems Transport and Session Support (OTSS) [46] provides an implementation of the OSI Transport and Session layers. As indicated in Fig. 12.5, user applications have access to all OSI service interfaces (i.e. Network, Transport and Session) if required.

The interconnection with the SNA environment can be performed at the application level, through an 'application bridge' function. Such a bridge is provided in the IBM GTMOSI (General Teleprocessing Monitor for OSI) which makes subsystem services, similar to those of the CICS

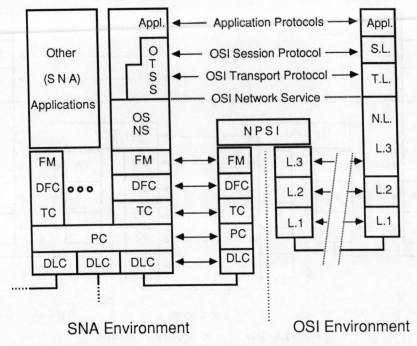

Fig. 12.5 SNA support for Open Systems Interconnection

subsystem, available to the users [47]. It allows connection of an application to both the SNA and the OSI environment. The reader is referred to the appropriate IBM literature, since further discussion is outside the scope of this book.

It should be noted that the interconnection described here is a 'bridge' function at the application level and not an interconnection as mentioned in the introduction to this chapter, in which equivalent protocols are mapped. As was already indicated, that type of interconnection is much more difficult, but there is no reason why it could not be provided in the future.

Acronyms

ABM	Asynchronous Balanced Mode
ACF	Advanced Communications Function
ACK	Acknowledgement
ACTCDRM	Activate Cross-Domain Resource Manager
ACTLU	Activate Logical Unit
ACTPU	Activate Physical Unit
AMP	Active Monitor Present
API	Application Program Interface
APPC	Advanced Program-to-Program Communication
APPN	Advanced Peer-to-Peer Networking
ARI	Address Recognized Indicator
ARPA	Advanced Research Project Agency
ARR	Asynchronous Reply Requested
ASM	Address Space Manager
BAC	Balanced Asynchronous Class of Procedures
BB	Begin Bracket
BBIU	Begin of Basic Information Unit
BC	Begin of Chain
BIU	Basic Information Unit
BTU	Basic Transmission Unit
CCITT	International Telegraph and Telephone Consultative Committee
CCN	Communications Controller Node
CD	Change Direction
CDCINIT	Cross-Domain Control Initiate
CDINIT	Cross-Domain Initiate
CDRM	Cross-Domain Resource Manager
CDSESSST	Cross-Domain Session Started
CEB	Conditional End-of-Bracket
CEBI	Conditional End-of-Bracket Indicator
CICS	Customer Information Control System
CINIT	Control Initiate
CNOS	Change Number of Sessions
CORR	Correlation
COS	Class of Service
COTP	Control Operator Transaction Program
CP	Control Point
CPMGR	Connection Point Manager
CPMS	Control Point Management Services
CRV	Cryptography Verification
CS	Configuration Services
CS	Connectivity Services
CSI	Code Selection Indicator

CTCP	Communication and Transmission Control Program
CWI	Change Window Indicator
CWRI	Change Window Reply Indicator
DAF	Destination Address Field
DATE	Dedicated Access to X.25 Transport Extension
DC	Direct Current
DCA	Document Content Architecture
DCF	Data Count Field
DEF	Destination Element Field
DEN	Distribution Element Name
DES	Data Encryption Standard
DFC	Data Flow Control
DGN	Distribution Group Name
DIA	Document Interchange Architecture
DIS	Draft International Standard
DISC	Disconnect
DIU	Document Interchange Unit
DIU-ID	DIU Identifier
DLC	Data Link Control
DM	Disconnected Mode
DR	Definite Response
DRM	Domain Resource Manager
DS	Data Stream
DS	Directory Services
DSAF	Destination Subarea Field
DSAP	Destination Service Access Point
DSU	Distribution Service Unit
DSUN	Distribution Service Unit Name
DTS	Data Transport Services
DUN	Distribution User Name
EB	End Bracket
EBCDIC	Extended Binary-Coded Decimal Interchange Code
EBI	End Bracket Indicator
EBIU	End of Basic Information Unit
EC	End of Chain
EDI	Enciphered Data Indicator
EDI	Error Detected Indicator
EFI	Expedited Flow Indicator
EN	End Node
ERI	Exception Response Indicator
ERN	Explicit Route Number
ERP	Error Recovery Procedure
EXR	Exception Request
F-bit	Final bit
FCI	Frame Copied Indicator
FCS	Frame Check Sequence
FI	Format Indicator
FID	Format Identifier
FIFO	First in, First out
FM	Function Management
FMD	Function Management Data
FMH	Function Management Header

FRMR	Frame Reject
GA	Go Ahead
GATE	General Access to X.25 Transport Extension
GDS	General Data Stream
GTMOSI	Generalized Transaction Monitor for OSI
HDLC	High-level Data Link Control
HDX	Half-Duplex
IBM	International Business Machines
ID	Identifier
IDP	Interchange Document Profile
IMS	Information Management System
IPR	Isolated Pacing Response
IS	International Standard
ISO	International Standardization Organization
LADN	Library Assigned Document Name
LAN	Local Area Network
LFSID	Local-Form Session Identifier
LL	Logical Record Length
LLC	Logical Link Control
LMS	Logical Message Stream
LMS	Local Management Services
LSID	Local Session Identifier
LT	Length-Type
LU	Logical Unit
LUSTAT	LU Status
MAC	Media Access Control
MC	Monitor Count
MOC	Middle of Chain
MPF	Mapping Field
N(R)	Receive Count
N(S)	Send Count
NAU	Network Addressable Unit
NAUN	Nearest Active Upstream Neighbor
NC	Network Control
NCP	Network Control Program
NIA	Network Interface Adapter
NMVT	Network Management Vector Transport
NN	Network Node
NPSI	NCP Packet Switching Interface
NRR	No Reply Requested
NSPE	Network Services Procedure Error
OAF	Origin Address Field
ODAI	OAF'-DAF' Assignor Indicator
OEF	Origin Element Field
OSAF	Origin Subarea Field
OSI	Open Systems Interconnection
OSN	Office System Node
P-bit	Poll-bit
PC	Path Control
PCNE	Protocol Converter for Non-SNA Equipment
PDI	Padded Data Indicator
PIU	Path Information Unit

PLU	Primary Logical Unit
PN	Peripheral Node
PNCP	Peripheral Node Control Point
PRID	Procedure Related Identifier
PS	Presentation Services
PU	Physical Unit
PUCP	Physical Unit Control Point
PUMS	Physical Unit Management Services
QEC	Quiesce at End of Chain
RD	Request Disconnect
REJ	Reject
REN	Routing Element Name
RERN	Reverse Explicit Route Number
RH	Request Header
RIM	Request Initialization Mode
RNAA	Request Network Address Assignment
RNR	Receive Not Ready
RQD	Request for Definite Response
RQE	Request for Exception Response only
RQN	Request No Response
RR	Receive Ready
RSCV	Route Selection Control Vector
RSET	Reset
RSHUTD	Request Shutdown
RSS	Route Selection Services
RTI	Response Type Indicator
RTR	Ready To Receive
RU	Request Unit
RWI	Reset Window Indicator
S/R	Source/Recipient
SA	Subarea
SABM	Set Asynchronous Balanced Mode
SAP	Service Access Point
SARM	Set Asynchronous Response Mode
SAS	Session Activation Services
SC	Session Control
SCB	String Control Byte
SCS	SNA Character String
SDI	Sense Data Included
SDLC	Synchronous Data Link Control
SDT	Start Data Traffic
SESSST	Session Started
SETCV	Set Control Vector
SHUTC	Shutdown Complete
SHUTD	Shutdown
SID	Session Identifier
SIM	Set Initialization Mode
SLU	Secondary Logical Unit
SMP	Standby Monitor Present
SNA	Systems Network Architecture
SNA/LEN	SNA Low Entry Networking
SNA/XI	SNA to X.25 Interconnection

SNADS	SNA Distribution Services
SNF	Sequence Number Field
SNI	SNA Network Interconnection
SNRM	Set Normal Response Mode
SPS	Sync Point Services
SREJ	Selective Reject
SRR	Synchronous Reply Requested
SSAP	Source Service Access Point
SSCP	System Services Control Point
SSCP-GW	SSCP-Gateway
STSN	Set and Test Sequence Numbers
TA	Turn Around
TCE	Transmission Control Element
TDU	Topology Database Update
TG	Transmission Group
TH	Transmission Header
TP	Transaction Program
TPF	Transmission Priority Field
TS	Transmission Services
TWA	Two-Way Alternate
TWS	Two-Way Simultaneous
UA	Unnumbered Acknowledgement
UAC	Unbalanced Asynchronous Class of Procedures
UI	Unnumbered Information
UNC	Unbalanced Normal Response Mode Class of Procedures
UP	Unnumbered Poll
VLSI	Very Large Scale Integration
VR	Virtual Route
VRN	Virtual Route Number
VRPRI	Virtual Route Pacing Response Indicator
VTAM	Virtual Telecommunications Access Method
XID	Exchange Identification

References

[1] Schultz, G. D. and Sundstrom, R. J., SNA's first six years: 1974–1980, *Proc. 5th Int. Conf. Computer Commun.*, Atlanta, 1980, pp. 578–585

[2] Atkins, J. D., Path Control: the Transport Network of SNA, *IEEE Trans. Commun.*, vol. Com-28, no. 4, pp. 527–538

[3] Ahuja, V., Routing and flow control in Systems Network Architecture, *IBM Syst. J.*, vol. 18, no. 2, 1979, pp. 298–314

[4] IBM Corporation, *Systems Network Architecture Technical Overview*, GC30-3073

[5] IBM Corporation, *Systems Network Architecture Format and Protocol Reference Manual : Architectural Logic,* SC30-3112

[6] IBM Corporation, *IBM Synchronous Data Link Control— Concepts*, GA27-3093

[7] International Standards Organization, ISO 3309: *Data Communication. High-level Data Link Control procedures—Frame Structure*

[8] International Standards Organization, ISO 4335: *Data Communication. High-level Data Link Control procedures—Consolidation of Elements of Procedures.*

[9] International Standards Organization, ISO 7809: *Data Communication. High-level Data Link Control procedures—Consolidation of Classes of Prodecures*

[10] Davies, D. W., Barber, D. L. A., Price, W. L. and Solomonides, C. M., *Computer Networks and their Protocols*, Wiley, 1979

[11] Tanenbaum, A. S., *Computer Networks*, Prentice Hall, 1981

[12] IBM Corporation, *Systems Network Architecture: Formats*, GA27-3136

[13] IBM Corporation, *Systems Network Architecture Format and Protocol Reference Manual: Architecture Logic For Type 2.1 Nodes,* SC30-3422

[14] IBM Corporation, *A Token Ring Network Architecture Reference Manual*, SC30-3374.

[15] International Standards Organization, DIS8802/5: *Information*

processing systems—*Local area networks—Part 5 : Token ring access method and physical layer specification*

[16] International Standards Organization, DIS8802/2: *Information processing systems—Local area networks—Part 2: Logical Link Control*

[17] Jueneman, R. R. and Kerr, G. S., Explicit path routing in communication networks, *Proc. 3rd Int. Conf. Computer Commun.*, Toronto, 1976, pp. 340–342

[18] Maruyama, K., Defining routing tables for SNA networks, *IBM Syst. J.*, vol. 22, no. 4, 1983, pp. 435–450.

[19] Deaton, G. A. Jr., Flow control in packet-switched networks with explicit path routing, *Proc. Flow Control in Computer Networks Conf.*, Paris, 1979

[20] IBM Corporation, *Systems Network Architecture—sessions between Logical Units*, GC20-1868

[21] IBM Corporation, *Systems Network Architecture Format and Protocol Reference Manual: Management Services*, SC30-3374

[22] IBM Corporation, *Systems Network Architecture—introduction to sessions between Logical Units*, GC20-1869

[23] IBM Corporation, *Systems Network Architecture Transaction Programmer's Reference Manual For LU Type 6.2*, GC30-3084

[24] IBM Corporation, *Systems Network Architecture Format and Protocol Reference Manual: Architecture Logic For LU Type 6.2*, SC30-3269

[25] Gray, J. P., Hansen, P. J., Homan, O., Lerner, M. A. and Pozefsky, M., Advanced program-to-program communication in SNA, *IBM Syst. J.*, vol. 22, no. 4, 1983, pp. 298–318

[26] IBM Corporation, *Document Interchange Architecture: Concepts and Structures*, SC23-0759

[27] Benjamin, J. H., Hess, M. L., Weingarten, R. A. and Wheeler, W. R., Interconnecting SNA networks, *IBM Syst. J.*, vol. 22, no. 4, 1983, pp. 344–366

[28] IBM Corporation, *Document Content Architecture: Final-Form-Text Reference*, SC23-0757

[29] IBM Corporation, *Document Content Architecture: Revisable-Form-Text Reference*, SC23-0758

[30] IBM Corporation, *Document Interchange Architecture: Document Distribution Services Reference*, SC23-0762

[31] IBM Corporation, *Document Interchange Architecture: Document Library Services Reference*, SC23-0760

[32] IBM Corporation, *Document Interchange Architecture: Application Processing Services Reference*, SC23-0761

[33] IBM Corporation, *Document Interchange Architecture: Interchange Document Profile Reference,* SC23-0764

[34] IBM Corporation, *Systems Network Architecture Format and Protocol Reference Manual: Distribution Services*, SC30-3098

[35] Housel, B. C. and Scopinich, C. J., SNA Distribution Services, *IBM Syst. J.,* vol. 22, no. 4, 1983, pp. 319–343

[36] Baratz, A. E., Gray, J. P., Green, P. E., Jaffe, J. M. and Pozefsky, D. P., SNA networks of small systems, *IEEE Journal on Selected Areas in Communications, SAC-3*, no. 3, 1985
Also published as IBM Technical Bulletin GG66-0216, IBM Corporation, 1985

[37] Sundstrom, R. J., Staton, J. B., Schultz, G. D., Hess, M. L., Deaton, G. A., Cole, L. D. and Amy, R. N., SNA directions—a 1985 perspective, *National Computer Conference 1985, AFIPS Conference Proc.,* vol. 54, pp. 589–603

[38] Dijkstra, E. W., A note on two problems in connexion with graphs, *Numer. Math.,* vol. 1, pp. 269–271, Oct. 1959

[39] Aho, A. V., Hopcroft, J. E. and Ullman, J. D., *The Design and Analysis of Computer Algorithms*, Addison-Wesley, 1974.

[40] Jaffe, J. M., Moss, F. H. and Weingarten, R. A., SNA routing: past, present, and possible future, *IBM Syst. J.,* vol. 22, no. 4, 1983, pp 417–434

[41] Meijer, A. and Peeters, P., *Computer Network Architectures*, Pitman, 1982

[42] Corr, F. P. and Neal, D. H., SNA and emerging international standards, *IBM Syst. J.,* vol. 18, no. 2, 1979, pp. 244–262

[43] Deaton, G. A. and Hippert, R. O., X.25 and related recommendations in IBM products, *IBM Syst. J.,* vol. 22, nrs. 1/2, 1983, pp. 11–29

[44] IBM Corporation, *X.25 NCP Packet Switching Interface—General Information,* GC30-3189

[45] IBM Corporation, *Open Systems Network Support—General Information,* GH12-5145

[46] IBM Corporation, *Open Systems Transport and Session Support—General Information,* GH12-5450

[47] IBM Corporation, *General Teleprocessing Monitor for Open Systems Interconnect—General Information,* GB11-8201

Index